Data Mining and
Machine Learning
in Cybersecurity

Data Mining and Machine Learning in Cybersecurity

Sumeet Dua and Xian Du

CRC Press
Taylor & Francis Group
Boca Raton   London   New York

CRC Press is an imprint of the
Taylor & Francis Group, an **informa** business
AN AUERBACH BOOK

Auerbach Publications
Taylor & Francis Group
6000 Broken Sound Parkway NW, Suite 300
Boca Raton, FL 33487-2742

Library of Congress Cataloging-in-Publication Data

Dua, Sumeet.
    Data mining and machine learning in cybersecurity / Sumeet Dua, Xian Du.
      p. cm.
    Summary: "Introducing basic concepts of machine learning and data mining methodologies for cyber security, this book provides a unified reference for specific machine learning solutions and cybersecurity problems. The authors focus on how to apply machine learning methodologies in cybersecurity, categorizing methods for detecting, scanning, profiling, intrusions, and anomalies. The text presents challenges and solutions in machine learning along with cybersecurity fundamentals. It also describes advanced problems in cybersecurity in the machine learning domain and examines privacy-preserving data mining methods as a proactive security solution"-- Provided by publisher.
    Includes bibliographical references and index.
    ISBN 978-1-4398-3942-3 (hardback)
    1. Data mining. 2. Machine learning. 3. Computer security. I. Du, Xian. II. Title.

QA76.9.D343D825 2011
005.8--dc22
                                               2011006228

**Visit the Taylor & Francis Web site at
http://www.taylorandfrancis.com**

**and the Auerbach Web site at
http://www.auerbach-publications.com**

Contents

List of Figures

List of Tables

Preface

In the emerging era of Web 3.0, securing cyberspace has gradually evolved into a critical organizational and national research agenda inviting interest from a multidisciplinary scientific workforce. There are many avenues into this area, and, in recent research, machine-learning and data-mining techniques have been applied to design, develop, and improve algorithms and frameworks for cybersecurity system design. Intellectual products in this domain have appeared under various topics, including machine learning, data mining, cybersecurity, data management and modeling, and privacy preservation. Several conferences, workshops, and journals focus on the fragmented research topics in this area. However, transcendent and interdisciplinary assessment of past and current works in the field and possible paths for future research in the area are essential for consistent research and development.

This interdisciplinary assessment is especially useful for students, who typically learn cybersecurity, machine learning, and data mining in independent courses. Machine learning and data mining play significant roles in cybersecurity, especially as more challenges appear with the rapid development of information discovery techniques, such as those originating from the sheer dimensionality and heterogeneous nature of the network data, the dynamic change of threats, and the severe imbalanced classes of normal and anomalous behaviors. In this book, we attempt to combine all the above knowledge for a single advanced course.

This book surveys cybersecurity problems and state-of-the-art machine-learning and data-mining solutions that address the overarching research problems, and it is designed for students and researchers studying or working on machine learning and data mining in cybersecurity applications. The inclusion of cybersecurity in machine-learning research is important for academic research. Such an inclusion inspires fundamental research in machine learning and data mining, such as research in the subfields of imbalanced learning, feature extraction for data with evolving characteristics, and privacy-preserving data mining.

Organization

In Chapter 1, we introduce the vulnerabilities of cyberinfrastructure and the conventional approaches to cyber defense. Then, we present the vulnerabilities of these conventional cyber protection methods and introduce higher-level methodologies that use advanced machine learning and data mining to build more reliable cyber defense systems. We review the cybersecurity solutions that use machine-learning and data-mining techniques, including privacy-preservation data mining, misuse detection, anomaly detection, hybrid detection, scan detection, and profiling detection. In addition, we list a number of references that address cybersecurity issues using machine-learning and data-mining technology to help readers access the related material easily.

In Chapter 2, we introduce machine-learning paradigms and cybersecurity along with a brief overview of machine-learning formulations and the application of machine-learning methods and data mining/management in cybersecurity. We discuss challenging problems and future research directions that are possible when machine-learning methods are applied to the huge amount of temporal and unbalanced network data.

In Chapter 3, we address misuse/signature detection. We introduce fundamental knowledge, key issues, and challenges in misuse/signature detection systems, such as building efficient rule-based algorithms, feature selection for rule matching and accuracy improvement, and supervised machine-learning classification of attack patterns. We investigate several supervised learning methods in misuse detection. We explore the limitations and difficulties of using these machine-learning methods in misuse detection systems and outline possible problems, such as the inadequate ability to detect a novel attack, irregular performance for different attack types, and requirements of the intelligent feature selection. We guide readers to questions and resources that will help them learn more about the use of advanced machine-learning techniques to solve these problems.

In Chapter 4, we provide an overview of anomaly detection techniques. We investigate and classify a large number of machine-learning methods in anomaly detection. In this chapter, we briefly describe the applications of machine-learning methods in anomaly detection. We focus on the limitations and difficulties that encumber machine-learning methods in anomaly detection systems. Such problems include an inadequate ability to maintain a high detection rate and a low false-alarm rate. As anomaly detection is the most concentrative application area of machine-learning methods, we perform in-depth studies to explain the appropriate learning procedures, e.g., feature selection, in detail.

In Chapter 5, we address hybrid intrusion detection techniques. We describe how hybrid detection methods are designed and employed to detect unknown intrusions and anomaly detection with a lower false-positive rate. We categorize the hybrid intrusion detection techniques into three groups based on combinational methods. We demonstrate several machine-learning hybrids that raise detection accuracies in the intrusion detection system, including correlation techniques, artificial neural networks, association rules, and random forest classifiers.

In Chapter 6, we address scan detection techniques using machine-learning methods. We explain the dynamics of scan attacks and focus on solving scan detection problems in applications. We provide several examples of machine-learning methods used for scan detection, including the rule-based methods, threshold random walk, association memory learning techniques, and expert knowledge-rule-based learning model. This chapter addresses the issues pertaining to the high percentage of false alarms and the evaluation of efficiency and effectiveness of scan detection.

In Chapter 7, we address machine-learning techniques for profiling network traffic. We illustrate a number of profiling modules that profile normal or anomalous behaviors in cyberinfrastructure for intrusion detection. We introduce and investigate a number of new concepts for clustering methods in intrusion detection systems, including association rules, shared nearest neighbor clustering, EM-based clustering, subspace, and informatics theoretic techniques. In this chapter, we address the difficulties of mining the huge amount of streaming data and the necessity of interpreting the profiling results in an understandable way.

In Chapter 8, we provide a comprehensive overview of available machine-learning technologies in privacy-preserving data mining. In this chapter, we concentrate on how data-mining techniques lead to privacy breach and how privacy-preserving data mining achieves data protection via machine-learning methods. Privacy-preserving data mining is a new area, and we hope to inspire research beyond the foundations of data mining and privacy-preserving data mining.

In Chapter 9, we describe the emerging challenges in fixed computing or mobile applications and existing and potential countermeasures using machine-learning methods in cybersecurity. We also explore how the emerging cyber threats may evolve in the future and what corresponding strategies can combat threats. We describe the emerging issues in network monitoring, profiling, and privacy preservation and the emerging challenges in intrusion detection, especially those challenges for anomaly detection systems.

Authors

Dr. Sumeet Dua is currently an Upchurch endowed associate professor and the coordinator of IT research at Louisiana Tech University, Ruston, Louisiana. He received his PhD in computer science from Louisiana State University, Baton Rouge, Louisiana.

His areas of expertise include data mining, image processing and computational decision support, pattern recognition, data warehousing, biomedical informatics, and heterogeneous distributed data integration. The National Science Foundation (NSF), the National Institutes of Health (NIH), the Air Force Research Laboratory (AFRL), the Air Force Office of Sponsored Research (AFOSR), the National Aeronautics and Space Administration (NASA), and the Louisiana Board of Regents (LA-BoR) have funded his research with over $2.8 million. He frequently serves as a study section member (expert panelist) for the National Institutes of Health (NIH) and panelist for the National Science Foundation (NSF)/CISE Directorate. Dr. Dua has chaired several conference sessions in the area of data mining and is the program chair for the *Fifth International Conference on Information Systems, Technology, and Management* (ICISTM-2011). He has given more than 26 invited talks on data mining and its applications at international academic and industry arenas, has advised more than 25 graduate theses, and currently advises several graduate students in the discipline. Dr. Dua is a coinventor of two issued U.S. patents, has (co-)authored more than 50 publications and book chapters, and has authored or edited four books. Dr. Dua has received the Engineering and Science Foundation Award for Faculty Excellence (2006) and the Faculty Research Recognition Award (2007), has been recognized as a distinguished researcher (2004–2010) by the Louisiana Biomedical Research Network (NIH-sponsored), and has won the Outstanding Poster Award at the NIH/NCI caBIG—NCRI Informatics Joint Conference; Biomedical Informatics without Borders: From Collaboration to Implementation. Dr. Dua is a senior member of the IEEE Computer Society, a senior member of the ACM, and a member of SPIE and the American Association for Advancement of Science.

Dr. Xian Du is a research associate and postdoctoral fellow at the Louisiana Tech University, Ruston, Louisiana. He worked as a postdoctoral researcher at the Centre National de la Recherche Scientifique (CNRS) in the CREATIS Lab, Lyon, France, from 2007 to 2008 and served as a software engineer in Kikuze Solutions Pte. Ltd., Singapore, in 2006. He received his PhD from the Singapore–MIT Alliance (SMA) Programme at the National University of Singapore in 2006.

Dr. Xian Du's current research focus is on high-performance computing using machine-learning and data-mining technologies, data-mining applications for cyber-security, software in multiple computer operational environments, and clustering theoretical research. He has broad experience in machine-learning applications in industry and academic research at high-level research institutes. During his work in the CREATIS Lab in France, he developed a 3D smooth active contour technology for knee cartilage MRI image segmentation. He led a small research and development group to develop color control plug-ins for an RGB color printer to connect to the Windows® system through image processing GDI functions for Kikuze Solutions. He helped to build an intelligent e-diagnostics system for reducing mean time to repair wire-bonding machines at National Semiconductor Ltd., Singapore (NSC). During his PhD dissertation research at the SMA, he developed an intelligent color print process control system for color printers. Dr. Du's major research interests are machine-learning and data-mining applications, heterogeneous data integration and visualization, cybersecurity, and clustering theoretical research.

Chapter 1

Introduction

> Many of the nation's essential and emergency services, as well as our critical infrastructure, rely on the uninterrupted use of the Internet and the communications systems, data, monitoring, and control systems that comprise our cyber infrastructure. A cyber attack could be debilitating to our highly interdependent Critical Infrastructure and Key Resources (CIKR) and ultimately to our economy and national security.
>
> **Homeland Security Council**
> *National Strategy for Homeland Security, 2007*

The ubiquity of cyberinfrastructure facilitates beneficial activities through rapid information sharing and utilization, while its vulnerabilities generate opportunities for our adversaries to perform malicious activities within the infrastructure.* Because of these opportunities for malicious activities, nearly every aspect of cyberinfrastructure needs protection (Homeland Security Council, 2007).

Vulnerabilities in cyberinfrastructure can be attacked horizontally or vertically. Hence, cyber threats can be evaluated horizontally from the perspective of the attacker(s) or vertically from the perspective of the victims. First, we look at cyber threats vertically, from the perspective of the victims. A variety of adversarial agents such as nation-states, criminal organizations, terrorists, hackers, and other malicious users can compromise governmental homeland security through networks.

---

* Cyberinfrastructure consists of digital data, data flows, and the supportive hardware and software. The infrastructure is responsible for data collection, data transformation, traffic flow, data processing, privacy protection, and the supervision, administration, and control of working environments. For example, in our daily activities in cyberspace, we use health Supervisory Control and Data Acquisition (SCADA) systems and the Internet (Chandola et al., 2009).

For example, hackers may utilize personal computers remotely to conspire, proselytize, recruit accomplices, raise funds, and collude during ongoing attacks. Adversarial governments and agencies can launch cyber attacks on the hardware and software of the opponents' cyberinfrastructures by supporting financially and technically malicious network exploitations.

Cyber criminals threaten financial infrastructures, and they could pose threats to national economies if recruited by the adversarial agents or terrorist organizations. Similarly, private organizations, e.g., banks, must protect confidential business or private information from such hackers. For example, the disclosure of business or private financial data to cyber criminals can lead to financial loss via Internet banking and related online resources. In the pharmaceutical industry, disclosure of protected company information can benefit competitors and lead to market-share loss. Individuals must also be vigilant against cyber crimes and malicious use of Internet technology.

As technology has improved, users have become more tech savvy. People communicate and cooperate efficiently through networks, such as the Internet, which are facilitated by the rapid development of digital information technologies, such as personal computers and personal digital assistants (PDAs). Through these digital devices linked by the Internet, hackers also attack personal privacy using a variety of weapons, such as viruses, Trojans, worms, botnet attacks, rootkits, adware, spam, and social engineering platforms.

Next, we look at cyber threats horizontally from the perspective of the victims. We consider any malicious activity in cyberspace as a cyber threat. A cyber threat may result in the loss of or damage to cyber components or physical resources. Most cyber threats are categorized into one of three groups according to the intruder's purpose: stealing confidential information, manipulating the components of cyberinfrastructure, and/or denying the functions of the infrastructure. If we evaluate cyber threats horizontally, we can investigate cyber threats and the subsequent problems. We will focus on intentional cyber crimes and will not address breaches caused by normal users through unintentional operations, such as errors and omissions, since education and proper habits could help to avoid these threats.* We also will not explain cyber threats caused by natural disasters, such as accidental breaches caused by earthquakes, storms, or hurricanes, as these threats happen suddenly and are beyond our control.

1.1 Cybersecurity

To secure cyberinfrastructure against intentional and potentially malicious threats, a growing collaborative effort between cybersecurity professionals and researchers from institutions, private industries, academia, and government agencies has engaged in

---

* We define a normal cyber user as an individual or group of individuals who do not intend to intrude on the cybersecurity of other individuals.

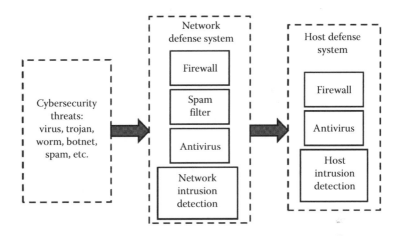

Figure 1.1 Conventional cybersecurity system.

exploiting and designing a variety of cyber defense systems. Cybersecurity researchers and designers aim to maintain the confidentiality, integrity, and availability of information and information management systems through various cyber defense systems that protect computers and networks from hackers who may want to intrude on a system or steal financial, medical, or other identity-based information.*

As shown in Figure 1.1, conventional cybersecurity systems address various cybersecurity threats, including viruses, Trojans, worms, spam, and botnets. These cybersecurity systems combat cybersecurity threats at two levels and provide network- and host-based defenses. Network-based defense systems control network flow by network firewall, spam filter, antivirus, and network intrusion detection techniques. Host-based defense systems control upcoming data in a workstation by firewall, antivirus, and intrusion detection techniques installed in hosts.

Conventional approaches to cyber defense are mechanisms designed in firewalls, authentication tools, and network servers that monitor, track, and block viruses and other malicious cyber attacks. For example, the Microsoft Windows® operating system has a built-in Kerberos cryptography system that protects user information. Antivirus software is designed and installed in personal computers and cyberinfrastructures to ensure customer information is not used maliciously. These approaches create a protective shield for cyberinfrastructure.

However, the vulnerabilities of these methods are ubiquitous in applications because of the flawed design and implementation of software and network

---

* The three requirements of cybersecurity correspond to the three types of intentional threats: confidentiality signifies the ability to prevent sensitive data from being disclosed to third parties; integrity ensures the infrastructure is complete and accurate, and availability refers to the accessibility of the normal operations of cyberinfrastructures, such as delivering and storing data.

infrastructure. Patches have been developed to protect the cyber systems, but attackers continuously exploit newly discovered flaws. Because of the constantly evolving cyber threats, building defense systems for discovered attacks is not enough to protect users. Higher-level methodologies are also required to discover the embedded and lurking cyber intrusions and cyber intrusion techniques, so that a more reliable security cyberinfrastructure can be utilized.

Many higher-level adaptive cyber defense systems can be partitioned into components as shown in Figure 1.2. Figure 1.2 outlines the five-step process for those defense systems. We discuss each step below.

Data-capturing tools, such as Libpcap for Linux®, Solaris BSM for SUN®, and Winpcap for Windows®, capture events from the audit trails of resource information sources (e.g., network). Events can be host-based or network-based depending on where they originate. If an event originates with log files, then it is categorized as a host-based event. If it originates with network traffic, then it is categorized as a network-based event. A host-based event includes a sequence of commands executed by a user and a sequence of system calls launched by an application, e.g., send mail. A network-based event includes network traffic data, e.g., a sequence of internet protocol (IP) or transmission control protocol (TCP) network packets. The data-preprocessing module filters out the attacks for which good signatures have been learned.

A feature extractor derives basic features that are useful in event analysis engines, including a sequence of system calls, start time, duration of a network flow, source IP and source port, destination IP and destination port, protocol,

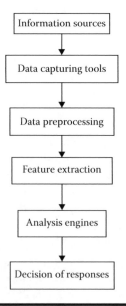

Figure 1.2 Adaptive defense system for cybersecurity.

number of bytes, and number of packets. In an analysis engine, various intrusion detection methods are implemented to investigate the behavior of the cyberinfrastructure, which may or may not have appeared before in the record, e.g., to detect anomalous traffic. The decision of responses is deployed once a cyber attack is identified. As shown in Figure 1.2, analysis engines are the core technologies for the generation of the adaptation ability of the cyber defense system. As discussed above, the solutions to cybersecurity problems include proactive and reactive security solutions.

Proactive approaches anticipate and eliminate vulnerabilities in the cyber system, while remaining prepared to defend effectively and rapidly against attacks. To function correctly, proactive security solutions require user authentication (e.g., user password and biometrics), a system capable of avoiding programming errors, and information protection [e.g., privacy-preserving data mining (PPDM)]. PPDM protects data from being explored by data-mining techniques in cybersecurity applications. We will discuss this technique in detail in Chapter 8. Proactive approaches have been used as the first line of defense against cybersecurity breaches. It is not possible to build a system that has no security vulnerabilities. Vulnerabilities in common security components, such as firewalls, are inevitable due to design and programming errors.

The second line of cyber defense is composed of reactive security solutions, such as intrusion detection systems (IDSs). IDSs detect intrusions based on the information from log files and network flow, so that the extent of damage can be determined, hackers can be tracked down, and similar attacks can be prevented in the future.

1.2 Data Mining

Due to the availability of large amounts of data in cyberinfrastructure and the number of cyber criminals attempting to gain access to the data, data mining, machine learning, statistics, and other interdisciplinary capabilities are needed to address the challenges of cybersecurity. Because IDSs use data mining and machine learning, we will focus on these areas. Data mining is the extraction, or "mining," of knowledge from a large amount of data. The strong patterns or rules detected by data-mining techniques can be used for the nontrivial prediction of new data. In nontrivial prediction, information that is implicitly presented in the data, but was previously unknown is discovered. Data-mining techniques use statistics, artificial intelligence, and pattern recognition of data in order to group or extract behaviors or entities. Thus, data mining is an interdisciplinary field that employs the use of analysis tools from statistical models, mathematical algorithms, and machine-learning methods to discover previously unknown, valid patterns and relationships in large data sets, which are useful for finding hackers and preserving privacy in cybersecurity.

Data mining is used in many domains, including finance, engineering, biomedicine, and cybersecurity. There are two categories of data-mining methods: supervised and unsupervised. Supervised data-mining techniques predict a hidden function using training data. The training data have pairs of input variables and output labels or classes. The output of the method can predict a class label of the input variables. Examples of supervised mining are classification and prediction. Unsupervised data mining is an attempt to identify hidden patterns from given data without introducing training data (i.e., pairs of input and class labels). Typical examples of unsupervised mining are clustering and associative rule mining.

Data mining is also an integral part of knowledge discovery in databases (KDDs), an iterative process of the nontrivial extraction of information from data and can be applied to developing secure cyberinfrastructures. KDD includes several steps from the collection of raw data to the creation of new knowledge. The iterative process consists of the following steps: data cleaning, data integration, data selection, data transformation, data mining, pattern evaluation, and knowledge representation, as described below.

Step 1. During data cleaning, which is also known as data cleansing, noise and irrelevant data are removed from the collection.

Step 2. Data integration combines data from multiple and heterogeneous sources into one database.

Step 3. Data-selection techniques allow the user to obtain a reduced representation of the data set to keep the integrity of the original data set in a reduced volume.

Step 4. In data transformation, the selected data is transformed into suitable formats.

Step 5. Data mining is the stage in which analysis tools are applied to discover potentially useful patterns.

Step 6. Pattern evaluation identifies interesting and useful patterns using given validation measures.

Step 7. In knowledge representation, the final phase of the knowledge-discovery process, discovered knowledge is presented to the users in visual forms.

Data-mining techniques are used to aid in the development of predictive models that enable a real-time cyber response after a sequence of cybersecurity processes, which include real-time data sampling, selection, analysis and query, and mining peta-scale data to classify and detect attacks and intrusions on a computer network (Denning, 1987; Lee and Stolfo, 1998; Axelsson, 2000; Chandola et al., 2006; Homeland Security Council, 2007). Learning user patterns and/or behaviors is critical for intrusion detection and attack predictions. Learning these behaviors is important, as they can identify and describe structural patterns in the data automatically and theoretically explain data and predict patterns. Automatic and theoretic learning require complex computation that calls for abundant machine-learning algorithms. We will discuss the concept of machine learning in Section 1.3.

1.3 Machine Learning

Learning is the process of building a scientific model after discovering knowledge from a sample data set or data sets. Generally, machine learning is considered to be the process of applying a computing-based resource to implement learning algorithms. Formally, machine learning is defined as the complex computation process of automatic pattern recognition and intelligent decision making based on training sample data.

Machine-learning methods can be categorized into four groups of learning activities: symbol-based, connectionist-based, behavior-based, and immune system-based activities. Symbol-based machine learning has a hypothesis that all knowledge can be represented in symbols and that machine learning can create new symbols and new knowledge, based on the known symbols. In symbol-based machine learning, decisions are deducted using logical inference procedures. Connectionist-based machine learning is constructed by imitating neuron net connection systems in the brain. In connectionist machine learning, decisions are made after the systems are trained and patterns are recognized. Behavior-based learning has the assumption that there are solutions to behavior identification, and is designed to find the best solution to solve the problem. The immune-system-based approach learns from its encounters with foreign objects and develops the ability to indentify patterns in data. None of these machine-learning methods has noticeable advantages over the others. Thus, it is not necessary to select machine-learning methods based on these fundamental distinctions, and within the machine-learning process, mathematical models are built to describe the data randomly sampled from an unseen probability distribution.

Machine learning has to be evaluated empirically because its performance heavily depends on the type of training experience the learning machine has undergone, the performance evaluation metrics, and the strength of the problem definition. Machine-learning methods are evaluated by comparing the learning results of methods applied on the same data set or quantifying the learning results of the same methods applied on sample data sets. The measure metrics will be discussed in Section 2.2.4. In addition to the accuracy evaluation, the time complexity and feasibility of machine learning are studied (Debar et al., 1999). Generally, the feasibility of a machine-learning method is acceptable when its computation time is polynomial.

Machine-learning methods use training patterns to learn or estimate the form of a classifier model. The models can be parametric or unparametric. The goal of using machine-learning algorithms is to reduce the classification error on the given training sample data. The training data are finite such that the learning theory requires probability bounds on the performance of learning algorithms. Depending on the availability of training data and the desired outcome of the learning algorithms, machine-learning algorithms are categorized into supervised learning and unsupervised learning. The first two groups include most machine-learning applications in cybersecurity. In supervised learning, pairs of input and target output are given to train a function, and a learning model is trained such that the output of the function can be predicted at a minimum cost. The supervised learning methods are categorized based on the structures and objective functions of learning algorithms. Popular categorizations include artificial neural network (ANN), support vector machine (SVM), and decision trees.

In unsupervised learning, no target or label is given in sample data. Unsupervised learning methods are designed to summarize the key features of the data and to form the natural clusters of input patterns given a particular cost function. The most famous unsupervised learning methods include *k*-means clustering, hierarchical clustering, and self-organization map. Unsupervised learning is difficult to evaluate, because it does not have an explicit teacher and, thus, does not have labeled data for testing.

We will discuss a number of classic machine-learning methods in Chapter 2. Readers who are familiar with this topic may skip that material.

1.4 Review of Cybersecurity Solutions

A number of surveys and review articles have focused on intrusion detection technologies (Debar et al., 1999; Axelsson, 2000; Homeland Security Council, 2007; Patcha and Park, 2007) or data mining in specific applications (Stolfo et al., 2001; Chandola et al., 2006). Hodge and Austin (2004) categorized anomaly detection techniques in statistics, neural networks, machine learning, and hybrid approaches. Meza et al. (2009) highlighted important cybersecurity problems such as cybersecurity for mathematical and statistical solutions. Siddiqui et al. (2008) categorized data-mining techniques for malware detection based on file features and analysis (static or dynamic) and detection types. Lee and Fan (2001) described a data-mining framework for mining audit data using IDSs.

In Section 1.4.1, we provide a broad structural review of the uses of machine learning for data mining in cybersecurity in the past 10 years. Besides the traditional intrusion detection (adaptive defense system) technologies, we also review proactive cybersecurity solutions. We focus on PPDM, which is designed to protect data from being explored by machine learning for data mining in cybersecurity applications. Scan detection, profiling, and hybrid detection are added to the traditional misuse and anomaly detection technologies in reactive security solutions.

1.4.1 Proactive Security Solutions

Traditionally, proactive security solutions (Canetti et al., 1997; Barak et al., 1999) are designed to maintain the overall security of a system, even if individual components of the system have been compromised by an attack.

Recently, the improvement of data-mining techniques and information technology brings unlimited chances for Internet and other media users to explore new information. The new information may include sensitive information and, thus, incur a new research domain where researchers consider data-mining algorithms from the viewpoint of privacy preservation. This new research, called PPDM

Table 1.1 Examples of PPDM

Data-Mining Techniques	Privacy-Preservation Methods	References
A.1 Statistical methods	Heuristic-based	Du et al. (2004)
A.2 Bayesian networks (BNs)	Reconstruction-based	Wright and Yang (2004)
A.3 Unsupervised clustering algorithm	Heuristic-based	Vaidya and Clifton (2003)
A.4 Association rules	Reconstruction-based	Evfimievski et al. (2002)
A.5 ANNs	Cryptography-based	Barni et al. (2006)
A.6 Decision tree	Cryptography-based	Du and Zhan (2002), Agrawal and Srikant (2000)
A.7 k-nearest neighbor (KNN)	Cryptography-based	Kantarcioglu and Clifton (2004)
A.8 SVM	Reconstruction-based	Yu et al. (2006)

Note: The privacy-preservation techniques, the most important techniques for the selective modification of the data, are categorized into three groups: heuristic-based techniques, cryptography-based techniques, and reconstruction-based techniques (see details in Verykios et al., 2004).

(Agrawal and Srikant, 2000; Verykios et al., 2004), is designed to protect private data and knowledge in data mining. PPDM methods can be characterized by data distribution, data modification, data-mining algorithms, rule hiding, and privacy-preservation techniques. We categorize the principle PPDM methods in Table 1.1 according to machine-learning algorithms for data mining and present their privacy-preservation methods. We discuss these methods in Chapter 8.

At this point in its research history, PPDM algorithms are developed for individual various machine-learning methods. The PPDM algorithms include privacy-preserving decision tree (Chebrolu et al., 2005), privacy-preserving association rule mining (Evfimievski et al., 2002), privacy-preserving clustering (Vaidya and Clifton, 2003), and privacy-preserving SVM classification (Yu et al., 2006) (see Table 1.1). We address PPDM and its application studies in Chapter 8.

1.4.2 Reactive Security Solutions

Since the principles of intrusion detection were first introduced by Denning in 1987, large numbers of reactive security systems have been developed. Such systems include RIPPER (Lee and Stolfo, 2000), EMERALD (Porras and Neumann, 1997),

MADAM ID (Lee and Stolfo, 2000), LERAD (Mahoney and Chan, 2002), and MINDS (Chandola et al., 2006).

Cyber intrusion is defined as any unauthorized attempt to access, manipulate, modify, or destroy information or to use a computer system remotely to spam, hack, or modify other computers. An IDS intelligently monitors activities that occur in a computing resource, e.g., network traffic and computer usage, to analyze the events and to generate reactions. In IDSs, it is always assumed that an intrusion will manifest itself in a trace of these events, and the trace of an intrusion is different from traces left by normal behaviors. To achieve this purpose, network packets are collected, and the rule violation is checked with pattern recognition methods. An IDS system usually monitors and analyzes user and system activities, accesses the integrity of the system and data, recognizes malicious activity patterns, generates reactions to intrusions, and reports the outcome of detection.

The activities that the IDSs trace can form a variety of patterns or come from a variety of sources. According to the detection principles, we classify intrusion detection into the following modules: misuse/signature detection, anomaly detection algorithms, hybrid detection, and scan detector and profiling modules. Furthermore, IDSs recognize and prevent malicious activities through network- or host-based methods. These IDSs search for specific malicious patterns to identify the underlying suspicious intent. When an IDS searches for malicious patterns in network traffic, we call it a network-based IDS. When an IDS searches for malicious patterns in log files, we call it host-based IDS.

1.4.2.1 Misuse/Signature Detection

Misuse detection, also called signature detection, is an IDS triggering method that generates alarms when a known cyber misuse occurs. A signature detection technique measures the similarity between input events and the signatures of known intrusions. It flags behavior that shares similarities with a predefined pattern of intrusion. Thus, known attacks can be detected immediately and realizably with a lower false-positive rate. However, signature detection cannot detect novel attacks. Examples of data mining in misuse detection are listed in Table 1.2. We address misuse detection techniques in Chapter 3.

1.4.2.2 Anomaly Detection

Anomaly detection triggers alarms when the detected object behaves significantly differently from the predefined normal patterns. Hence, anomaly detection techniques are designed to detect patterns that deviate from an expected normal model built for the data. In cybersecurity, anomaly detection includes the detection of malicious activities, e.g., penetrations and denial of service. The approach consists of two steps: training and detection. In the training step, machine-learning

Table 1.2 Examples of Data Mining and Machine Learning for Misuse/Signature Detection

Technique Used	Input Data Format	Levels	References
B.1 Rule-based signature analysis	Frequency of system calls, off line	Host	Lee et al. (1999)
B.2 ANN	TCP/IP data, offline	Host	Ghosh and Schwartzbard (1999), Cannady (1998)
B.3 Fuzzy association rules	Frequency of system calls, online	Host	Abraham et al. (2007b), Su et al. (2009)
B.4 SVM	TCP/IP data, offline	Network	Mukkamala and Sung (2003)
B.5 Linear genetic programs (LGP)	TCP/IP data, offline	Network	Mukkamala and Sung (2003), Abraham et al. (2007a,b), Srinivas et al. (2004)
B.6 Classification and regression trees	Frequency of system calls, offline	Host	Chebrolu et al. (2005)
B.7 Decision tree	TCP/IP data, online	Network	Kruegel and Toth (2003)
B.8 BN	Frequency of system calls, offline	Host	Chebrolu et al. (2005)
B.9 Statistical method	Executables, offline	Host	Schultz et al. (2001)

techniques are applied to generate a profile of normal patterns in the absence of an attack. In the detection step, the input events are labeled as attacks if the event records deviate significantly from the normal profile. Subsequently, anomaly detection can detect previously unknown attacks. However, anomaly detection is hampered by a high rate of false alarms. Moreover, the selection of inappropriate features can hurt the effectiveness of the detection result, which corresponds to the learned patterns. In extreme cases, a malicious user can use anomaly data as normal data to train an anomaly detection system, so that it will recognize malicious patterns as normal. Examples of data mining in anomaly detection are listed in Table 1.3. We will address anomaly detection techniques in Chapter 4.

Table 1.3 Examples of Data Mining and Machine Learning for Anomaly Detection

Technique Used	Input Data Format	Levels	References
C.1 Statistical methods	Sequences of system calls, offline	Host	Ye et al. (2001), Feinstein et al. (2003), Smaha (1988), Ye et al. (2002)
C.2 Statistical methods	TCP/IP data, online	Network	Yamanishi and Takeuchi (2001), Yamanishi et al. (2000), Mahoney and Chan (2002, 2003), Soule et al. (2005)
C.3 Unsupervised clustering algorithm	TCP/IP data, offline	Network	Portnoy et al. (2001), Leung and Leckie (2005), Warrender et al. (1999), Zhang and Zulkernine (2006a,b)
C.4 Subspace	TCP/IP data offline	Network	Li et al. (2006)
C.5 Information theoretic	TCP/IP, online	Network	Lakhina et al. (2005)
C.6 Association rules	Frequency of system calls, online	Host	Lee and Stolfo (1998), Abraham et al. (2007a,b), Su et al. (2009), Lee et al. (1999)
C.7 Kalman filter	TCP/IP data, online	Network	Soule et al. (2005)
C.8 Hidden Markov model (HMM)	Sequences of system calls, offline	Host	Warrender et al. (1999)
C.9 ANN	Sequences of system calls, offline	Host	Ghosh et al. (1998, 1999), Liu et al. (2002)
C.10 Principal component analysis (PCA)	TCP/IP data, online	Network	Lakhina et al. (2004), Ringberg et al. (2007)
C.11 KNN	Frequency of system calls, offline	Host	Liao and Vemuri (2002)
C.12 SVM	TCP/IP data, offline	Network	Hu et al. (2003), Chen et al. (2005)

Table 1.4   Examples of Data Mining for Hybrid Intrusion Detection

Technique Used	Input Data Format	Levels	References
D.1 Correlation	TCP/IP data, online	Network	Ning et al. (2004), Cuppens and Miège (2002), Dain and Cunningham (2001a,b)
D.2 Statistical methods	Sequences of system calls, offline	Host	Endler (1998)
D.3 ANN	Sequences of system calls, offline	Host	Endler (1998)
D.4 Association rules	Frequency of system calls, online	Host	Lee and Stolfo (2000)
D.5 ANN	TCP/IP data, online	Network	Ghosh et al. (1999)
D.6 Random forest	TCP/IP data, online	Network	Zhang and Zulkernine (2006a,b)

1.4.2.3 Hybrid Detection

Most current IDSs employ either misuse detection techniques or anomaly detection techniques. Both of these methods have drawbacks: misuse detection techniques lack the ability to detect unknown intrusions; anomaly detection techniques usually produce a high percentage of false alarms. To improve the techniques of IDSs, researchers have proposed hybrid detection techniques to combine anomaly and misuse detection techniques in IDSs. Examples for hybrid detection techniques are listed in Table 1.4. We address hybrid detection techniques in Chapter 5.

1.4.2.4 Scan Detection

Scan detection generates alerts when attackers scan services or computer components in network systems before launching attacks. A scan detector identifies the precursor of an attack on a network, e.g., destination IPs and the source IPs of Internet connections. Although many scan detection techniques have been proposed and declared to be able to detect the precursors of cyber attacks, the high false-positive rate or the low scan detection rate limits the application of these solutions in practice. Some examples of scan detection techniques are categorized in Table 1.5. We address scan and scan detection techniques in Chapter 6.

1.4.2.5 Profiling Modules

Profiling modules group similar network connections and search for dominant behaviors using clustering algorithms. Examples of profiling are categorized in Table 1.6. We address profiling techniques in Chapter 7.

Table 1.5   Examples of Data Mining for Scan Detection

Technique Used	Granularity	Levels	References
E.1 Statistical methods	Batch	Both	Staniford et al. (2002a,b)
E.2 Rule-based	Batch	Both	Staniford-Chen et al. (1996)
E.3 Threshold random walk	Continues	Host	Jung et al. (2004)
E.4 Expert knowledge—rule based	Batch	Network	Simon et al. (2006)
E.5 Associative memory	Continuous	Network	Muelder et al. (2007)

Table 1.6   Examples of Data Mining for Profiling

Technique Used	Input Data Format	Levels	References
F.1 Association rules	Set of network flow, offline	Network	Apiletti et al. (2008)
F.2 Shared nearest neighbor clustering (SNN)	Set of network flow, offline	Network	Ertöz et al. (2003), Chandola et al. (2006)
F.3 EM-based clustering	Set of network flow, offline	Network	Patcha and Park (2007)
F.4 Subspace	Set of network flow, offline	Network	Lakhina et al. (2004), Erman et al. (2006)
F.5 Information theoretic	Set of network flow, offline	Network	Xu et al. (2008)

1.5 Summary

In this chapter, we have introduced what we believe to be the most important components of cybersecurity, data mining, and machine learning. We provided an overview of types of cyber attacks and cybersecurity solutions and explained that cyber attacks compromise cyberinfrastructures in three ways: They help cyber criminals steal information, impair componental function, and disable services. We have briefly defined cybersecurity defense strategies, which consist of proactive and reactive solutions.

We highlighted proactive PPDM, and the reactive misuse detection, anomaly detection, and hybrid detection techniques. PPDM is rising in popularity as operative computation and data sharing in cyber space creates more concerns about privacy leaks, and misuse detection, anomaly detection, and hybrid detection techniques compose many IDSs. Misuse detection methods attempt to match test data with the profiled anomalous patterns, while anomalous detection solutions profile normal patterns to search for outliers. Hybrid detection systems combine misuse and anomalous detection techniques to improve the detection rate and reduce the false-alarm rate. In addition, we discuss two specific research areas in cybersecurity: scan detection and network profiling. Scan detection is used to detect the precursor of attacks, such that its use can lead to the earlier deterrence of attacks or defenses. Profiling networks facilitate the administration and monitoring of cybersecurity through extraction, aggregation, and visualization tools.

1.6 Further Reading

Throughout this book, we assume that the readers are familiar with cyberinfrastructures, with network intrusions, and with elementary probability theory, information theory, and linear algebra. Although we present a readable product for readers to solve cybersecurity problems using data-mining and machine-learning paradigms, we will provide further reading that we feel is related to our content to supplement that basic knowledge.

The resources in the areas of data mining and machine learning in cyber security are rich and rapidly growing. We provide a succinct list of the principal references for data mining, machine learning, cybersecurity, and privacy. We also list related books at the end of this chapter for readers to access the related material easily. In the later chapters of the book, we list readings that address the specific problems corresponding to the chapter topics. Our general reading list follows. If you are familiar with the material, you can skip to Chapter 2.

The key important forums on cybersecurity include the *ACM International Conference on Computer Security (S&P)*, the *IEEE Symposium on Security and Privacy*, the *International Conference on Security and Management*, the *ACM Special Interest Group on Management of Data* (SIGMOD), the *National Computer Security Conference*, the *USENIX Security Symposium*, the *ISOC Network and Distributed System Security Symposium* (NDSS), the *International Conference on Security in Communication Networks*, the *Annual Computer Security Applications Conference*, the *International Symposium on Recent Advances in Intrusion Detection*, the *National Information Security Conference*, and the *Computer Security Foundations Workshop*.

The most important data-mining conferences include *ACM Knowledge Discovery and Data Mining, ACM Special Interest Group on Management of Data, Very Large Data Bases, IEEE International Conference on Data Mining, ACM Special Interest Group on Information Retrieval, IEEE International Conference on Data Engineering, International Conference on Database Theory*, and *Extending Database Technology*.

The most important machine-learning conferences include *American Association for AI National Conference (AAAI), (NIPS), (IJCAI), CVPR*, and *ICML*.

The most important journals on cybersecurity include *ACM Transactions on Information and System Security, IEEE Transactions on Dependable and Secure Computing, IEEE Transactions on Information Forensics and Security, Journal of Computer Security,* and the *International Journal of Information Security.*

The most important journals on data mining and machine learning include *IEEE Transactions on Pattern Analysis and Machine Learning, IEEE Transactions on Systems, Man and Cybernetics, IEEE Transactions on Software Engineering, IEEE/ACM Transactions on Networking, IEEE Transactions on Computers, IEEE Transactions on Knowledge and Data Engineering, Machine Learning Journal, Journal of Machine Learning Research, Neural Computation, Pattern Recognition,* and *Pattern Recognition Letters.*

We list a number of books that contain complementary knowledge in data mining, machine learning, and cybersecurity. These books provide readable and explanatory materials for readers to access.

Stuart J. Russell and Peter Norvig, *Artificial Intelligence: A Modern Approach* (3rd edition), Prentice Hall, Upper Saddle River, NJ, 2009.

Stephen Northcutt and Judy Novak, *Network Intrusion Detection* (3rd edition), New Riders, Indianapolis, IN, 2003.

Daniel Barbará and Sushil Jajodia, *Applications of Data Mining in Computer Security*, Kluwer, Norwell, MA, 2002.

Tom Mitchell, *Machine Learning*, McGraw Hill, New York, 1997.

Richard O. Duda, Peter E. Hart, and David G. Stork, *Pattern Classification* (2nd edition), Wiley, New York, 2001.

Christopher M. Bishop, *Pattern Recognition and Machine Learning*, Springer, Heidelberg, 2006.

Jiawei Han and Micheline Kamber, *Data Mining Concepts and Techniques*, Morgan Kaufmann, San Francisco, CA, 2001.

David J. Hand, Heikki Mannila, and Padhraic Smyth, *Principles of Data Mining*, MIT Press, Cambridge, MA, 2001.

David J. C. MacKay, *Information Theory, Inference, and Learning Algorithms*, Cambridge University Press, Cambridge, U.K., 2003.

Jaideep Vaidya, Christopher W. Clifton, and Yu Michael Zhu, *Privacy Preserving Data Mining*, Springer, New York, 2006.

References

Abraham, A., C. Grosan, and C. Martin-Vide. Evolutionary design of intrusion detection programs. In: *International Journal of Networks Security* 4 (3) (2007a): 328–339.

Abraham, A., R. Jain, J. Thomas, and S.Y. Han. DSCIDS: Distributed softcomputing intrusion detection system. *Journal of Network and Computer Applications* 30 (1) (2007b): 381–398.

Agrawal, R. and R. Srikant. Privacy-preserving data mining. In: *Proceedings of the ACM SIGMOD Conference on Management of Data*, Dallas, TX, 2000, pp. 439–450.

Apiletti, D., E. Baralis, T. Cerquitelli, and V. D'Elia. Characterizing network traffic by means of the NetMine framework. *Computer Networks* 53 (6) (2008): 774–789.

Axelsson, S. *Intrusion Detection Systems: A Survey and Taxonomy*. Göteborg, Sweden: Department of Computer Engineering, Chalmers University, 2000.

Barak, B., A. Herzberg, D. Naor, and E. Shai. The proactive security toolkit and applications. In: *Proceedings of the 6th ACM Conference on Computer and Communications Security*, Singapore, 1999, pp. 18–27.

Barni, M., C. Orlandi, and A. Piva. A privacy-preserving protocol for neural-network-based computation. In: *Proceedings of the 8th Workshop on Multimedia and Security*, Geneva, Switzerland, 2006, pp. 146–151.

Canetti, R., R. Gennaro, A. Herzberg, and D. Naor. Proactive security: Long-term protection against break-ins. *CryptoBytes* 3 (1997): 1–8.

Cannady, J. Artificial neural networks for misuse detection. In: *Proceedings of the 1998 National Information Systems Security Conference (NISSC'98)*, Arlington, VA, 1998, pp. 443–456.

Chandola, V., E. Banerjee et al. Data mining for cyber security. In: *Data Warehousing and Data Mining Techniques for Computer Security*, edited by A. Singhal. Springer, New York, 2006.

Chebrolu, S., A. Abraham, and J.P. Thomas. Feature deduction and ensemble design of intrusion detection systems. *Computers & Security* 24 (2005): 1–13.

Chen, W.H., S.H. Hsu, and H.P. Shen. Application of SVM and ANN for intrusion detection. *Computers & Operations Research* 32 (2005): 2617–2634.

Cuppens, F. and A. Miège. Alert correlation in a cooperative intrusion detection framework. *IEEE Symposium on Research in Security and Privacy*, Oakland, CA, 2002.

Dain, O. and R. Cunningham. Building scenarios from a heterogeneous alert stream. In: *Proceedings of the 2001 IEEE Workshop on Information Assurance and Security*, West Point, NY, 2001a, pp. 231–235.

Dain, O. and R. Cunningham. Fusing a heterogeneous alert stream into scenarios. In: *Proceedings of the 2001, ACM Workshop on Data Mining for Security Applications*, Philadelphia, PA, 2001b, pp. 1–13.

Debar, H., M. Dacier, and A. Wespi. Toward taxonomy of intrusion detection systems. *Computer Networks* 31 (1999): 805–822.

Denning, D. An intrusion-detection model. *IEEE Transactions on Software Engineering* 13 (2) (1987): 118–131.

Du, W. and Z. Zhan. Building decision tree classifier on private data. In: *Proceedings of the IEEE ICDM Workshop on Privacy, Security and Data Mining*, Maebashi City, Japan, 2002.

Du, W., Y.S. Han, and S. Chen. Privacy-preserving multivariate statistical analysis: Linear regression and classification. In: *Proceedings of SIAM International Conference on Data Mining (SDM)*, Lake Buena Vista, FL, 2004.

Endler, D. Intrusion detection: Applying machine learning to solaris audit data. In: *Proceedings of the 1998 Annual Computer Security Applications Conference (ACSAC)*, Los Alamitos, CA, 1998, pp. 268–279.

Erman, J., M. Arlitt, and A. Mahanti. Traffic classification using clustering algorithms. In: *Proceedings of the 2006 ACM SIGCOMM Workshop on Mining Network Data*, Pisa, Italy, 2006.

Ertöz, L., M. Steinbach, and V. Kumar. Finding clusters of different sizes, shapes, and densities in noisy, high dimensional data. In: *Proceedings of the Third SIAM International Conference on Data Mining*, San Francisco, CA, 2003, pp. 47–58.

Evfimievski, A., R. Srikant, R. Agrawal, and J. Gehrke. Privacy preserving mining of association rules. In: *Proceedings of the 8th ACM SIGKDDD International Conference on Knowledge Discovery and Data Mining*, Edmonton, Canada, 2002.

Feinstein, L., D. Schnackenberg, R. Balupari, and D. Kindred. Statistical approaches to DdoS attack detection and response. In: *Proceedings of DARPA Information Survivability Conference and Exposition*, Washington, DC, 2003, pp. 303–314.

Ghosh, A.K., J. Wanken, and F. Charron. Detecting anomalous and unknown intrusions against programs. In: *Proceedings of the 1998 Annual Computer Security Applications Conference (ACSAC)*, Scottsdale, AZ, 1998.

Ghosh, A.K., and A. Schwartzbard. A study in using neural networks for anomaly and misuse detection. In: *Proceedings of the 8th USENIX Security Symposium*, Washington, DC, 1999, pp. 141–152.

Ghosh, A.K., A. Schwartzbard, and M. Schatz. Learning program behavior profiles for intrusion detection USENIX Association. In: *Proceedings of the 1st USENIX Workshop on Intrusion Detection and Network Monitoring*, Santa Clara, CA, 1999.

Hodge, V.J. and J. Austin. A survey of outlier detection methodologies. *Artificial Intelligence Review* 22 (2) (2004): 85–126.

Homeland Security Council. *National Strategy for Homeland Security*. 2007, p. 36, http://www.dhs.gov/xlibrary/assets/nat_strat_homeland-security_2007.pdf

Hu, W.J., Y.H. Liao, and V.R. Vemuri. Robust support vector machines for anomaly detection in computer security. In: *Proceedings of the International Conference on Machine Learning*, 2003, pp. 282–289.

Jung, J., V. Paxson, A.W. Berger, and H. Balakrishnan. Fast portscan detection using sequential hypothesis testing. In: *IEEE Symposium on Security and Privacy*, Oakland, CA, 2004.

Kantarcioglu, M. and C. Clifton. Privately computing a distributed k-nn classifier. In: *Proceedings of the 8th European Conference on Principles and Practice of Knowledge Discovery in Databases*, Pisa, Italy, 2004, pp. 279–290.

Kruegel, C. and T. Toth. Using decision trees to improve signature-based intrusion detection. In: *Proceedings of the 6th International Workshop on the Recent Advances in Intrusion Detection*, West Lafayette, IN, 2003, pp. 173–191.

Lakhina, A., M. Crovella, and C. Diot. Characterization of network-wide anomalies in traffic flows. In: *Proceedings of the 4th ACM SIGCOMM Conference on Internet Measurement*, Taormina, Sicily, Italy, 2004, pp. 201–206.

Lakhina, A., M. Crovella, and C. Diot. Mining anomalies using traffic feature distributions. In: *Proceedings of the 2005 Conference on Applications, Technologies, Architectures, and Protocols for Computer Communications*, Philadelphia, PA, 2005.

Lee, W. and W. Fan. Mining system audit data: Opportunities and challenges. *SIGMOD Record* 30 (4) (2001): 33–44.

Lee, W. and S.J. Stolfo. Data mining approaches for intrusion detection. In: *Proceedings of the 7th USENIX Security Symposium*, San Antonio, TX, 1998.

Lee, W. and S.J. Stolfo. A framework for constructing features and models for intrusion detection systems. *ACM Transactions on Information and System Security (TISSEC)* 2 (4) (2000): 227–261.

Lee, W., S.J. Stolfo, and K.W. Mok. A data mining framework for building intrusion detection models. In: *Proceedings of the IEEE Symposium on Security and Privacy*, 1999, pp. 120–132.

Leung, K. and C. Leckie. Unsupervised anomaly detection in network intrusion detection using clusters. In: *Proceedings of the Twenty-Eighth Australasian Conference on Computer Science*, 2005, pp. 333–342.

Li, X., F. Bian, M. Crovella, C. Diot, R. Govindan, G. Iannaccone, and A. Lakhina. Detection and identification of network anomalies using sketch subspaces. In: *Proceedings of the 6th ACM SIGCOMM Conference on Internet Measurement*, 2006, pp. 147–152.

Liao, Y.H. and V.R. Vemuri. Use of K-nearest neighbor classifier for intrusion detection. *Computers & Security* 21 (5) (2002): 439–448.

Liu, Z., G. Florez, and S.M. Bridges. A comparison of input representations in neural networks: A case study in intrusion detection. In: *Proceedings of the 2002 International Joint Conference on Neural Networks*, Honolulu, HI, 2002.

Mahoney, M.V. and P.K. Chan. Learning nonstationary models of normal network traffic for detecting novel attacks. In: *Proceedings of the Eighth ACM SIGKDD International Conference on Knowledge Discovery and Data Mining*, Edmonton, Canada, 2002, pp. 376–386.

Mahoney, M.V. and P.K. Chan. Learning rules for anomaly detection of hostile network traffic. In: *Proceedings of the 3rd International Conference on Data Mining*, Melbourne, FL, 2003, pp. 601–603.

Meza, J., S. Campbell, and D. Bailey. *Mathematical and Statistical Opportunities in Cybersecurity*, Paper LBNL-1667E, Lawrence Berkeley National Laboratory, Berkeley, CA, 2009.

Muelder, C., L. Chen, R. Thomason, K.L. Ma, and T. Bartoletti. Intelligent classification and visualization of network scans. In: *Proceedings of the Workshop on Visualization for Computer Security*, Sacramento, CA, 2007.

Mukkamala, S. and A.H. Sung. A comparative study of techniques for intrusion detection. In: *Proceedings of the 15th IEEE International Conference on Tools with Artificial Intelligence*, 2003, pp. 570–577.

Ning, P., D. Xu, C. Healey, and R.S. Amant. Building attack scenarios through integration of complementary alert correlation method. In: *Proceedings of the 11th Annual Network and Distributed System Security Symposium*, San Diego, CA, 2004.

Patcha, A. and J.M. Park. An overview of anomaly detection techniques: Existing solutions and latest technological trends. *Computer Networks* 51 (12) (2007): 3448–3470.

Porras, P.A. and P.G. Neumann. EMERALD: Event monitoring enabling responses to anomalous live disturbances. In: *Proceedings of the Nineteenth Computer Security*, Baltimore, MD, 1997, pp. 353–365.

Portnoy, L., E. Eskin, and S. Stolfo. Intrusion detection with unlabeled data using clustering. In: *Proceedings of ACM CSS Workshop on Data Mining Applied to Security (DMSA)*, Philadelphia, PA, 2001.

Ringberg, H., A. Soule, J. Rexford, and C. Diot. Sensitivity of PCA for traffic anomaly detection. *ACM SIGMETRICS Performance Evaluation Review* 35 (1) (2007): 109–120.

Schultz, M.G., E. Eskin, E. Zadok, and S.J. Stolfo. Data mining methods for detection of new malicious executables. In: *DARPA Information Survivability Conference and Exposition (DISCEX)*, Anaheim, CA, 2001.

Siddiqui, M., M.C. Wang, and J. Lee. A survey of data mining techniques for malware detection using file features. In: *Proceedings of the 46th Annual Southeast Regional Conference*, Auburn, Canada, 2008.

Simon, G., H. Xiong, E. Eilertson, and V. Kumar. Scan detection: A data mining approach. In: *Proceedings of the Sixth SIAM International Conference on Data Mining (SDM)*, Bethesda, MD, 2006, pp. 118–129.

Smaha, S.E. Haystack: An intrusion detection system. In: *IEEE Fourth Aerospace Computer Security Applications Conference*, Orlando, FL, 1988, pp. 37–44.

Soule, A., K. Salamatian, and N. Taft. Combining filtering and statistical methods for anomaly detection. In: *Proceedings of the Fifth ACM SIGCOMM Conference on Internet Measurement*, Berkeley, CA, 2005.

Srinivas, M., S. Andrew, A. Ajith, and R. Vitorino. Intrusion detection systems using adaptive regression splines. In: *The Sixth International Conference on Enterprise Information Systems*, Porto, Portugal, 2004.

Staniford, S., J.A. Hoagland, and J.M. McAlerney. Practical automated detection of stealthy portscans. *Journal of Computer Security* 10 (2002a): 105–136.

Staniford, S., J.A. Hoagland, and J.M. McAlerney. Practical automated detection of stealthy portscans. In: *Proceedings of the 7th ACM Conference on Computer and Communications Security*, Athens, Greece, 2002b.

Staniford-Chen, S., S. Cheung, R. Crawford, M. Dilger, J. Frank, J. Hoagland, K. Levitt, C. Wee, R. Yip, and D. Zerkle. GrIDS: A graph-based intrusion detection system for large networks. In: *The 19th National Information Systems Security Conference*, Baltimore, MD, 1996.

Stolfo, S.J., W. Lee, P.K. Chan, W. Fan, and E. Eskin. Data mining-based intrusion detectors: An overview of the Columbia IDS project. *ACM SIGMOD Record* 30 (4) (2001): 5–14.

Su, M., G. Yu, and C. Lin. A real-time network intrusion detection system for large-scale attacks based on an incremental mining approach. *Computers and Security* 28 (5) (2009): 301–309.

Vaidya, J. and C. Clifton. Privacy-preserving k-means clustering over vertically partitioned data. In: *Proceedings of the Ninth ACM SIGKDD International Conference on Knowledge Discovery and Data Mining*, Washington, DC, 2003.

Verykios, V.S., E. Bertino, I.N Fovino, L.P. Provenza, Y. Saygin, and Y. Theodoridis. State-of-the-art in privacy preserving data mining. *ACM SIGMOD Record* 33 (1) (2004): 50–57.

Warrender, C., S. Forrrest, and B. Pearlmutter. Detecting intrusions using system calls: Alternative data models. In: *IEEE Symposium on Security and Privacy*, Oakland, CA, 1999, pp. 133–145.

Wright, R. and Z. Yang. Privacy-preserving Bayesian network structure computation on distributed heterogeneous data. In: *Proceedings of the tenth ACM SIGKDD International Conference on Knowledge Discovery and Data Mining*, Seattle, WA, 2004.

Xu, K., X.L. Zhang, and S. Bhattachayya. Internet traffic behavior profiling for network security monitoring. *IEEE/ACM Transactions on Networking (TON)* 16 (6) (2008): 1241–1252.

Yamanishi, K. and J.I. Takeuchi. Discovering outlier filtering rules from unlabeled data: Combining a supervised learner with an unsupervised learner. In: *Proceedings of the Seventh ACM SIGKDD International Conference on Knowledge Discovery and Data Mining*, San Francisco, CA, 2001, pp. 389–394.

Yamanishi, K., J.I. Takeuchi, G. Williams, and P. Milne. On-line unsupervised outlier detection using finite mixtures with discounting learning algorithms. In: *Proceedings of the Sixth ACM SIGKDD International Conference on Knowledge Discovery*, Boston, MA, 2000.

Ye, N., X.Y. Li, Q. Chen, S.M. Emran, and M.M Xu. Probabilistic techniques for intrusion detection based on computer audit data. *IEEE Transactions on Systems, Man, and Cybernetics—Part A: Systems and Humans* 31 (4) (2001): 266–274.

Ye, N., S.M. Emran, Q. Chen, and S. Vilbert. Multivariate statistical analysis of audit trails for host-based intrusion detection. *IEEE Transactions on Computers* 51 (2002): 810–820.

Yu, H., X. Jiang, and J. Vaidya. Privacy-preserving SVM using nonlinear kernels on horizontally partitioned data. In: *Proceedings of the 2006 ACM Symposium on Applied Computing*, Dijon, France, 2006.

Zhang, J. and M. Zulkernine. A hybrid network intrusion detection technique using random forests. In: *Proceedings of the First International Conference on Availability, Reliability and Security*, 2006a, pp. 262–269.

Zhang, J. and M. Zulkernine. Anomaly based network intrusion detection with unsupervised outlier detection. In: *IEEE International Conference on Communications*, Istanbul, Turkey, 2006b.

Chapter 2

Classical Machine-Learning Paradigms for Data Mining

We are drowning in information but starved for knowledge.

John Naisbitt
Megatrends: Ten New Directions Transforming Our Lives

Data mining flourishes because the information influx in ubiquitous applications calls for data management, pattern recognition and classification, and knowledge discovery. Cyberinfrastructures generate peta-scale data sets for daily monitoring and pattern profiling in cybersecurity models. To facilitate the application of data-mining techniques in cybersecurity protection systems, we comprehensively study the classic data-mining and machine-learning paradigms. In this chapter, we introduce the fundamental concepts of machine learning in Section 2.1. We categorize classic machine-learning methods into supervised learning and unsupervised learning, and present the respective methodologies, which will be used in cybersecurity techniques. In Section 2.2, we highlight a variety of techniques, such as resampling, feature selection, cost-effective learning, and performance evaluation metrics, that can be used to improve and evaluate the quality of machine-learning methods in mining cyberinfrastructure data. Since malicious behaviors occur either rarely or infrequently among cyberinfrastructures, classic machine-learning techniques must adopt machine-learning techniques to perform unbalanced learning accurately. In Section 2.3, we address several challenges that arise when we apply the classic data-mining and machine-learning methods to discovering cyberinfrastructures. Finally, we summarize the emerging research directions in machine learning for cybersecurity in Section 2.4.

2.1 Machine Learning

Machine learning is the computational process of automatically inferring and generalizing a learning model from sample data. Learning models use statistical functions or rules to describe the dependences among data and causalities and correlations between input and output (Jain et al., 2000). Theoretically, given an observed data set X, a set of parameters θ, and a learning model $f(\theta)$, a machine-learning method is used to minimize the learning errors $E(f(\theta), X)$, between the learning model $f(\theta)$ and the ground truth. Without loss of generalization, we obtain the learning errors using the difference between the predicted output $f(\hat{\theta})$ and the observed sample data, where $\hat{\theta}$ is the set of approximated parameters derived from the optimization procedures for minimization of the objective function of learning errors. Machine-learning methods differentiate from each other because of the selection of the learning model $f(\theta)$, the parameters θ, and the expression of learning error $E(f(\theta), X)$.

To make a clear representation in the following review, we start with some notations used in the book. Given a training data set S with m samples ($|S| = m$), d dimensional feature space F, and a l-dimensional class label set $C = \{C_1, ..., C_l\}$, we have paired samples and target labels $S = \{(x_i, y_i)\}$, $i = 1, ..., m$, and $F = \{f_1, f_2, ..., f_d\}$, where $x_i \in X$ is an instance and $y_i \in Y$ is the class label of instance x_i.

2.1.1 Fundamentals of Supervised Machine-Learning Methods

In supervised machine learning, an algorithm is fed sample data that are labeled in meaningful ways. The algorithm uses the labeled samples for training and obtains a model. Then, the trained machine-learning model can label the data points that have never been used by the algorithm. The objective of using a supervised machine-learning algorithm is to obtain the highest classification accuracy. The most popular supervised machine-learning methods include artificial neural network (ANN), support vector machine (SVM), decision trees, Bayesian networks (BNs), k-nearest neighbor (KNN), and the hidden Markov model (HMM).

2.1.1.1 Association Rule Classification

An association rule can be seen as an extension of the correlation property to more than two dimensions, since it can find associated isomorphisms among multiple attributes. We explain the basics of association rules as follows.

Let $E = \{I_1, I_2, \ldots, I_k\}$ be a set of items and D be a database consisting of N transactions $T_1, T_2, \ldots, T_N$. Each transaction T_j, $\forall 1 \leq j \leq N$ is a set of items such that $T_j \subseteq E$. We present an association rule $A \Rightarrow B$ with the following constraints:

1. $\exists T_j, A, B \in T_j$,
2. $A \subseteq E$, $B \subseteq E$, and
3. $A \cap B \in \varphi$.

In the above rule, A (left-hand side of rule) is called the antecedent of the rule, and B (right-hand side of rule) is called the precedent of the rule. Since many such rules may be presented in the database, two interestingness measures, *support* and *confidence*, are provided for association rules. *Support* indicates the percentage of data in the database that shows the correlation, and *confidence* indicates the conditional probability of a precedent if the antecedent has already occurred. Using the notations above, we define the *support* and *confidence* below

$$Support(A \Rightarrow B) = \frac{\left|\#T_i \mid A, B \in T_i\right|}{N},$$

$$Confidence(A \Rightarrow B) = \frac{\left|\#T_i \mid A, B \in T_i\right|}{\left|\#T_i \mid A \in T_i\right|}.$$

An association rule is considered strong if the support and confidence of a rule are greater than user-specified minimum support and minimum confidence thresholds.

Let the above A describe frequent patterns of attribute-value pairs, and let B describe class labels. Then, association rules can conduct effective classification of A. Association rules have advantages in elucidating interesting relationships, such as causality between the subsets of items (attributes) and class labels. Strong association rules can classify frequent patterns of attribute-value pairs into various class labels. However, elucidation of all interesting relationships by rules can lead to computational complexity, even for moderate-sized data sets. Confining and pruning the rule space can guide association rule mining at a fast speed.

2.1.1.2 Artificial Neural Network

An ANN is a machine-learning model that transforms inputs into outputs that match targets, through nonlinear information processing in a connected group of artificial neurons (as shown in Figure 2.1), which make up the layers of "hidden" units. The activity of each hidden unit and output $\hat{Y}$ is determined by the composition of its input X and a set of neuron weights W: $\hat{Y} = f(X, W)$, where W refers to the matrix of weight vectors of hidden layers. For example, Figure 2.1 presents an ANN structure with four inputs, one output, and two hidden layers. W^1 and W^2

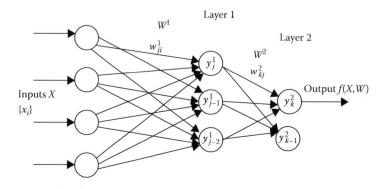

Figure 2.1 Example of a two-layer ANN framework.

are weight vectors for layer 1 and layer 2, respectively. Layer 1 has three neurons, and layer 2 has two neurons.

When ANN is used as a supervised machine-learning method, efforts are made to determine a set of weights to minimize the classification error. One well-known method that is common to many learning paradigms is the least mean-square convergence. The objective of ANN is to minimize the errors between the ground truth Y and the expected output $f(X; W)$ of ANN as $E(X) = (f(X; W) - Y)^2$. The behavior of an ANN depends on both the weights and the transfer function T_f, which are specified for the connections between neurons. For example, in Figure 2.1, the net activation at the jth neuron of layer 1 can be presented as

$$y_j^1 = T_f \left(\sum_i x_i \cdot w_{ji}^1 \right). \tag{2.1}$$

Subsequently, the net activation at the kth neuron of layer 2 can be presented as

$$y_k^2 = T_f \left(\sum_j y_j^1 \cdot w_{kj}^2 \right). \tag{2.2}$$

This transfer function typically falls into one of three categories: linear (or ramp), threshold, or sigmoid. Using the linear function, the output of T_f is proportional to the weighted output. Using the threshold method, the output of T_f depends on whether the total input is greater than or less than a specified threshold value. Using the sigmoid function, the output of T_f varies continuously but not linearly, as the input changes. The output of the sigmoid function bears a greater resemblance to real neurons than do linear or threshold units. In any application of these three functions, we must consider rough approximations.

ANN encompasses diverse types of learning algorithms, the most popular of which include feed-forward back-propagation (BP), radial basis function (RBF) networks, and self-organizing map (SOM). SOM ANN is an unsupervised learning technique, and we discuss it in Section 2.1.2.4.

In feed-forward BP ANN, information is transformed from an input layer through hidden layers to an output layer in a straightforward direction without any loop included in the structure of network (e.g., Figure 2.1). In feed-forward BP ANN, we train the ANN structure as follows. First, we feed input data to the network and the activations for each level of neurons are cascaded forward. We compare the desired output and real output to update BP ANN structure, e.g., weights in different layers, layer-by-layer in a direction of BP from the output layer to the input layer.

RBF ANN has only one hidden layer and uses a linear combination of nonlinear RBFs in the transfer function T_f. For instance, we can express the output of a RBF ANN as follows:

$$f(X,W) = \sum_{i=1}^{n} w_i \cdot T_f \left(\|X - c_i\| \right), \tag{2.3}$$

where

w_i and c_i are the weight and center vectors for neuron i

n is the number of neurons in the hidden layer

Typically, the center vectors can be found by using k-means or KNN. The norm function can be Euclidean distance, and the transfer function T_f can be Gaussian function.

ANN methods perform well for classifying or predicting latent variables that are difficult to measure and solving nonlinear classification problems and are insensitive to outliers. ANN models implicitly define the relationships between input and output, and, thus, offer solutions for tedious pattern recognition problems, especially when users have no idea what the relationship between variables is. ANN may generate classification results that are harder to interpret than those results obtained from the classification methods that assume functional relationships between data points, such as using associate rules. However, ANN methods are data dependent, such that the ANN performance can improve with increasing sample data size.

2.1.1.3 Support Vector Machines

Given data points X in an n dimensional feature space, SVM separates these data points with an $n - 1$ dimensional hyperplane. In SVM, the objective is to classify the data points with the hyperplane that has the maximum distance to the nearest

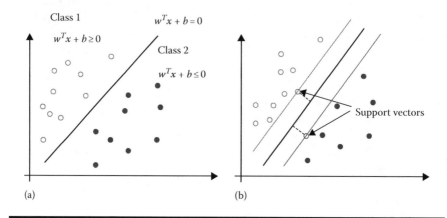

Figure 2.2   SVM classification. (a) Hyperplane in SVM. (b) Support vector in SVM.

data point on each side. Subsequently, such a linear classifier is also called the maximum margin classifier. As shown in Figure 2.2a, any hyperplane can be written as the set of points X satisfying $w^T x + b = 0$, where the vector w is a normal vector perpendicular to the hyperplane and b is the offset of the hyperplane $w^T x + b = 0$ from the original point along the direction of w.

Given labels of data points X for two classes: class 1 and class 2, we present the labels as $Y = +1$ and $Y = -1$. Meanwhile, given a pair of (w^T, b), we classify data X into class 1 or class 2 according the sign of the function $f(x) = sign(w^T x + b)$, as shown in Figure 2.2a. Thus, the linear separability of the data X in these two classes can be expressed in the combinational equation as $y \cdot (w^T x + b) \geq 1$. In addition, the distance from data point to the separator hyperplane $w^T x + b = 0$ can be computed as $r = (w^T x + b)/\|w\|$, and the data points closest to the hyperplane are called support vectors. The distance between support vectors is called the margin of the separator (Figure 2.2b). Linear SVM is solved by formulating the quadratic optimization problem as follows:

$$\arg\min_{w,b}\left(\frac{1}{2}\|w\|^2\right),$$

$$\text{s.t.} \quad y\left(w^T x + b\right) \geq 1. \tag{2.4}$$

Using kernel functions, nonlinear SVM is formulated into the same problem as linear SVM by mapping the original feature space to a higher-dimensional feature space where the training set is separable by using kernel functions. Nonlinear SVM is solved by using a soft margin to separate classes or by adding slack variables, as shown in Equation 2.4.

SVM is better than ANN for achieving global optimization and controlling the overfitting problem by selecting suitable support vectors for classification.

SVM can find linear, nonlinear, and complex classification boundaries accurately, even with a small training sample size. SVM is extensively employed for multi-type data by incorporating kernel functions to map data spaces. However, selecting kernel functions and fine-tuning the corresponding parameters using SVM are still trial-and-error procedures. SVM is fast, but its running time quadruples when a sample data size doubles.

Unfortunately, SVM algorithms root in binary classification. To solve multi-class classification problems, multiple binary-class SVMs can be combined by classifying each class and all the other classes or classifying each pair of classes.

2.1.1.4 Decision Trees

A decision tree is a tree-like structural model that has leaves, which represent classifications or decisions, and branches, which represent the conjunctions of features that lead to those classifications. A binary decision tree is shown in Figure 2.3, where C is the root node of the tree, A_i (i = 1, 2) are the leaves (terminal nodes) of the tree, and B_j (j = 1, 2, 3, 4) are branches (decision point) of the tree.

Tree classification of an input vector is performed by traversing the tree beginning at the root node, and ending at the leaf. Each node of the tree computes an inequality based on a single input variable. Each leaf is assigned to a particular class. Each inequality that is used to split the input space is only based on one input variable. Linear decision trees are similar to binary decision trees, except that the inequality computed at each node takes on an arbitrary linear form that may depend on multiple variables. With the different selections of splitting criteria, classification and regression trees and other tree models are developed.

As shown in Figure 2.3, a decision tree depends on if–then rules, but requires no parameters and no metrics. This simple and interpretable structure allows decision trees to solve multi-type attribute problems. Decision trees can also manage missing values or noise data. However, they cannot guarantee the optimal accuracy that other machine-learning methods can. Although decision trees are easy

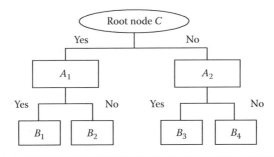

Figure 2.3 Sample structure of a decision tree.

to learn and implement, they do not seem to be popular methods of intrusion detection. A possible reason for the lack of popularity is that seeking the smallest decision tree, which is consistent with a set of training examples, is known to be NP-hard.

2.1.1.5 Bayesian Network

The BN, also called the belief network, uses factored joint probability distribution in a graphical model for decisions about uncertain variables. The BN classifier is based on the Bayes rule that gives a hypothesis H of classes and data x, we have, then

$$P(H \mid x) = \frac{P(x \mid H)P(H)}{P(x)}, \tag{2.5}$$

where
$P(H)$ denotes prior probability of each class without information about a variable x
$P(H \mid x)$ denotes posterior probability of variable x over the possible classes
$P(x \mid H)$ denotes the conditional probability of x given likelihood H

As shown in Figure 2.4, BNs are presented with nodes representing random variables and arcs representing probabilistic dependencies between variables, and conditional probabilities encoding the strength of the dependencies, while unconnected nodes refer to variables that are independent of each other. Each node is associated with a probability function corresponding to the node's parent variables. The node always computes posterior probabilities given proof of the parents for

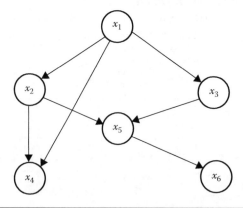

Figure 2.4   Bayes network with sample factored joint distribution.

the selected nodes. For example, in Figure 2.4, the factored joint probability of the network is computed as

$$\mathbf{p}(x_1, x_2, x_3, x_4, x_5, x_6) = \mathbf{p}(x_6 \mid x_5)\ \mathbf{p}(x_5 \mid x_3, x_2)\ \mathbf{p}(x_4 \mid x_2, x_1)\ \mathbf{p}(x_3 \mid x_1)\ \mathbf{p}(x_2 \mid x_1)\ \mathbf{p}(x_1),$$

where

$\mathbf{p}(\cdot)$ denotes probability of a variable
$\mathbf{p}(\cdot|\cdot)$ denotes conditional probability of variables

Naïve Bayes is a simple BN model that assumes all variables are independent. Using the Bayes rule for Naïve Bayes classification, we need to find the maximum likelihood hypothesis, which determines the class label, for each testing data x. Given observed data x and a group of class labels $C = \{c_j\}$, a Naïve Bayes classifier can be solved by maximum a posteriori probability (MAP) hypothesis for the data as follows:

$$\arg\max_{c_j \in C} P(x|c_j)P(c_j). \tag{2.6}$$

Naïve Bayes is efficient for inference tasks. However, Naïve Bayes is based on a strong independence assumption of the variables involved. Surprisingly, the method gives good results even if the independence assumption is violated.

2.1.1.6 Hidden Markov Model

In the previous sections, we have discussed machine-learning methods for data sets that consist of independent and identically distributed (iid) samples from sample space. In some cases, data may be sequential, and the sequences may have correlation. To solve the sequential learning problems, a dynamic BN method, HMM has been proposed for supervised learning of the sequential patterns, e.g., speech recognition (Rabiner, 1989).

In HMM, the observed samples y_t, $t = 1, \ldots, T$, have an unobserved state x_t at time t (as shown in Figure 2.5). Figure 2.5 shows the general architecture of an HMM. Each node represents a random variable with the hidden state x_t and observed value y_t at time t. In HMM, it is assumed that state x_t has a probability distribution over the observed samples y_t and that the sequence of observed samples embed information about the sequence of states. Statistically, HMM is based on the Markov property that the current true state x_t is conditioned only on the value of the hidden variable x_{t-1} but is independent of the past and future states. Similarly,

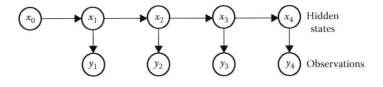

Figure 2.5 Architecture of HMM.

the observation y_t only depends on the hidden state x_t. The most famous solution to HMM is the Baum–Welch algorithm, which derives the maximum likelihood estimate of the parameters of the HMM given a data set of output sequences.

Let us formulate the HMM using the above notations as follows. Given that Y and X are the fixed observed samples and state the sequence of length T defined above, $Y = (y_1, ..., y_T)$ and $X = (x_1, ..., x_T)$, then, we have the state set S and the observable data set O, $S = (s_1, ..., s_M)$ and $O = (o_1, ..., o_N)$. Let us define A as the state transition array $[A_{i,j}]$, $i = 1, ..., M$, $j = 1, ..., M$, where each element $A_{i,j}$ represents the probability of state transformation from s_i to s_j. The transformation can be calculated as follows:

$$A_{i,j} = \text{prob}(x_t = s_j \mid x_{t-1} = s_i). \tag{2.7}$$

Let us define B as the observation array $[B_{j,k}]$, $j = 1, ..., M$, $k = 1, ..., N$, where each element B_{jk} represents the probability of the observation o_k has the state s_j. The observation array can then be calculated as follows:

$$B_{j,k} = \text{prob}(y_t = o_k \mid x_t = s_j). \tag{2.8}$$

Let us define π as the initial probability array $[\pi_t]$, $t = 1, ..., T$, where π_t represents the probability that the observation y_t has the state s_i, $i = 1, ..., \pi$ can be expressed as

$$\pi_i = \text{prob}(x_1 = s_i). \tag{2.9}$$

We then define an HMM using the above definitions, as follows:

$$\lambda = (A, B, \pi). \tag{2.10}$$

The above analysis is the evaluation of the probability of observations, which can be summarized in the algorithm in four steps as follows:

Step 1. Initialize for $t = 1$, according to the initial state distribution π.
Step 2. Deduct the observation value at time t corresponding to Equation 2.8.
Step 3. Deduct the new state at time $t + 1$ according to Equation 2.9.
Step 4. Iterate Steps 2 through 4 until $t = T$.

Given the HMM described in Equation 2.10, we can predict the probability of observations Y for a specific state sequence X and the probability of the state sequence X as

$$\text{prob}(Y \mid X, \lambda) = \prod_{t=1}^{T} \text{prob}(y_t \mid x_t, \lambda), \tag{2.11}$$

and

$$\text{prob}(X \mid \lambda) = \pi_1 \cdot A_{12} \cdot A_{23} \dots A_{T-1T}. \tag{2.12}$$

Then, we obtain the probability of observation sequence Y for state sequence X as follows:

$$\text{prob}(Y\mid\lambda)=\sum_{X}\text{prob}(Y\mid X,\lambda)\cdot\text{prob}(X\mid\lambda). \qquad (2.13)$$

Users are generally more interested in predicting the hidden state sequence for a given observation sequence. This decoding process has a famous solution known as the Viterbi algorithm, which uses the maximized probability at each step to obtain the most probable state sequence for the partial observation sequence. Given an HMM model λ, we can find the maximum probability of the state sequence $(x_1, \dots, x_t)$ for the observation sequence $(y_1, \dots, y_t)$ at time t as follows:

$$\rho_t(i)=\max_{x_1,\dots x_{t-1}}\ \big(\text{prob}(x_1,\dots,x_t=s_i,y_1,\dots,y_t\mid\lambda)\big). \qquad (2.14)$$

The Viterbi algorithm follows the steps listed below:

Step 1. Initialize the state for $t = 1$, according to the initial state distribution π:

$$\rho_1(i)=\pi_i B_i(y_1),\quad 1\le i\le M,\quad \psi_1(i)=0. \qquad (2.15)$$

Step 2. Deduct the observation value at time t corresponding to the following equation:

$$\rho_t(j)=\max_i[\rho_t(i)A_{ij}]B_j(y_t),\quad 2\le t\le T,\quad 1\le j\le M, \qquad (2.16)$$

and

$$\psi_t(j)=\arg\max_i[\rho_{t-1}(i)A_{ij}],\quad 2\le t\le T,\quad 1\le j\le M. \qquad (2.17)$$

Step 3. Iterate Steps 2 through 4 until $t = T$.

HMM can solve sequential supervised learning problems. It is an elegant and sound method to classify or predict the hidden state of the observed sequences with a high degree of accuracy when data fit the Markov property. However, when the true relationship between hidden sequential states does not fit the proposed HMM structure, HMM will result in poor classification or prediction. Meanwhile, HMM suffers from large training data sets and complex computation, especially when sequences are long and have many labels. The assumption of the independency between the historical states, or future states and the current states also hampers the development of HMM in achieving good classification or prediction accuracy. For further discussion and a detailed analysis of the above algorithms in HMM, readers should refer to Roweis and Ghahramani (1999) and Dietterich (2002).

2.1.1.7 Kalman Filter

Unlike HMM, the Kalman filter performs based on the assumption that the true state is dependent on and evolved from the previous state. This state transition is expressed as follows:

$$x_t = A_t x_{t-1} + B_t u_t + w_t, \quad w_t \sim N(0, Q_t), \tag{2.18}$$

$$y_t = H_t x_t + v_t, \quad v_t \sim N(0, R_t), \tag{2.19}$$

where
   A_t is the state transition array between states x_t and x_{t-1} at time t and $t-1$
   B_t refers to the control model for control vector u_t
   w_t presents the process noise
   H_t is the observation transition array between the hidden state x_t and the observation y_t at time t
   v_t denotes the measurement noise in observation
   Q_t denotes the variance of noise of hidden state x_t
   R_t denotes the variance of noise of observation y_t

As shown in Equations 2.18 and 2.19, the Kalman model recursively estimates the present current systematic state x_t based on the previous state x_{t-1} and present observation y_t.

The Kalman filter estimates the posterior state using a minimum mean-square error estimator. Two phases are included in Kalman filter algorithms: apriori estimate phase, in which the current state is estimated from the previous state, and a posteriori estimate phase, in which the current apriori estimate is combined with current observation information to refine the state estimate. In the apriori estimate phase, the model is assumed to be perfect and without process noise, and the error covariance of the next state is estimated. In the posteriori estimate phase, a gain factor, called Kalman gain, is computed to correct state estimation and minimize the error covariance. The above is presented in detail in Figure 2.6.

The most employed Kalman filters include the basic Kalman filter, the extended Kalman filter, the unscented Kalman filter, and the Stratonovich–Kalman–Bucy filter (Dietterich, 2002). The Kalman filter enables the online continuous estimation of state vectors for updating observations. Implicatively, the Kalman filter uses all the historical and current information for state prediction, which results in the smooth interpretation and estimation of states. However, the accuracy of the Kalman filter most relies on the assumption that noises and initial states have normal distributions. The loss of the normality assumption can result in biased estimators.

2.1.1.8 Bootstrap, Bagging, and AdaBoost

In complex machine-learning scenarios, a single machine-learning algorithm cannot guarantee satisfactory accuracy. Researchers attempt to ensemble a group of

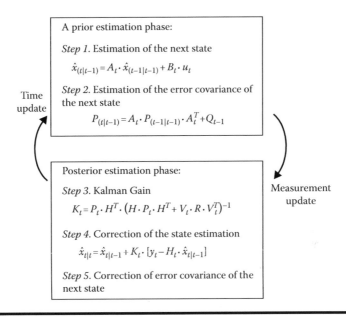

Figure 2.6   Workflow of Kalman filter.

learning algorithms to improve the learning performance over single algorithms. In the next sections, we will introduce several popular ensemble learning methods, including random forest, bagging, bootstrap, and AdaBoost.

Bootstrap is most employed to yield a more informative estimate of a general statistics, such as bias and variance of an estimator. Given sample set $X = \{x_i\}$, $i = 1, \ldots, m$, a set of parameters θ, and a learning model $f(\theta)$, a machine-learning method minimizes the learning errors $E(f(\theta), X)$. In bootstrap, m data points are selected randomly with replacements from data set X. By repeating this sampling process independently B times, we obtain B Bootstrap sample sets. The parameters in function $f(\theta)$ can be estimated by each sample set, and we obtain a set of bootstrap estimate $\{\hat{\theta}_j\}$, $j = 1, \ldots, B$. Then, the estimate on bootstrap samples is

$$\hat{\theta}^B = \sum_{j=1}^{B} \hat{\theta}_j. \qquad (2.20)$$

As the bootstrap selects samples repeatedly from X, each data sample has $1/m$ probability of being chosen in each selection. When m is big enough, the probability that x_i is selected m_{boot} times is Poisson distribution with mean unity. We can obtain its unbiased estimate of parameters $\hat{\theta}$ statistically over sample data X. Then, we can obtain the bootstrap estimate of the parameter bias at

$$\text{bias}_b(\theta) = \hat{\theta}^B - \hat{\theta}, \qquad (2.21)$$

and the bootstrap estimate of the parameter variance,

$$\text{var}_b(\theta) = \frac{1}{B}\sum_{j=1}^{B}\left(\hat{\theta}_j - \hat{\theta}\right)^2. \tag{2.22}$$

Bootstrap aggregating (bagging) aims to sample data sets for an ensemble of classifiers. In bagging, $m' < m$ data points are selected randomly with replacement from the data set X. Repeating this sampling process multiple times, we obtain different training sample sets for each member of the ensemble of classifiers. The final decision is the average of the member-model decisions by voting. Bagging is commonly used to improve the stability of decision trees or other machine-learning models. However, bagging can result in redundant and lost information because of replacement.

Boosting is used to boost a strong machine-learning algorithm with an arbitrarily high accuracy by using a weighted training data set. Boosting algorithms start by finding a weak machine-learning algorithm that performs better than random guessing. Then, member classifiers are integrated into an accurate classification ensemble over the most informative subset of the training data. Boosting modifies bagging in two ways: weighting the sample and weighting the vote. Boosting can result in higher accuracy than bagging when a data set is noise free, although bagging stays more robust in noisy data.

Adaptive boosting (AdaBoost) is the most popular variant of boosting algorithms. Given training data set S with m examples ($|S| = m$), and an l-dimensional class label set $C = \{C_1, \ldots, C_l\}$, we have a paired data set $S = \{(x_i, y_i)\}$, $i = 1, \ldots, m$, where $x_i \in X$ is an instance and $y_i \in Y$ and $y_i \in C$ form the class label of sample x_i. We assign a sample weight $w_t(i)$, $t = 1, \ldots T$, to each sample x_i to determine its probability of being selected as the training set for a member classifier at iterative step t. This weight will be raised if the sample is not accurately classified. Likewise, it will be lowered if the sample is accurately classified. In this way, boosting will select the most informative or difficult samples over each iterative step k. AdaBoost algorithms can be summarized in the following steps (as shown in Figure 2.7):

Step 1. Initialize the sample weight $w_1(i) = 1/m$, $i = 1, \ldots, m$.

Step 2. Train the weak learner $h_t : X \rightarrow Y$ by the weighted samples S_t defined by $w_t(i)$ and S, where h_t is assigned label $+ 1$ when $h_t(x_i) = y_i$, else -1.

Step 3. Calculate the learning error of h_t by $\varepsilon_t = \displaystyle\sum_{i:h_t(x_i)(\neq y_i)} w_t(i)$ and the weight $\alpha_t = (1/2)\ln[(1 - \varepsilon_t)/\varepsilon_t]$.

Step 4. Update sample weights over the training set: $w_{t+1}(i) = (w_t(i)\exp(-w_t y_i h_t(x_i)))/Z_t$, where Z_t denotes the normalization factor to ensure that $w_t(i)$ is a distribution.

Step 5. Iterate Steps 2 through 4 until $t = T$, weighted voting among the ensemble of classifiers: $H(x) = \text{sign}\left(\displaystyle\sum_{t=1}^{T}\alpha_t h_t(x)\right)$.

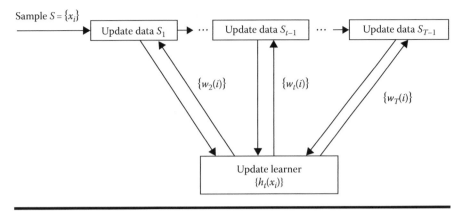

Figure 2.7   Workflow of AdaBoost.

In the above steps, α_t measures the confidence when assigning those samples to the classifier h_t at step t.

AdaBoost offers accurate machine-learning results without overfitting problems that are common in machine-learning algorithms. AdaBoost is simple for implementation and has a solid theoretical background and good generalization. Therefore, AdaBoost has been employed for various learning tasks, e.g., feature selection. However, Adaboost can only guarantee suboptimal learning solutions after greedy learning. Readers should refer to Freund and Schapire (1999), Breiman (1996), and Freund and Schapire (1997) for a better understanding of the underlying theory and algorithms of AdaBoost.

2.1.1.9 Random Forest

The random forest algorithm is the most popular bagging ensemble classifier (Breiman, 2001). Random forest consists of many decision trees. The output of random forest is decided by the votes given by all individual trees. Each decision tree is built by classifying the bootstrap samples of the input data using a tree algorithm. Then, every tree will be used to classify testing data. Each tree has a decision to label any testing data. This label is called a vote. Finally, the forest decides the classification result of the testing data after collecting the most votes among trees.

Let us review the random forests using some definitions given by Breiman (2001). Given a forest consisting of K trees $\{T_1, \ldots, T_K\}$, a random vector θ_k is generated for the kth tree, $k = 1, \ldots, K$. The vectors $\{\theta_k\}$ are iid random vectors for tree modeling. These vectors are defined in tree construction. For instance, in random selection, these vectors are composed of random integers randomly selected from $\{1, \ldots, N\}$ where N is the split number. Using training data set and the vectors $\{\theta_k\}$, a tree grows and casts a unit vote for the most popular class at input x. We present the kth tree classifier as $f(x, \theta_k)$ and obtain a random forest consisting of the collection of those trees, $\{ f(x, \theta_k)\}$, $k = 1, \ldots, K$.

The accuracy of random forest depends on the strength of the individual trees and a measure of the dependence between the trees. Moreover, the random forest algorithm uses bootstrap to avoid biases in tree building, such that cross validation (CV) is not needed in training and testing. However, random forest suffers from the class imbalance due to the maximization of the prediction accuracy in its algorithm. Tree-based methods have a high variance. The hierarchical structure of trees can produce an unstable result. The average of many trees, e.g., using bagging, can improve stability of ensemble learning algorithms.

2.1.2 Popular Unsupervised Machine-Learning Methods

2.1.2.1 k-Means Clustering

Clustering is the assignment of objects into groups (called clusters) so that objects from the same cluster are more similar to each other than objects from different clusters. The sameness of the objects is usually determined by the distance between the objects over multiple dimensions of the data set. Clustering is widely used in various domains like bioinformatics, text mining, pattern recognition, and image analysis. Clustering is an approach of unsupervised learning where examples are unlabeled, i.e., they are not pre-classified.

k-Means clustering partitions the given data points X into k clusters, in which each data point is more similar to its cluster centroid than to the other cluster centroids. The k-means clustering algorithm generally consists of the steps described as follows:

Step 1. Select the k initial cluster centroids, $c_1, c_2, c_3 \dots, c_k$.
Step 2. Assign each instance x in S to the cluster that has a centroid nearest to x.
Step 3. Recompute each cluster's centroid based on which elements are contained in it.
Step 4. Repeat Steps 2 through 3 until convergence is achieved.

Two key issues are important for the successful implementation of the k-means method: the cluster number k for partitioning and the distance metric. Euclidean distance is the most employed metric in k-means clustering. Unless the cluster number k is known before clustering, no evaluation methods can guarantee the selected k is optimal. However, researchers have tried to use stability, accuracy, and other metrics to evaluate clustering performance.

2.1.2.2 Expectation Maximum

The expectation maximization (EM) method is designed to search for the maximum likelihood estimates of the parameters in a probabilistic model. The EM methods assume that parametric statistical models, such as the Gaussian mixture model (GMM), can describe the distribution of a set of data points. For example, when the histogram of the data points is regarded as an estimate of the probability density function (PDF), the parameters of the function can be estimated by using the histogram.

Correspondingly, in EM, the expectation (E) step and the maximization (M) step are performed iteratively. The E step computes an expectation of the log likelihood with respect to the current estimate of the distribution for the latent variables, and M step computes the parameters that maximize the expected log likelihood found on the E step. These parameters are then used to determine the distribution of the latent variables in the next E step. The two steps are described as follows:

Step 1. (Expectation step) Given sample data x and undiscovered or missed data z, the expected log likelihood function of parameters θ can be estimated by θ^t:

$$f\left(\theta|\theta^t\right) = E[\log L(\theta; x, z)]. \tag{2.23}$$

Step 2. (Maximization step) Using the estimated parameter at step t, the maximum likelihood function of the parameters can be obtained through

$$\theta^{t+1} = \arg\max_{\theta}\left(f\left(\theta|\theta^t\right)\right). \tag{2.24}$$

In the above, the maximum likelihood function is determined by the marginal probability distribution of the observed data $L(\theta; x)$. In the following, we formulate the EM mathematically and describe the iteration steps in depth.

Given a set of data points $S = \{x_1, \ldots, x_m\}$, we describe the mixture of PDFs as follows:

$$p(x_i) = \sum_{j=1}^{K} \alpha_j p_j(x_i; \theta_j). \tag{2.25}$$

In the above, α_j is the proportion of the jth density in the mixture model, and $\sum_{j=1}^{K} \alpha_j = 1$. $p_j(x_i; \theta_j)$ is the jth density function with parameter set θ_j. The GMM is the most employed, and has two parameters, mean μ_j and covariance Σ_j, such that $\theta_j = (\mu_j, \Sigma_j)$. If we assume that θ_j^t is the estimated value of parameters (μ_j, Σ_j) at the t-th step, then θ_j^{t+1} can be obtained iteratively. The EM algorithm framework follows:

$$\alpha_j^{t+1} = \frac{1}{r} \sum_{i=1}^{m} a_{ij}^t, \tag{2.26}$$

$$u_j^{t+1} = \frac{\sum_{i=1}^{m} a_{ij}^t x_j}{\sum_{j=1}^{m} a_{ij}^t}, \tag{2.27}$$

$$\sum_{j}^{t+1} = \frac{\sum_{i=1}^{m} d_{ij}^{t} \left[\left(x_i - u_j^t \right) \left(x_i - u_j^t \right)^T \right]}{\sum_{i=1}^{m} d_{ij}^{t}}, \tag{2.28}$$

$$d_{ij}^{t} = \frac{a_i \cdot p\left(x_j; u_i^t, \Sigma_i^t \right)}{\sum_{i=1}^{m} a_i \cdot p\left(x_j; u_i^t, \Sigma_i^t \right)}. \tag{2.29}$$

These equations state that the estimated parameters of the density function are updated according to the weighted average of the data point values where the weights are the weights from the E step for this partition. The EM cycle starts at an initial setting of $\theta_j^0 = \left(u_j^0, \Sigma_j^0 \right)$ and updates the parameters using Equations 2.26 through 2.29 iteratively. The EM algorithm converges until its estimated parameters cannot change.

The EM algorithm can result in a high degree of learning accuracy when given data sets have the same distribution as the assumption. Otherwise, the clustering accuracy is low because the model is biased.

2.1.2.3 k-Nearest Neighbor

In KNN, each data point is assigned the label that has the highest confidence among the k data points nearest to the query point. As shown in Figure 2.8, $k = 5$, the query point X_{query}, is classified to the negative class with a confidence of 3/5, because there are three negative and two positive points inside the circle. The numbers of nearest neighbors (k) and the distance measure are key components for the KNN algorithm. The selection of the number k should be based on a CV over a number of k settings. Generally, a larger number k reduces the effect of data noise on

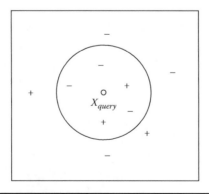

Figure 2.8 KNN classification (k = 5).

classification, while it may blur the distinction between classes. A good rule-of-thumb is that k should be less than the square root of the total number of training patterns. In two-class classification problems, k should be selected among odd numbers to avoid tied votes.

The most employed distance metric is Euclidean distance. Given two data points in n dimensional feature space: $x_1 = (x_{11}, \ldots, x_{1n})$ and $x_2 = (x_{21}, \ldots, x_{2n})$, the Euclidean distance between these points is given by

$$dist(x_1, x_2) = \left(\sum_{i=1}^{n} (x_{1i} - x_{2i})^2 \right)^{0.5}. \tag{2.30}$$

Because KNN does not need to train parameters for learning while it remains powerful for classification, it is easy to implement and interpret. However, KNN classification is time consuming and storage intensive.

2.1.2.4 SOM ANN

SOM ANN, also known as Kohonen, characterizes ANN in visualizing low-dimensional views of high-dimensional data by preserving neighborhood properties of the input data. For example, a two-dimensional SOM consists of lattices. Each lattice corresponds to one neuron. Each lattice contains a vector of weights of the same dimension as the input vectors, and no neurons connect with each other. Each weight of a lattice corresponds to an element of the input vector. The objective of SOM ANN is to optimize the area of lattice to resemble the data for the class that the input vector belongs to. The SOM ANN algorithms consist of the following steps:

Step 1. Initialize neuron weights.
Step 2. Select a vector randomly from training data for the lattice.
Step 3. Find the neuron that has the weights most matching the input vector.
Step 4. Find the neurons inside the neighborhood of the matched neurons in Step 3
Step 5. Fine-tune the weight of each neighboring neuron obtained in Step 4 to increase the similarity of these neurons and the input vector
Step 6. Iteratively run Steps 1 through 5 until convergence

SOM ANN forms a semantic map where similar samples are mapped close together and dissimilar samples are mapped further apart. We can visualize the similarity by the Euclidean distance between weight vectors of neighboring cells. SOM preserves the topological relationships between input vectors.

2.1.2.5 Principal Components Analysis

The principal components analysis (PCA) represents the raw data in a lower dimensional feature space to convey the maximum useful information. The extracted principal feature components are located in the dimensions that represent the variability of the data. Given data set $\{x_1, \ldots, x_n\}$ in d-dimensional feature space, we put these data points in matrix X with each row presenting a data point and each column denoting a feature. We present the matrix X as $X = [x_1, \ldots, x_n]^T$, and transpose as T. Then, we adjust the data points to be centered around zero by $X - \overline{X}$, where $\overline{X}$ denotes the matrix in space $\mathbb{R}^{n \times d}$, with each row presenting the mean of all rows in matrix X. Such an operation ensures that the PCA result will not be skewed due to the difference between features.

Then, an empirical covariance matrix of $X - \overline{X}$ can be obtained by $C = (1/d)$ $\sum (X - \overline{X})(X - \overline{X})^T$. After we obtain the empirical covariance matrix of $X - \overline{X}$, we then obtain a matrix V, $V = [v_1, \ldots, v_d]$, of eigenvectors in space $\mathbb{R}^d$, which consists of a set of d principal components in d dimensions. Each eigenvector v_i, $i = 1, \ldots, m$, in matrix V corresponds to an eigenvalue λ_i in the diagonal matrix D, where $D = V^{-1}CV$ and $D_{ij} = \lambda_i$, if $i = j$; else $D_{ij} = 0$. Finally, we rank eigenvalues and reorganize the corresponding eigenvectors such that we can find the significance of variance along the different orthogonal directions (denoted by eigenvectors). Then, we can present the ith principal component or eigenvector v_i as follows:

$$v_i = \arg\max_{\|v\|=1} \left\| \left((X - \overline{X}) - \sum (X - \overline{X}) v_j v_j^T \right) v \right\|. \tag{2.31}$$

In the above equation, $(X - \overline{X})v_j$ captures the amount of variance projected along the direction of v_j. This variance is also denoted by the corresponding eigenvalue λ_i. The application of the PCA method can be summarized in four steps as follows:

Step 1. Subtract the mean in each of the dimensions to produce a data set with a mean of zero.

Step 2. Calculate the covariance matrix.

Step 3. Calculate the eigenvectors and eigenvalues of the covariance matrix.

Step 4. Rank the eigenvectors by eigenvalues from highest to lowest to get the components in order of significance.

As shown in Figure 2.9, v_1 and v_2 are the first and second principal components obtained by PCA. λ_1 and λ_2 are the corresponding first and second eigenvalues. The principal components are orthogonal in feature space, while v_1 represents the original variance in the data set and v_2 represents the remaining variance.

PCA projects original data on a lower dimensional data space while retaining data variance as much as possible. PCA can extract uncorrelated features to describe the embedded statistical information of data sets. PCA has assumption that input data distribute continuously and normally, although non-normally distributed data may also result in good projection. However, when data spread in a complicated manifold, PCA can fail. PCA provides little visualization implications of the features in the original data sets.

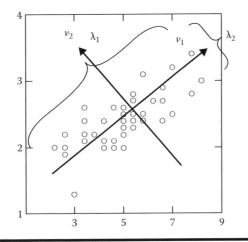

Figure 2.9 Example of PCA application in a two-dimensional Gaussian mixture data set.

2.1.2.6 Subspace Clustering

In clustering methods, e.g., *k*-means, similar objects are grouped by measuring the distance between them. For high-dimensional data, objects are dispersed in space and distance, as the measure of "sameness" becomes meaningless (referred as the "curse of dimensionality"). Irrelevant dimensions act as noise, masking the clusters in a given data set. In order to reduce the number of dimensions, feature transformation (e.g., PCA in the next section) combines some attributes to produce a new attribute. However, since dimensions are not essentially eliminated, subspace clustering is not useful for clustering high-dimensional data with a number of irrelevant attributes. Feature selection is used to find the subset that contains the most relevant attributes. However, even this subset may have irrelevant attributes for some clusters. In addition, overlapping clusters will be ignored.

Subspace clustering, which performs a localization search and focuses on only a subset of dimensions, is an effective technique in such cases. This technique is similar to feature selection, except that instead of searching the entire data set, the subspace search is localized. The localization of the search makes it possible to find clusters from multiple and overlapping subspaces. The motivation for using subspace clustering is to remove the data that are not coherent with the clustered data. These data can be found by plotting data in the histogram charts with the dimensions as coordinate references.

Subspace clustering algorithms can be categorized as top-down or bottom-up. There are various bottom-up search methods like CLIQUE, MAFIA, cell-based clustering, CLTree, and density-based optimal projective clustering. All of the methods use the apriori style approach. In this style, if there are "*n*" units in "*s*" dimensions, then the *s*-dimensional data will be projected in $(s - 1)$ dimensions. CLIQUE forms a cluster, and it discards the data in the cluster that are repeated during input. The cluster that is formed is represented using the disjunctive normal form (DNF). ENCLUS inherits all the characteristics of CLIQUE, except that it uses entropy to evaluate the clusters. MAFIA inherits all the characteristics of CLIQUE, and it introduces a new concept called parallelism. The cell-based clustering method fixes all the efficiency problems of the previous methods, and it uses an index structure to retrieve data from the clusters. The CLTree method evaluates by considering each cluster separately, unlike the previous methods. In the density-based method, the Monte Carlo algorithm is used to find the subset of data clusters that are not in coherence with other data in the cluster. In top-down subspace search methods, we have different types of methods such as PROCLUS, ORCLUS, FINDIT, and COSA. Readers should refer to L. Parsons, E. Haque, and H. Liu (2004) for details.

2.2 Improvements on Machine-Learning Methods

As discussed above, given a sample data set, a machine-learning algorithm can output a class label. The machine-learning methods have hypothesis that there exist unknown functions for a given sample data set. Using the given training data set, a family of hypotheses can be built, and then functions can be trained. A machine-learning model can be applied on the new data for classification or prediction. These classic machine-learning methods have common drawbacks when applied in cybersecurity applications. For example, classic machine-learning methods cannot use anomaly detection or other cyber defense analysis and decision procedures due to specific problems embedded in the cyber network data, e.g., imbalanced class distributions of normal and anomaly data.

2.2.1 New Machine-Learning Algorithms

Various new learning algorithms have been proposed to classify imbalanced data sets. The objective of these algorithms is to ensure the classification methods achieve optimal performance on unseen data. The representatives of the methods include one-class learners, ensemble methods, and cost-sensitive learners. One-class learners are trained to recognize samples from one class while rejecting samples from another class. In the training process, one-class data are used primarily to identify the minority class successfully. One-class learners are not stable, and the performance of one-class learners is strongly affected by the parameters and kernel used.

Cost-sensitive learners maximize a loss function associated with a data-based cost matrix in which misclassification costs are different, e.g., the costs

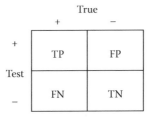

Figure 2.10 Confusion matrix for machine-learning performance evaluation.

for classification results in confusion matrix in Figure 2.10. In the confusion matrix, TP denotes true positive, TN denotes true negative, FP denotes false positive, and FN denotes false negative. The cost-sensitive methods improve the classification performance in imbalanced learning, although it is assumed that the cost matrix is available. Ensemble machine learning integrates the classification results of various classifiers into one classification result in a suitable fashion, such as by voting. This method attempts to generalize the task by training individual classifiers using randomly selected subsets of the data set. As long as each data subset is different, ensemble methods can provide a good discovery of the machine-learning task.

Two methods, bagging and boosting, resample the data set in ensemble classifiers. In the bagging ensemble, each classifier is trained using a different bootstrap of the data set. (Section 2.1.1.9 contains a detailed explanation of the bagging, boosting, and bootstrap methods.) The average bootstrap contains roughly 62% of the samples in the original data. Once each classifier is trained, the final classification result is determined by counting the majority of classifiers' votes. Bagging performs well when individual classifiers can identify large differences in the classifications in the training data.

Boosting is used to weight the most difficult samples that are easily misclassified. In boosting, the probability of misclassification is increased, or vice versa for the series of classifiers. Ensemble methods can be valid only if there is disagreement among classifiers. A combination of classifiers cannot guarantee better performance than an individual classifier.

Additionally, researchers attempt to apply semi-supervised machine-learning methods to combat challenges in using labeled data sets for supervised learning, such as time consumption, expensiveness, limitation of expertise, and the accuracy of labels in collecting labeled data. Especially, semi-supervised learning has applications in cyber anomaly detection (Lakhina et al., 2004). Reinforced learning is a branch of machine learning, which considers the feedback from the finite states in an environment to adapt actions in the environment. Reinforced learning methods particularly have applications in multiagent environments in cyberinfrastructures. We recommend (Kaelbling et al., 1996; Chapelle et al., 2006) for more detailed analyses of semi-supervised learning.

2.2.2 Resampling

As shown in Section 2.1.1.8, bootstrap, bagging, and AdaBoost are supervised machine-learning methods that use resampling. Similarly, other resampling methods are designed to improve classifier accuracies when used in conjunction with algorithms for training classifiers. For example, resampling is commonly used for imbalanced learning. Resampling adds samples to minority classes or reduces samples in majority classes in imbalanced data sets by using artificial mechanisms. The resampling data distribution is closer to a balanced data distribution.

Resampling methods can be classified into the following groups: random oversampling and undersampling, informed undersampling, and synthetic sampling with data generation. Undersampling is performed by reducing samples in the majority class. This technique may miss important information pertaining to the majority class. Oversampling replicates the minority samples, which causes overfitting. The synthetic sampling method generates synthetic data samples for the minority class by using clustering methods, such as finding the nearest neighbors to the current minority samples. This method may increase overlap between classes. Although none of these methods is perfect, studies have shown that sampling methods can improve the overall classification performance of classifiers over unbalanced data sets (H. He and E.A. Garcia, 2009).

2.2.3 Feature Selection Methods

Imbalanced data is commonly accompanied by high-dimensional feature space. Among the high-dimensional features, the existence of many noisy features can hinder and downgrade classifier performance. In the last few years, feature selection and subspace methods have been proposed and evaluated to solve this problem. Feature subset selection methods are used to select a small feature subset among high-dimensional features according to feature selection metrics. It has been demonstrated that feature selection methods perform better than classification algorithms when imbalanced data have the characteristics of high-dimensional feature space.

Feature selection methods can be divided into two categories, feature scalar selection, which selects features individually, and feature vector selection, which selects features based on the mutual correlation between features. Feature scalar selection has the advantage of computation simplification and may not be effective for a data set with mutually correlated features. Feature vector selection methods select the best feature vector combinations.

Feature vector selection methods can be further divided into wrapper and filter-based methods. Wrappers use machine-learning methods, such as black box, and select the features that are most relevant, so that the learning method performs optimally. The search strategies include exhaustive search, beam search, branch and bound, genetic algorithms, greedy search methods, and so on. When wrappers are used, the selected features are prone to overfitting the data. In the filter-based feature selection method, the feature is correlated with a class of features and its corresponding feature subset.

Using a correlation measure leads to an optimal solution in feature selection. Thus, the method focuses on two issues: the correlation measure criteria and the feature selection algorithm. The correlation criteria can be Pearson's correlation coefficient (PCC), mutual information (MI), and other relevant criterions. PCC is a measure of linear dependency between variables and features. It is versatile to continuous or binary variables.

MI can measure nonlinear dependency, which measures the irrelevance of individual variables using the Kullback-leibler divergence. However, MI is harder than PCC to estimate, especially for continuous data. A typical filter-based feature selection method is sequential forward floating selection (SFFS), which finds the best approximation solution with regard to the number of selected features. SFFS starts from an empty feature selection pool and increases the pool using the local optimal feature set in two steps: inclusion and conditional exclusion steps. The heuristic basis of the SFFS algorithm is the assumption that the feature selection criteria are monotonic with the change of feature size and feature set information. SFFS approximates the optimal solution at an affordable computational cost.

2.2.4 Evaluation Methods

The traditional classification metrics include classification accuracy and error, defined as follows:

$$\text{accuracy} = \frac{\#\,\text{TP} + \#\,\text{TN}}{|S|}, \tag{2.32}$$

$$\text{error} = 1 - \text{accuracy}. \tag{2.33}$$

The metrics are sensitive to the change in the data set and are effective when data are not balanced. For example, we have a data set that has a distribution in which 95% of samples are negative and 5% of samples are positive. If 5 of a given test data set of 100 samples are positive and 95 samples are negative, then, even if all test results are classified as negative, the accuracy is 95%. This value is preserved when the number of TN increases while the number of TP decreases the same amount. When the positive result is more important for researchers, the above metrics cannot provide the exact information of the class labels.

To comprehensively evaluate imbalanced learning, especially for minority classification, other metrics are used including precision, recall, *F*-score, *Q*-score, *G*-mean, receiver operating characteristics (ROC), areas under receiver operating characteristics, precision recall curves, and cost curves. The metrics are defined as follows:

$$\text{Precision} = \frac{\#\,\text{TP}}{\#\,\text{TP} + \#\,\text{FP}}, \tag{2.34}$$

$$\text{Recall} = \frac{\#\,\text{TP}}{\#\,\text{TP} + \#\,\text{FN}}, \tag{2.35}$$

$$F\text{-score} = \frac{(1+\beta)^2 \cdot \text{Recall} \cdot \text{Precision}}{\beta^2 \cdot \text{Recall} \cdot \text{Precision}}, \tag{2.36}$$

or

$$F\text{-score} = \frac{(1+\beta)^2 \cdot \#\,\text{TP}}{(1+\beta)^2 \cdot \#\,\text{TP} + \beta^2 \cdot \#\,\text{FN} + \#\,\text{FP}}, \tag{2.37}$$

and

$$G\text{-mean} = \sqrt{\frac{\#\,\text{TP}}{\#\,\text{TP} + \#\,\text{FN}} \cdot \frac{\#\,\text{TN}}{\#\,\text{TN} + \#\,\text{FP}}}. \tag{2.38}$$

Precision, as shown in Equation 2.34, measures the exactness of positive labeling, the coverage of the correct positive labels among all positive-labeled samples. Recall, as shown in Equation 2.36, measures the completeness of positive labeling, the percentage of the correctly labeled positive samples among all positive class samples. Precision is sensitive to data distribution, while recall is not (as shown in the confusion matrix in Figure 2.10). Recall does not reflect how many samples are labeled positive incorrectly, and precision does not provide any information about how many positive samples are labeled incorrectly. *F*-measure combines the above two metrics and assigns the weighted importance on either precision or recall using the coefficient β. Consequently, the *F*-measure provides more insight into the accuracy of a classifier than recall and precision, while remaining sensitive to data distribution. The *G*-mean evaluates the inductive bias of the classifier using the ratio of positive to negative accuracy.

ROC curves provide more insight into the relative balance between the gains (true positive) and costs (false positive) of classification on a given data set. Two evaluation metrics are used in ROC curves as follows:

$$\text{TP}_{\text{rate}} = \frac{\#\,\text{TP}}{|S_{mi}|}, \tag{2.39}$$

$$\text{FP}_{\text{rate}} = \frac{\#\,\text{FP}}{|S_{ma}|}. \tag{2.40}$$

As shown in Figure 2.11, ROC curves are composed of the combinational values of TP_{rate} and FP_{rate}. Each point on the ROC curve (the gray line in Figure 2.11)

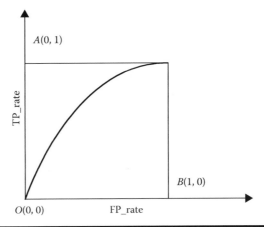

Figure 2.11   ROC curve representation.

corresponds to the performance of a classifier on a given data set. Point A is the perfect classification result with no errors. Point B is the worst classification result, in which all positive labels are incorrect. The point located nearer to point A has a better classification result than the point nearer to point B.

2.2.5 Cross Validation

CV assesses how the results provided by machine-learning methods will generalize to an independent data set. CV is used when the goal of machine learning is prediction, and it is critical to evaluate the performance of a machine-learning method. The purpose of CV is to predict the fit of a model to a validation data set. For example, when parametric machine-learning methods are applied on a data set, generally, the model parameters are optimized to fit the model with the training data as well as possible. When the size of the training data set is small, or when the number of parameters in the model is large, the trained model above does not always fit the validation data as well as it fits the training data, due to the overfitting caused in training.* Using CV methods, sample data is subdivided into disjointed subsets, and machine-learning methods perform the training phase on one subset and the validating phase on the other subset. To reduce variability, multiple rounds of CV are performed using different subdivisions, and the validation results from the rounds are averaged. The most employed CV methods include repeated random subsampling validation, *k*-fold CV, and leave-one-out CV.

---

* Overfitting occurs when a machine-learning model has not captured the true knowledge underlying the sample data, but only describes random error or noise.

2.3 Challenges

Machine learning for data-mining applications in cybersecurity face challenges due to the amount and complexity of growing data in cyberinfrastructures. Intrusions (e.g., network anomalies) are moving targets and are difficult to detect precisely and in a predefined way. Meanwhile, large false alarms make analysis overwhelming due to the lack of labels for intrusion.

2.3.1 Challenges in Data Mining

The challenges are classified into four areas for data-mining applications in cybersecurity: modeling large-scale networks, intrusion discovery, network dynamics, and privacy preserving in data mining.

2.3.1.1 Modeling Large-Scale Networks

Modeling a cyberinfrastructure is challenging, as many common graph measures are difficult to compute for the underlying networks. It is difficult to build the explanatory model of networks due to the requirements for accurate learning and prediction: Realistic networks at different scales are simulated for testing algorithms for defense, and anomalies that do not conform to the model and potentially represent an intrusion or other network problem are detected.

A network model can be extracted partially and amenably for advanced analysis, and a network can be built in a real-world, meaningful way but may not follow the assumption of iid random variables. Moreover, challenges exist in the computation of graphic measures in the network model. Examples of these graphic models have the dynamic network of telecommunications, e-mail communication networks through which viruses spread, and the network of hyperlinks between Web sites. One example of a graphic measure is the graph diameter, i.e., the greatest distance between two nodes in a graph. The computation difficulties call for a data-mining model that discovers the nature of real data using a simpler model.

2.3.1.2 Discovery of Threats

Data-mining cyberinfrastructure for the discovery of threats suffers from the sheer volume and heterogeneous network data, the dynamic change of threats, and the severe imbalanced classes of normal and anomalous behaviors. The above challenges call for the methods that can aggregate information dynamically and locally and across the networks to detect complex multistage attacks and predict potential and rare threats based on the behavior analysis of network event data. The most employed methods for detecting malicious code or behavior use rule-based or statistical models to identify threats in real-time, using adaptive threat detection with temporal data modeling and missing data. The sampling of big-scale network data has to be adaptive to the uncertainty of physical changes of networks, malicious code, and malicious behavior. Adaptive and dynamic modeling is necessary for the temporally evolving data structure and features.

2.3.1.3 Network Dynamics and Cyber Attacks

Many cyber attacks spread malware to vulnerable computers. Due to the conditions triggering the malware, the malware may infect computers in a network in varying degrees. Once the cyber defenders detect the malware, the spread of malware infections is investigated to build the protection system. Novel data-mining methods are necessary to predict future attacks by constantly evolving malware and launch defenses correspondingly. However, the detailed structure of the network is unknown, limiting the knowledge of infection evolution.

2.3.1.4 Privacy Preservation in Data Mining

Data-mining techniques are critical for discovering intrusions in cybersecurity systems. However, data mining can also be used maliciously in cyberinfrastructures to breach privacy. In principle, the more complete data is available for data mining, the more accurate the mining result that will be obtained. However, the comprehensive and accurate data may also raise privacy breach issues. Furthermore, the data-mining result can potentially reveal private information. Privacy preserving data mining (PPDM) protects private data from being stolen or misused by malicious users, while allowing the other data to be extracted for use.

2.3.2 Challenges in Machine Learning (Supervised Learning and Unsupervised Learning)

Machine learning faces challenges that are common for researchers in any application. First, it is difficult to select a good machine-learning algorithm that is amenable for the new data by the comparative evaluation of machine-learning methods. Insufficient knowledge about the performance of the given machine-learning methods in different data sets makes such evaluation difficult. Second, there is no way to provide the exact quantity requirement for training data and validation data. No methods exist to demonstrate that a given machine-learning method can converge.

Third, the relationship between the stability of machine-learning methods and their optimal settings of parameters has not been established. For example, the selection of a cluster number k in k-means clustering is empirical. Normally, researchers believe the best k should be accompanied by the stable performance of the k-means in available data. When the data is not enough to reflect the ground truth in the data distribution, the selected number k is wrong. Meanwhile, another question arises even if this k reflects the small sample data well: What is the relation between the sample data distribution and the true data distribution.

In cybersecurity, machine learning is formulated to classify event data into normal or anomaly classes. Machine learning has two formulations according to the classification objectives. In the first formulation, machine learning detects anomaly patterns by employing a learning mechanism and classifying new network event data into normal or anomaly classes. Inversely, in the second formulation, machine learning detects normal patterns. The first implementation of machine learning is most employed in misuse detection while the second is most employed in anomaly detection. As one of the most used methods in data-mining applications in cybersecurity, machine learning faces pertinent challenges as stated in Section 2.3.1. Machine learning also faces the following obstacles: online learning methods for the dynamic modeling of network data and malware, modeling data with skewed class distributions to handle rare event detection, and feature selection/extraction for data with evolving characteristics.

2.3.2.1 Online Learning Methods for Dynamic Modeling of Network Data

The most employed method for finding the temporal or sequential patterns of an audit data stream is to slide a window across the audit trace and determine whether the short sequence within the sliding window is anomalous or not. Sequences of the same window size are used in training and testing. The primary difficulty with using this method is selecting the appropriate window size for anomaly detection using a good learning method instead of trial-and-error.

Information-theoretic measures have been proposed to describe the regularity of an audit data set and determine the best sliding window size based on the conditional entropy and information cost measures. However, a simple trained detector based on instance cannot be generalized, and the conditional entropy does not affect the appropriate window size. Consequently, a good learning method is needed to find the optimum window size for sequence learning in anomaly detection and dynamic modeling in network.

2.3.2.2 Modeling Data with Skewed Class Distributions to Handle Rare Event Detection

There is a fundamental asymmetry in anomaly detection problems: normal activity is common, and intrusive activity in the network is typically a small fraction of the total network data. One often faces a training set consisting of a handful of attack examples and plenty of normal examples, or no attack example at all. Standard machine-learning classification methods have been found to be biased toward recognizing the majority class in an imbalanced data set. Because classic learning algorithms have the assumption that data distribute equally among classes, the mining accuracy can be represented by the overall classification accuracy across the classes of data. These classification algorithms generalize well to the overall predictive accuracy of training data when data equally distribute across classes.

When a data set is highly skewed, a classifier attempts to classify both the majority and minority samples into the majority class for better classification accuracy over all samples. It has been shown that high predictive accuracy over all samples cannot guarantee the correct classification of minority samples. Because of the lack of attack examples, improved imbalanced machine-learning approaches are needed to generate a meaningful and general classification of the intrusive behavior for intrusion detection. Classification should be focused toward classifying the minority behavior as attack or anomalous.

2.3.2.3 Feature Extraction for Data with Evolving Characteristics

In anomaly detection, there are many different levels at which an intrusion detection system (IDS) can monitor activities in a computer system. Anomalies may be undetectable at one level of granularity or abstraction but easy to detect at another level. For example, a worm attack might escape detection at the level of a single host, but be detectable when the traffic of the whole network is observed and analyzed. One of the biggest challenges in anomaly detection is to choose features (i.e., attributes) that best characterize the user or system usage patterns so that intrusive behavior will be perceived, whereas nonintrusive activities will not be classified as anomalous.

Even at a certain level of monitoring granularity, one often faces a large number of features representing the monitored object's behavior. For instance, a network connection can be characterized with numerous attributes, including basic features such as source and destination IPs, ports, protocols, and other secondary attributes. Meanwhile, an audit trail usually consists of sequences of categorical symbols generated from a large discrete alphabet. A program may issue several hundred unique system calls. The high dimensionality of the data or the large alphabet size gives rise to a large hypothesis search space. This, in turn, not only increases the complexity of the problem of learning normal behavior, but also can lead to large classification errors. Therefore, selecting relevant features and eliminating redundant features is vital to the effectiveness of the machine-learning technique employed. Like other machine-learning applications, anomaly detection often needs an expert to use his or her domain knowledge to select relevant features manually.

2.4 Research Directions

As shown in the above literature review, a significant amount of research has been done in cybersecurity using machine-learning and data-mining methods. However, many fundamental problems await solutions, and the complexity of cybersecurity problems present new research challenges in the domains of machine learning and data mining. The complexity of many learning problems in cybersecurity goes well beyond the capabilities of current machine-learning methods.

In the cybersecurity area, the machine-learning technologies that are being used are not adequate to handle challenges from the huge amount of dynamic and severely imbalanced network data. Machine-learning technologies should be revolutionized so that their potential can be leveraged to address those challenges in cybersecurity. We briefly discuss several aspects for the future research directions in this domain.

2.4.1 Understanding the Fundamental Problems of Machine-Learning Methods in Cybersecurity

Most of the research efforts in machine-learning applications in cybersecurity focus on specific machine-learning algorithms and case studies; only a limited number of principal and consequence theories have been investigated. We have discussed several fundamental problems existing in machine-learning methods, and similarly, fundamental questions await answers in the challenges posed in Section 2.3. For example, an imbalanced learning problem exists in cybersecurity.

The following are the critical questions that remain unanswered in this domain. First, what assumptions make imbalanced learning algorithms work better than algorithms that learn from the original distribution? Second, to what degree should data be balanced such that ordinary machine-learning methods work well? Third, given imbalanced data, what is the optimal solution for an imbalanced machine-learning method, and how can we define the best performance metric for imbalanced learning? Fourth, is there theoretical evaluation of different imbalanced learning methods, such as between resampling and cost-effective learning. The answers to these questions can vastly improve results.

2.4.2 Incremental Learning in Cyberinfrastructures

Theoretically, there is an inadequate understanding of the characteristics and normal behavior of an attack. Without this information, it is difficult to detect excursions from the norm. However, cyberinfrastructure contains a huge amount of data streaming continuously and dynamically. These data are required for incremental learning. Dynamic information challenges machine-learning modeling, whereas "time" adds important information for the understanding and learning of anomalies. New machine-learning principles, methodologies, algorithms, and tools are required for such dynamic modeling to transform raw data into the useful information about their own normal and anomaly behaviors.

2.4.3 Feature Selection/Extraction for Data with Evolving Characteristics

Feature selection/extraction methods partially solve the problems that cybersecurity encounters with imbalanced data sets. However, the existing feature selection/extraction methods extract static information without perturbation.

Cyberinfrastructure is characterized with a large amount of evolving dynamic information. This evolving information requires feature selection/extraction, not only to reduce the dimensionality for machine learning, but also to capture the evolving characteristics. To discover the evolving patterns in data, machine-learning methods have to be combined into feature selection. New machine-learning and feature-selection techniques are required to indentify continuous behavior in data.

2.4.4 Privacy-Preserving Data Mining

PPDM techniques address concerns that the broad use of data mining will threaten the privacy of individuals, industries, and even countries. Meanwhile, PPDM opens opportunities for data mining to protect private data from disclosure. The interaction between legally protected data and data mining has never been explored. PPDM is relatively new and has not been adopted in real-world applications. At this point, it is not clear how much or little private information data-mining methods can disclose. Thus, machine-learning and data-mining methods should be fundamentally investigated to answer this question. Meanwhile, the developed PPDM methods need to be evaluated for researchers to determine how much privacy they can protect.

2.5 Summary

In this chapter, we introduced the fundamental background of machine learning and provided a brief overview of machine-learning formulations and methods for data mining in cybersecurity. We discussed challenging and critical problems that occur when machine-learning methods are applied in the huge amount of temporal and unbalanced network data. We hope that our discussions of the nature of the network data, fundamental problems existing in machine learning, the recommended solutions used to address the problems, and the evaluation methods used to explore the problems will serve as a comprehensive resource for researchers in machine learning, data mining, and cybersecurity. We also hope that our insights into the new research area will help guide potential research in the future.

References

Breiman, L. Bagging predictors. *Machine Learning* 24 (2) (1996): 123–140.
Breiman, L. Random forests. *Machine Learning* 45 (1) (2001): 5–32.
Chapelle, O., B. Schölkopf, and A. Zien, eds. *Semi-Supervised Learning*. Cambridge, MA: The MIT Press, 2006.
Dietterich, T.G. Machine learning for sequential data: A review. In: *Proceedings of the Joint IAPR International Workshop on Structural, Syntactic, and Statistical Pattern Recognition*, Windsor and Ontario, Canada, 2002, pp. 15–30.

Freund, Y. and R.E. Schapire. A decision-theoretic generalization of on-line learning and an application to boosting. *Journal of Computer and System Sciences* 55 (1) (1997): 119–139.

Freund, Y. and R.E. Schapire. A short introduction to boosting (in Japanese, translation by Naoki Abe). *Journal of Japanese Society for Artificial Intelligence* 14 (5) (1999): 771–780.

He, H. and E.A. Garcia. Learning from imbalanced data. *IEEE Transactions on Knowledge and Data Engineering* 21(9) (2009): 1263–1284.

Jain, A.K., R.P.W. Duin, and J. Mao. Statistical pattern recognition: A review. *IEEE Transactions on Pattern Analysis and Machine Intelligence* 22 (1) (2000): 4–37.

Kaelbling, L.P., M.L. Littman, and A.W. Moore. Reinforcement learning: A survey. *Journal of Artificial Intelligence Research* 4 (1996): 237–285.

Lakhina, A., M. Crovella, and C. Diot. Diagnosing network-wide traffic anomalies. In: *Proceedings of the 2004 Conference on Applications, Technologies, Architectures, and Protocols for Computer Communications*, Portland, OR, Vol. 34, No. 4, 2004, pp. 219–230.

Parsons, L., E. Haque, and H. Liu. Subspace clustering for high dimensional data: A review. *SIGKDD Exploration Newsletter* 6 (1) (2004): 90–105.

Rabiner, L.R. A tutorial on hidden Markov models and selected applications in speech recognition. *Proceedings of the IEEE* 77 (2) (1989): 257–286.

Roweis, S. and Z. Ghahramani. A unifying review of linear Gaussian models. *Neural Computation* 11 (2) (1999): 305–345.

Chapter 3

Supervised Learning for Misuse/Signature Detection

If you know both the enemy and yourself, you will fight a hundred battles without danger of defeat; if you are ignorant of the enemy but only know yourself, your chances of winning and losing are equal; if you know neither the enemy nor yourself, you will certainly be defeated in every battle.

Sun Zi
The Art of War

Cyberinfrastructures are vulnerable due to design and implementation flaws, such as errors in the procedure, code, and design of the software. Malicious users attack system vulnerabilities by using a sequence of events, which helps them to break into a cyberinfrastructure. These events result in distinct characteristics that are defined as patterns of attack. Misuse/signature detection techniques target these patterns for further analysis in order to develop protection against or to stop such threats.

We can eliminate all known vulnerabilities in cyberinfrastructures by using supervised learning approaches for misuse/signature detection. Because we have no way of knowing all vulnerabilities, the only resources we can use to learn attack patterns are the sequences of events correlated with the cyber attacks. Thus, the most convenient methods of threat elimination are measuring the similarity between the patterns recognized in the recent activity and the known patterns of various types

57

of cyber attacks, identifying which system vulnerabilities have been used in known attacks and determining what actions cyber administrators should take to defend against such attacks. Moreover, execution signatures vary substantially from one attack category to another, so that specific detection methods are required to classify attack patterns and, thus, to improve detection capability. Researchers have proposed many machine-learning algorithms for misuse detection systems. Reported results show that there is a great berth of room for improvement in detection performance.

In this chapter, we introduce fundamental knowledge, key issues, and challenges in misuse/signature detection systems, such as building efficient rule-based algorithms, feature selection for rule matching and accuracy improvement, and supervised machine-learning classification of attack patterns. First, we present a detailed description of the basic techniques and applications of several representative supervised machine-learning classifiers in a misuse detection system, such as association rules, fuzzy-rule-based method, artificial neural network (ANN), support vector machine (SVM), and genetic programming (GP). Second, we explore the machine-learning methods for feature selection. Such methods include decision trees, classification and regression tree (CART), and Bayesian network (BN). Third, we briefly analyze and discuss the accuracies of these techniques along with other machine-learning algorithms (maximum likelihood Gaussian classifiers, incremental radial basis function, fuzzy adaptive resonance theory mapping, and *k*-nearest neighbor [KNN]) for misuse detection. We explore the limitations and difficulties of using these machine-learning methods in misuse detection systems and outline possible problems such as inadequate ability to detect a novel attack, irregular performance for different attack types, and requirements of the intelligent feature selection. We will guide readers to learn more about the use of advanced machine-learning techniques to solve these problems.

3.1 Misuse/Signature Detection

Misuse detection, also called signature detection, is used to recognize specifically unique patterns of unauthorized behavior to predict and detect subsequent similar attempts. These specific patterns, called signatures, include patterns of specific log files or packets that have been identified as a threat. Each file is composed of signatures, which are unique arrangements of zeros and ones. For example, in a host-based intrusion detection system (IDS), a signature can be a pattern of system calls. In a network-based IDS, a signature can be a specific pattern of the packet such as packet content signatures and/or header content signatures that can indicate unauthorized actions such as improper FTP initiation. The packet includes source or destination IP addresses, source or destination TCP/UDP ports, and IP protocols such as UDP, TCP, and ICMP, and data payloads.

As shown in Figure 3.1, misuse/signature detection methods match the learned patterns and signature of attacks to identify malicious users. If the learned patterns

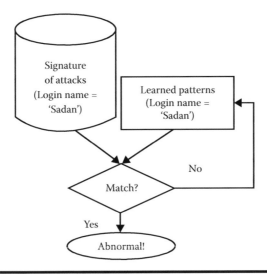

Figure 3.1   Misuse detection using "if–then" rules.

and signature of attacks match, the system will alert the system administrator that a cyber attack has been detected. Then, the administrator will attempt to label the attack. The related information will be delivered to an administrator. For example (see Figure 3.1), if we have an attack signature as "Login name = 'Sadan'," then, when any data matches this signature, the system will alert the administrator that anomalous events have been detected.

Signature detection methods typically search for known potentially malicious information by scanning cyberinfrastructure and, thus, make decisions based on a significant amount of prior knowledge of the attack signatures. For these solutions to work, the security software will need to obtain collections of known cyber attack characteristics. Therefore, the quality and reliability of the signature detection results rely on the frequent updating of the signature database. For example, antispyware tools usually use signature detection techniques to find malicious software embedded in a computational system. When a signature-based antispyware tool is active, it scans files and programs in the system and compares them with the signatures in the database. If there is a match, the tool will alert the system administrator that spyware has been detected and will provide information associated with the spyware, such as the name of the software, the danger level, and the location of the spyware, to cyber administrators.

This technique often locates known threats. However, this technique may cause false alarms. A false alarm is an instance in which an alert occurs although unauthorized access has not been attempted. For example, a user may forget a login password and make multiple attempts to sign into an account. Most site accounts lock for 24 h after three failed login attempts. Attempts after this point can be regarded as attacks. Depending on the robustness and seriousness of a triggered signature, an alarm or notification will be reported to the proper authorities.

The strength of a misuse/signature detection system depends on the sufficiency of the knowledge of the system vulnerabilities and known attack patterns. Traditionally, the construction of the knowledge of a cyberinfrastructure relies heavily on domain experts. Domain experts vary in experience and knowledge, which leads to the incomplete coverage and inaccurate detection of malicious behaviors. Moreover, any variation, evolution, or blending of known attacks can challenge the similarity learning process.

3.2 Machine Learning in Misuse/Signature Detection

As shown in Figure 3.2, a typical misuse/signature detection system consists of five steps: information collection, data preprocessing, misuse/signature identification by matching methods, rules regeneration, and denial of service (DoS) or other security response. The data resources include cyber attribute data such as audit log, network packet flow, and windows registry. Data preprocessing prepares input data for pattern learning by reducing noises and normalizing, selecting, and extracting features. Once these steps have been performed, domain experts or automatic intelligent learning systems build intrusive learning models, such as rule-based expert systems, based on prior knowledge of malicious code and data and vulnerabilities in cyberinfrastructures. Then, we can apply the learned classification models or rules to the incoming data for misuse pattern detection. *If* any cyber information is found to be similar to the attack patterns in an apriori rule, *then* decisions will be made automatically by software or manually by cyber administrators after further

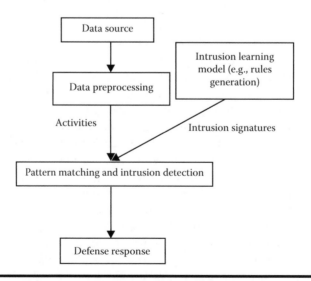

Figure 3.2 Workflow of misuse/signature detection system.

analysis. Consequently, misuse/signature detection can be simply understood as an "*if–then*" sequence as shown in Figure 3.1.

Machine-learning methods play several core roles in misuse detection systems. These approaches can provide feature selection in the data preprocessing step and help build rules or perform pattern classification and recognition in signature identifications. As shown in Figure 3.2, machine-learning algorithms can improve pattern matching and intrusion detection by intelligently comparing the misuse/signature patterns with the collected cyber information. As the training data for the buildup of rules or other machine-learning models are labeled as normal, anomalous, or as specific attack types, most of the machine-learning methods employed in misuse detection systems are supervised. Subsequently, these detection techniques rely on the similarity measure between input events and the signatures of known intrusions. They flag the event that is close to a predefined pattern of intrusion. Thus, known attacks can be detected immediately and realizably with a lower false-positive rate. However, signature detection is ineffective for detecting novel attacks.

3.3 Machine-Learning Applications in Misuse Detection

In this section, we present a variety of misuse techniques that are based on machine-learning methods. We have listed some examples of machine-learning methods applied in misuse detection systems in Table 1.2. Below, we introduce the fundamental techniques of rule-based classifiers, GP, decision tree, and BN. We also discuss the application of these methods, ANN, and SVM in misuse detection system along with examples. We begin with rule-based signature analysis.

3.3.1 Rule-Based Signature Analysis

Many misuse-detection techniques frequently utilize some form of rule-based analysis. Rules describe the correlation between attribute conditions and class labels. When applied to misuse detection, the rules become descriptive scenarios for network attacks. The intrusion detection mechanism identifies a potential attack if a user's activities are found to be consistent with the established rules for detecting a threat. The use of comprehensive rules is critical in the application of expert systems for intrusion detection. Below, we present the fundamentals of associative rules classification and associative rules classification application in misuse detection. In Section 3.3.1.1, we introduce associative classification and association rules. We discuss the application of association rules in misuse detection. In Section 3.3.1.2, we extend the above technique to fuzzy-rule-based classification.

3.3.1.1 Classification Using Association Rules

Agrawal et al. (1993) introduced association rules to capture and represent causal relationships among attributes in a multidimensional database. Association rules classification describes the frequent patterns in a data set, e.g., computer and anti-virus software that appear frequently together in a transaction data set.

For example, let us assume that an association rule from the shell command history file of a user, which is a stream of commands and their arguments, is trn → rec.humor, [0.3, 0.1]. This association rule indicates that 30% of the time when the user invokes trn, he or she is reading the news in rec.humor, and reading this newsgroup accounts for 10% of the activities recorded in his or her command history file. If minimum support is 0.25 and minimum confidence is 0.25, we can say that this rule is strong.

Association rules are generated in two steps. First, we find all frequent itemsets and identify the strong association rules in the frequent itemsets. Mining frequent itemsets from a large data set is challenging, because it generates a large number of itemsets, which satisfy the minimum support threshold, and if any itemset is frequent, its subset should also be frequent. Researchers have proposed many efficient algorithms for association rule mining. Among these methods, an apriori algorithm introduced by Agrawal et al. in 1993 is the most commonly used frequent association rule mining algorithm. This algorithm uses support and confidence measures of interestingness and improves rule mining efficiency by using the prior knowledge of frequent itemset properties that all nonempty subsets of a frequent itemset must also be frequent. Subsequently, the apriori algorithm consists of the following steps.

Step 1. Find all length 1 itemsets that satisfy the minimum support threshold.

Step 2. Iteratively generate sets of candidate length k itemsets by combining two length $k - 1$ frequent itemsets. Prune the infrequent length k candidate itemsets that include any infrequent length $k - 1$ subsets. Find all length k itemsets among the candidate pool, which satisfy the minimum support threshold.

Step 3. Generate all nonempty subsets for each of the frequent itemsets generated in Step 2.

Step 4. For each nonempty subset generated in Step 3, output the corresponding rules for the frequent itemsets that satisfy minimum confidence.

Application Study 1: Application of Association Rules in Audit Data for Misuse Detection

In this study, we demonstrate the application of association rules as a misuse detection technique. The following is an example, based on host-based record data, of one telnet session recorded by a mid-size company server (shown in Table 3.1). There are 15 transactions in this database. Using the apriori algorithm, we can obtain the association rules, which are extracted between items of time, hostname, command,

Table 3.1   Example of Shell Command Data

Time	Hostname	Command	Arg
am	Bluedawg	cd	home
am	Bluedawg	vi	tex
am	Bluedawg	mail	boss
am	Bluedawg	subject	conference
am	Bluedawg	vi	tex
am	Bluedawg	mail	boss
am	Bluedawg	subject	progress
am	Bluedawg	cd	work
am	Bluedawg	vi	tex
am	Bluedawg	mail	hotel
am	Bluedawg	subject	travel
am	Bluedawg	vi	tex
am	Bluedawg	mail	boss
am	Bluedawg	subject	plan
am	Bluedawg	logout	

and arg. Since the basic apriori algorithm does not consider domain knowledge, its application results in a large number of irrelevant rules. Given prior knowledge, we can reduce redundant rules in postprocessing or use item constraints over attribute values. For example, in our case study, Lee et al. (1999) proposed to use association rules and frequent episodes computed from audit data to guide further audit data gathering and feature selection. They then modified two algorithms using axis and reference attributes as item constraints to compute only the relevant patterns. In addition, an iterative approximate mining procedure was applied across each level to uncover the low frequency, important patterns. In Table 3.2, we list two interesting rules that we generated using the shell command records in Table 3.1.

We recommend readers find the detailed description of these methods in Lee et al. (1999).

Application Study 2: Application of Association Rules in Network Traffic Data for Misuse Detection

In Lee et al. (1999), the authors presented an example of network traffic data at a company. The association rules were extracted between items of label, service,

Table 3.2   Examples of Association Rules for Shell Command Data

Association Rules	Meaning
Command = vi ⇒ time = am	When using vi to edit a file, the user is always editing a tex file, in the morning and at host Bluedawg and 25% of the data has this pattern.
Host = Bluedawg	
Arg = tex	
(confident = 1.0, support = 0.25)	
Command = vi ⇒ time = am	The mail is 75% sent to boss, in the morning and at host Bluedawg and 19% of the data has this pattern.
Host = Bluedawg	
Arg = boss	
(support = 0.25, confident = 0.75)	

Table 3.3   Example of "Traffic" Connection Records

Label	Service	host_ count	srv_ count	host_ REJ_%	host_diff_ srv_%	...
Normal	ecr_i	1	1	0	1	...
DOS	ecr_i	350	350	0	0	...
PROBING	User-level	231	1	85	89	...
Normal	http	1	0	0	1	...
...	...	...	...	...	...	...

Source: Lee, W.K. et al., A data mining framework for building intrusion detection models, in: *Proceedings of the IEEE Symposium on Security and Privacy,* Oakland, CA, 1999, pp. 120–132. © [1999] IEEE.

host_count, srv_count, host_REJ_%, and host_diff_srv_% as shown in Table 3.3. The following were two association rules for DOS and PROBING attacks:

$$\{ \text{service} = \text{ecr\_i}, \text{host\_count} \geq 5, \text{host\_srv\_count} \geq 5 \Rightarrow \text{DOS} \},$$

and

$$\{ \text{host\_REJ\%} \geq 83\%, \text{host\_diff\_srv\%} \geq 87\% \Rightarrow \text{PROBING} \}.$$

The first rule refers to the transactions that occur when icmp echo request service is called, and the connections over the past two seconds on the same destination host with the same service provider as the current information source are equal to or more than five. The connection for these transactions was labeled a DOS attack.

The second rule refers to the transactions that occur on the same destination host when the rejected connections over the past two seconds account for not less than 83%, and the different services account for not less than 87%. The connection for these transactions was labeled a PROBING attack.

3.3.1.2 Fuzzy-Rule-Based

The rule-based misuse detection system can be outwitted by a slight variance in attacks, which can cause mismatches between anomalous data and signatures. This mismatch is due to the hard cutoff in the rules generated by experts or intelligent systems. Human experts can update rules after new attacks are detected and identified. However, the reliance on human expertise can lead to uncertain reasoning in a noisy and changing cyberinfrastructure environment. To generate human-like expertise in machine learning and the decision-making process, researchers have developed fuzzy-rule-based systems to exploit the tolerance for handling and manipulating uncertainty, robustness, and partial truth to achieve tractability. The most difficult task in building a fuzzy classification system is to find a set of fuzzy rules pertaining to the specific classification problem that you are trying to solve.

As discussed above, a rule-based system classifies the membership of data points in a binary term: a data point belongs to either a normal or an anomalous data set (or in a multiset system, a data point that has to fall into one and only one set). We can indicate the membership of any data point in a set by {0, 1}. In fuzzy set theory, the membership of any data point in a set is described by a value in the range [0.0, 1.0], with 0.0 representing absolute falseness and 1.0 representing absolute truth.

Given a set of data points $X = \{x\}$ and a fuzzy set A, the membership of each data point $x \in A$ can be denoted by a membership function m as $f(x)$, where A is a fuzzy set and $f: A \rightarrow [0, 1]$. For each data set, $x \in A$, $f(x)$ is the weight of membership of x. In particular, an element mapping to the value 0 means that the member is not included in the fuzzy set, while 1 describes a fully included member. Values strictly between 0 and 1 characterize the fuzzy members. The set $\{x \in A | m(x) > 0\}$ is called the support of the fuzzy set (A,m).

A fuzzy system is characterized by a set of linguistic statements based on expert knowledge. For example, a rule is in the form of "*if:* antecedent–*then: consequent*," e.g., rule: *if* (src_ip == dst_ip) *then* "land attack." Correspondingly, a fuzzy rule is presented in the form of "*if:* antecedent–*then:* consequent [weight]," e.g., *if* (src_ip == dst_ip) *then* "land attack" [0.6]. We present this rule as

$$FZ(\text{rule}) = FO(\text{src\_ip} == \text{dst\_ip}) * 0.6,$$

where $FO(\text{src\_ip} = = \text{dst\_ip})$ justifies and evaluates the input (src_ip, dst_ip) using a fuzzy operator function FO.* Then, the above result is applied to the consequent "land attack" by assigning the weight of the rule through the fuzzy membership function.

Given the data set $X = \{x_i\}$, $i = 1, \ldots, n$ in d-dimensional feature space, we denote each data point x_i as $x_i = (x_{i1}, \ldots, x_{id})$. Then, the pattern space can be represented as unit cube $[0, 1]^d$ and $x_i \in [0, 1]^d$. In Abraham et al. (2007a), each feature dimension is partitioned into K grids with interval $[\alpha_{k-1}, \alpha_k]$ denoting the kth interval and $\alpha_0 = 0$, $\alpha_K = 1$. Correspondingly, the 0.5-level set of the membership function $h_k(\cdot)$, $k = 1, \ldots, K$ is defined with $\alpha_k = (1/(K - 1))(k - 0.5)$. Given C classes in a data set,

$$m^c(x_i) = \frac{1}{n_c} \sum_{\substack{x_i \in c \\ j \in \{1, \ldots, d\}}} h_k(x_{ij}) \text{ for } x_{ij} \in [\alpha_{k-1}, \alpha_k] \text{ represents the membership weight}$$

of data point x_i in class c, $c \in \{1, \ldots, C\}$, where n_c denotes the number of data points classified in class c. Subsequently, a single fuzzy rule for class c can be presented as the following,

$$R_c: \text{if } x_{i1} \text{ is } A_1^c \text{ and } x_{i2} \text{ is } A_2^c \text{ and } \ldots x_{id} \text{ is } A_d^c, \text{ then the class } c.$$

In the above, A_i^c denotes the antecedent fuzzy set of ith rule for the ith feature. The membership function of A_i^c is defined as

$$A_i^c(x_i) = \exp\left(-\left(\frac{x_i - u_i^c}{\sqrt{2}\sigma_i^c}\right)^2\right), \tag{3.1}$$

where u_i^c and σ_i^c are the mean of the ith feature values of the data points in class c.

A drawback to the above approach is that the number of possible fuzzy if–then rules exponentially increases with dimensionality of feature space. Another problem with this approach is that it uses fuzzy if–then rules with certainty grades without using any local information about training patterns in the corresponding fuzzy subspace. To solve these problems, the following fuzzy rules can be used:

$$R_c: \text{if } x_{i1} \text{ is } A_1^c \text{ and } x_{i2} \text{ is } A_2^c \text{ and } \ldots x_{id} \text{ is } A_d^c, \text{ then the class } c,$$

$$\text{with } CF = CF_c, c \in \{1, \ldots, C\}.$$

In the above, CF_c is the grade of certainty for class c.

To achieve the consequent class and grade of certainty for each of these classes, we employ the following heuristic steps.

Step 1. For each training data point, $x_i = (x_{i1}, \ldots, x_{id})$, calculate the joint antecedent fuzzy set of the qth rule as

$$\Pi_q(x_i) = A_q^1(x_{i1}) \times \cdots \times A_q^d(x_{id}), \quad q = 1, \ldots, n.$$

---

* For example, the fuzzy operator function of logic function "A and B" is min{A,B}.

Step 2. For each class $c \in \{1, ..., C\}$, calculate the sum of the grades of the training data points in class c with the qth fuzzy rule R with the qth fuzzy rule R_q as

$$\beta_c(R_q) = \sum_{x_q \in c} \Pi_q(x_i). \tag{3.2}$$

Step 3. Seek the class that has the maximum value calculated in Step 2.

$$\beta_{c^*}(R_q) = \max\{\beta_c(R_q)\}, \quad c \in \{1, ..., C\}. \tag{3.3}$$

Step 4. Calculate the grade of certainty as following:

$$CF_q = \frac{\beta_{c^*}(R_q) - \bar{\beta}}{\sum_{c=1}^{C} \beta_c(R_q)}, \tag{3.4}$$

$$\bar{\beta} = \sum_{c \neq c^*} \frac{\beta_c(R_q)}{(C-1)}. \tag{3.5}$$

Application Study 3: Application of Fuzzy Rules in 1998 DARPA Intrusion Detection Data Sets for Misuse Detection

Abraham et al. applied fuzzy rules in 1998 DARPA intrusion detection data sets for misuse detection in (Abraham et al., 2007b). Forty-one features were extracted for each connection record, including 24 attack types, which also were categorized into four groups: DoS, remote to user attack (R2L), user to root (U2R), and probes. Thus, five classes are defined in the data set: normal, DoS, R2L, U2R, and probes.

Three phases were included in the experiments: feature selection, training, and testing. In the feature selection phase, 12 important attributes were selected for real-time intrusion detection using the decision-tree method. In the training phase, data were normalized to (0,1). Then, the grade of certainty was learned, so that the grade of certainty was increased if an attack was classified correctly, and when an attack was classified inaccurately, the grade of certainty was decreased. Triangular membership functions were used for all fuzzy-rule-based classifiers. Abraham et al. introduced three fuzzy-rule-based classifiers and compared the experimental performance with the results obtained using linear genetic program (LGP), SVM, and decision tree. Furthermore, they modeled a fuzzy ensemble IDS as a combination of classifiers to model lightweight and more accurate (heavyweight) IDS.

3.3.2 Artificial Neural Network

As described in Section 2.1.1.2, ANN matches samples through nonlinear information processing in a connected network. The constantly changing nature of network attacks requires a flexible misuse detection system that is capable of accurately identifying the variety of intrusions. In a misuse detection system, the application of ANN provides the capability of analyzing data, even if the data is incomplete or distorted. Because of this capability, ANN can learn misuse attacks and identify suspicious events that are unlikely to be accurately observed with other methods. This hypothesis is based on the knowledge that attackers often emulate the successes of others, and ANN can detect the similar attacks but not match the previous malicious behaviors exactly. Moreover, ANN provides faster speed, nonlinear data analysis, and predictive capability to detect instances of misuse.

Two main difficulties lie in the application of ANN in misuse detection. First, accurate ANN prediction needs a large number of attack data to ensure the training data are adequate and balanced with the normal data. As we explained in Chapter 1, malicious information is in nature infrequent and time consuming to collect. Thus, advanced methods are needed to solve this imbalanced learning problem. Second, ANN learns patterns in a black box, which consists of the connection weights and transfer functions of various net nodes. Hence, the success of ANN depends on the learning results of these weights. However, the accuracy of prediction cannot be interpreted using the complex network structure; therefore, we will not attempt to define it here.

We can implement ANN in misuse detection in two ways. First, we can incorporate ANN into existing or modified rule-based systems. Second, we can configure ANN to stand alone as a misuse detection system. When ANN is implemented with a rule-based system, it filters the input data of suspicious events before forwarding the misuse candidate data to a rule-based expert system. This method increases the sensitivity of misuse detection within the system. However, the use of ANN does have one drawback. The rule-based system has to be updated when ANN identifies new suspicious events, because this rule-based system cannot improve itself automatically with the incoming data. Instead of combining ANN and the rule-based system, ANN can be fed network data to identify the malicious events.

Application Study 4: Application of ANN in Network Traffic Data for Misuse Detection

Cannady applied ANN as a network misuse-detection technique in 1998. The prototype ANN was designed to identify signs of misuse by utilizing the analytical strengths of neural networks and the potential to identify and classify network activity based on limited, incomplete, and nonlinear data sources. The proposed feed-forward ANN architecture consisted of four fully connected layers with nine input nodes and two output nodes. The two output nodes indicated normal data with 1 and anomalous data with 0. The nine elements were selected in the event record data. (Event record data are present in network data packets and can cover all the information transmitted by the packet.) These nine elements include the protocol ID, source port, destination port, source address, destination address, ICMP type, ICMP code, raw data length, and raw data. Each of the elements was preprocessed into a standardized numeric representation.

The sigmoid transfer function was applied to the neuron connection weights in each hidden and output node. The output node was defined as

$$F(x) = \frac{1}{1 + e^{-x}}. \tag{3.6}$$

The author collected "normal" network activity data using RealSecure™ and simulated attacks generated by the Internet Scanner™ and the Satan scanner. The attacks varied from DoS attacks to portscans. Around 10,000 network data were generated for training and testing of ANN and approximately 3,000 belonged to anomalous data.

One-thousand testing data were selected randomly among the 9462 preprocessed records, and the remaining data served as training data. ANN was conducted with 10,000 iterations of the selected training data. The ANN model resulted in the desired root mean square error and correlation value. The prototype detected each of the imbedded attacks in the test data composed of three "normal" events and one simulated attack event.

3.3.3 Support Vector Machine

The SVM conducts structural risk minimization, e.g., true error on unseen examples, while ANN focuses on empirical risk minimization. Subsequently, SVM selects a number of parameters based on the requirement of the margin that separates the data points but not based on the number of feature dimensions. This feature allows SVM to be compatible with more applications. SVM has two significant advantages over ANN when applied in intrusion detection: speed and scalability. Speed is important for real-time detection, and scalability is important for the huge cyber-infrastructure information flow. In addition, SVM is capable of updating training patterns dynamically. This feature is important when attack patterns change.

Application Study 5: Application of SVM for Misuse Detection
In S. Mukkamala, G. Janoski, and A. H. Sung (2002), SVM was applied to identify attack and misuse patterns associated with computer security breaches, such as consequence of system software bugs, hardware or software failures, incorrect system administration procedures, or failure of the system authentication. SVM intrusion detection procedures include three steps: first, input and output pairs must be extracted from the user logs, web servers, and the authority log. Second, the SVM model is trained over the numerical data obtained in the first step, and third, the classification ability of SVM model is tested.

The raw information that originates in system log files of user activities consists of various types of attributes related to command, HTTP, and class labels—normal or anomalous. Weights were assigned to system commands and user activities to indicate the potential status as an anomaly. For example, an *rm* (command of remove) command received a weight of four and a *rm – r** was (remove everything in a directory and include the removed material in its subdirectory) assigned a weight of five, because the second weight posed a greater threat to the system. For example, in HTTP activities, "Read only actual html pages or images" were assigned weight of one, while "Read and attempt to access directory pages" were assigned a weight of two. "Read and attempt to access directory pages" received a higher weight because it may be related to malicious queries to the server.

Mukkamala et al. (2002) presented a training set of 699 data points that contained actual attacks, probable attacks, and normal patterns. Eight features were obtained after preprocessing, and all the data values were normalized to [0,1]. The testing set consists of 250 data points and eight features. The estimated precision was better than 85.53% on the training data set and 94% on the testing data set. SVM proved to be more efficient in the training and running processes than ANN. This experiment demonstrated that SVM could simulate security scenarios using the SVM component to adapt to individual information systems, to provide real-time detection, and to minimize false alarms immediately after detecting true attacks. Furthermore, the above advantages were also evaluated in Mukkamala and Sung (2003); in the comparative study, the authors used SVMs, ANNs, multivariate adaptive regression splines, and LGPs for intrusion detection.

3.3.4 Genetic Programming

The GP automatically breeds a population of computer programs according to the Darwin's theory of evolution by natural selection. The theory states that expressions should "evolve," so that the overall fitness of the population increases every generation. GP is a searching algorithm akin to the natural selection process, as shown in Figure 3.3. GP maintains an initial population of solutions. As with natural selection, the solutions in the candidate pool are evaluated, and fitness values are assigned to each solution according to the fitness of the solution to the problem. The fittest solutions in the population are more likely to perform the reproduction operation that creates a new generation of computer programs. The reproduction of the new population includes three operations: direct reproduction by copying the best existing programs, creation of new computer programs by a mutation operation, and creation of new computer programs by a crossover operation. The best solution in any generation thus far is designated as the result of the GP. Empirical results reveal that the GP technique is more accurate than some conventional machine learning-based IDSs.

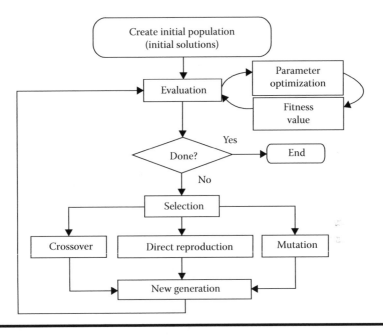

Figure 3.3   Workflow of a GP technique.

The workflow of GP is presented in Figure 3.3; GP techniques consist of the following steps:

Step 1. Randomly initialize a population of individual solutions.
Step 2. Randomly select the fittest individuals from the population by using a selection method. The fitness measure defines the problem the algorithm is expected to solve.
Step 3. Generate new variants by applying the following genetic operators for certain probabilities:
  – Reproduction—Copy an individual without change.
  – Recombination—Exchange substructures between individuals.
  – Mutation—Randomly replace a single atomic unit in an individual.
Step 4. Calculate the fitness of new the individual without change.
Step 5. Go to Step 2, if the termination criterion is not met.
Step 6. Stop. The best individual represents the best solution found.

In Step 3, three genetic operators use different techniques to produce the next generation of population in GP.

In the reproduction operation, a parent is selected probabilistically, based on fitness, and it is copied (unchanged) into the next generation of the population.

In the crossover operation, parent solutions are selected to generate new solutions. The crossover operation is composed of the following steps.

Step 1. Select two parents probabilistically based on fitness.
Step 2. Pick a number randomly from the first parent.
Step 3. Pick a number independently and randomly for the second parent. The result is a syntactically valid executable program.
Step 4. Deposit the offspring into the pool of the next generation of the population.
Step 5. Identify the subtrees rooted at the two data points of Step 2 and Step 3.

The following steps are included in the mutation operation:

Step 1. Select one parent probabilistically based on fitness.
Step 2. Pick a data point from the whole population.
Step 3. Delete the subtree at the data point of Step 2.
Step 4. Grow a new subtree at the mutation point using the same way as the generated trees for the initial random population.
Step 5. Put the offspring into the next generation of the population.

GP techniques have variants, such as LGP,* multiexpression programming (MEP), and gene expression programming (GEP). LGP evolves computer programs as sequences of imperative instructions. The sequences of instructions run on the registers of predefined sets. Successively removing the variables that start with the last effective instruction, we can represent an LGP chromosome in a functional way. The settings of LGP parameters, such as the restriction of the mitigation of individuals among subpopulations, which locate in the subdivision of population space and control diversity of population, are critical for the performance of the system. MGP chromosomes encode several expressions (computer program). We represent MEP genes using variable-length substrings. The length of the MGP chromosome corresponds to the number of genes of the chromosome. A function symbol presents a gene, which consists of pointers toward the function arguments. MGP is suitable for situations in which the target expression complexity is unknown. GEP uses character linear chromosomes with structurally organized heads and tails by genes. The head consists of symbols denoting the elements from both function and terminal sets, while the tail consists of only elements from terminal sets. We represent GEP individuals using fixed-length linear strings. The strings correspond to variable-size and shape chromosomes.

---

* In this definition, "linear" refers to the structures of the imperative programming representation but does not mean it only solves linear problems. LGP differs from tree-based GP in that the evolvable units are not the expressions of a functional programming language, such as LISP, but of a imperative language (native machine code), such a c/c++.

Application Study 6: Application of GP Variants for Misuse Detection

In Abraham et al. (2007b), the researchers evaluated the performance of three variants of GP techniques in IDS, LGP, MEP, and GEP. They performed five experiments on the test data from the 1998 DARPA program. The data set consists of normal data and 24 types of attack data. Each data has 41 features. They categorized the attack data into four groups: R2L, DoS, U2R, and probing (probes), so that finally a five-class classification was performed on the data set: normal, R2L, DoS, U2R, and probes. The training and testing data consisted of 5092 and 6890 records, respectively. Training data were normalized to (0, –1).

Experiments included two phases: training and testing. In the training phase, LGP structures were trained to generalize the unseen data with maximum data. In the testing phase, intrusion detection accuracies were measured using testing data for each class.

In the research, it was found that MEP performed better than LGP in detecting three attack types, while LGP outperformed MEP in the detection of the other two classes. For the three attack classes, MEP obtained classification accuracies of more than 99.75%. Meanwhile, for all five data types, MEP and GEP obtained classification accuracies better than 95%. As LGP and GEP can be performed at machine code levels, these two methods can potentially work properly for online IDSs.

3.3.5 Decision Tree and CART

Decision tree is an unparametric machine-learning method, which has no requirement for data types. In decision-tree algorithms, a data point is labeled by testing the feature values of the data against nodes of the decision tree. A decision of the classification of the data point can be traced from the root node to a leaf node. The decision traces can be converted into classification rules in which the terminal nodes (leaves) correspond to the final decision.

Because of its high classification accuracy, intuitive knowledge expression, simple implementation, efficiency, and strength in handling high dimensional data, decision-tree classifiers are popularly used in many applications, such as biomedical analysis, manufacturing and production, and clinical research.

Among the decision-tree algorithms, CART represents trees in a form of binary recursive partitioning. It classifies objects or predicts outcomes by selecting from a large number of variables. The most important of these variables determine the outcome variable.

In Section 3.3.5.1, we introduce the basic algorithms of decision tree and the important issues in those algorithms, such as split and split criteria, pruning, and scalability. In Section 3.3.5.2, we describe and discuss the application of decision trees for feature selection in misuse detection systems. In Section 3.3.3, we introduce CART algorithms and similar issues, as in Section 3.3.5.1. In Section 3.4.5.4, we describe and discuss the application of CART for feature selection in misuse detection systems.

3.3.5.1 Decision-Tree Techniques

In the decision-tree method, each internal node tests a feature, each branch corresponds to a feature value, and each leaf node assigns a classification. The methodology for using decision tree is described as follows:

Step 1. Split a variable at all of its split points. Sample sections into multiple nodes at each split point.

Step 2. Select the best split in the variable in terms of splitting criterion.

Step 3. Repeat Steps 1 and 2 for all variables at the root node.

Step 4. Rank the best splits and select the variable that achieves the highest purity at the root.

Step 5. Assign classes to the nodes according to a rule that minimizes misclassification costs.

Step 6. Repeat Steps 1–5 for each nonterminal node.

Step 7. Grow a large tree until each leaf is pure.

Step 8. Prune and choose the final tree using the cross validation (CV).

In the above steps, the splitting criterion plays a critical role in the feature selection process for splitting. The process employs a feature selection measure, such as information gain (IG). Below, we introduce the two most employed splitting criteria in decision trees: information gain and gini index.

Assume we have a discrete set of symbols $\{x_1, \ldots, x_n\}$ with an associated probability P_i for variable x. According to Shannon's information theory, the randomness of a sequence of symbols drawn from this symbol set can be measured by the entropy of the probability distribution as follows:

$$H(x) = -\sum_{i=1}^{m} P_i \log P_i. \tag{3.7}$$

Suppose we have two distributions over variables x and y, denoted by $P(x)$ and $P(y)$. Given condition y, the conditional entropy of x is defined as the average conditional entropy of y:

$$H(x \mid y) = \sum_i P(y = y_i) H(x \mid y = y_i). \tag{3.8}$$

Then, IG is defined as following:

$$IG(X \mid Y) = H(X) - H(X \mid Y). \tag{3.9}$$

IG describes the difference between the original information requirement and the new information requirement. Hence, IG tells us the reduction in uncertainty about one variable when we have the knowledge of the other correlated variable.

Given a set of training samples, S, with the respective m-class labels, we have s_i samples in class i. A feature with values $\{f_1, f_2, ..., f_l\}$ can classify S into l classes $\{s_1, s_2, ..., s_l\}$, where s_j denotes the subset of f_j. Moreover, given s_{ij} samples of class i in the sample set s_i, we obtain the expected information of s_i by

$$I(S) = \sum_{i=1}^{m} \left(\frac{s_i}{s}\right) * \log\left(\frac{s_i}{s}\right). \tag{3.10}$$

The entropy of feature F is

$$H(S \mid F) = -\sum_{i=1}^{l} \frac{s_{1j} + \cdots + s_{mj}}{s} * I(s_{1j}, ..., s_{mj}). \tag{3.11}$$

IG for feature F can be calculated as

$$\text{Gain}(F) = I(S) - H(S \mid F). \tag{3.12}$$

When we apply the above IG as a splitting criterion in the decision-tree algorithm, the feature with the highest IG is chosen as the splitting feature at a node.

The Gini index measures the impurity data distribution. It is defined as

$$\text{Gini}(x) = \sum_{i \neq j} p_i p_j = 1 - \sum_j p_j^2, \tag{3.13}$$

where p_i is the probability that a variable x has symbol x_i.

When we apply the Gini index in decision trees, the Gini index considers a binary split for each feature. As the Gini index is widely used by CART, we discuss it in details in Section 3.3.5.3.

Due to noise and outliers, many of the decision-tree branches reflect anomalies after the trees are built. To address this problem, tree-pruning methods are employed to remove the least reliable branches. Two methods are commonly used in tree-pruning: prepruning and postpruning. Prepruning is applied to halt splitting at a given node. Postprunning removes subtrees from a fully built tree.

3.3.5.2 Application of a Decision Tree in Misuse Detection

Empirical results have demonstrated that feature selection is critical in real-world IDSs, especially in improving the effectiveness of IDSs. In this section, we will describe how to use a decision tree for feature selection in IDSs.

In misuse detection techniques, it is tedious to test the match between an input element and a rule (signature) by sequentially comparing the input element to the corresponding constraints associated with the rule. The matching process covers the most resources intensively in the processes of signature detection. To improve the matching efficiency, a straightforward approach of clustering rules according to selected criteria can be used. For example, we can cluster the rules that have the same constraints in the same group. During signature detection, each rule in the group will be checked only when the common constraints of a rule group match any input element.

Application Study 7: Application of a Decision-Tree Feature Selection in Rule-Based Misuse Detection

Kruegel and Toth (2003) partitioned the set of rules in smaller subsets where only a single subset had to be analyzed for each input element in the signature detection system. They introduced a decision tree to detect the most discriminating features for a rule set and allowed it to perform a parallel evaluation of every feature. In the decision tree, the root node corresponded to the set consisting of all rules. The children nodes were the direct subsets that were partitioned from the rule set according to the first feature. Nodes were portioned further until each node had only one rule. Each node was labeled with the feature used for the corresponding partitioning. Each arrow leading from a node to a child was associated with the value of the feature specified in the child node. Each leaf node contained one rule or the rules that could not be distinguished by features. For example (as shown in Table 3.4), we have four rules {A, B, C, and D} described by three features {source address, destination address, and port} (Kruegel and Toth, 2003). As shown in Figure 3.4, we obtain a decision tree to describe the rules in the sequence of the features: source port, source address, and destination address. In the misuse detection process, an input data point is matched with the four rules in the feature sequence from root node to leaves.

During splitting, the sequence of features has impact on the shape and depth of the tree structure. The authors aimed to obtain an optimal decision tree to minimize the depth of the trees, which contained two-level nodes: root and leaves. Each of the leaves corresponds to one rule. They approached

Table 3.4 Example of Rules and Features of Network Packets

Rules	Source Addresses	Destination Addresses	Source Ports
A	100.100.0.1	100.100.0.3	80
B	100.100.0.2	100.100.0.4	80
C	100.100.0.2	100.100.0.3	80
D	100.100.0.2	100.100.0.5	88

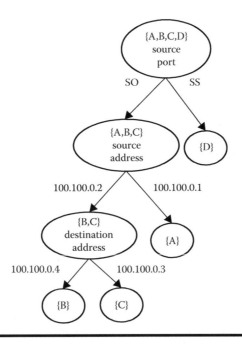

Figure 3.4 Example of a decision tree.

this optimization using iterative dichotomiser* clustering algorithm using the knowledge of IG† of the features.

In Kruegel and Toth (2003), an algorithm was designed to generate a decision tree. The algorithm detected malicious events with few redundant comparisons using the set of rules extracted in the tree. This theory has been applied to network-based IDS. The experimental evaluation presented by the authors reported that the detection process was significantly faster than previous methods, including Snort's recently released, fully revised detection engine.

3.3.5.3 CART

In CART, a decision tree *T* describes the collection of splits of subsets of *T* into two descendant subsets. From any subset *t* of *T* to *T*, *t* ∈ *T*, the relation can be described by the paired functions left(.) and right(.) In the above, *T* and its two functions satisfy two conditions as follows,

■ For each *t* ∈ *T*, either left(*t*) = right(*t*) = 0, or left(*t*) > *t* and right(*t*) > *t*.
■ For each *t* ∈ *T*, other than the smallest integer in *T*, there is exactly one *s* ∈ *T*, an ancestor of *t*, s.t. either *t* = left(*s*) or *t* = right(*s*).

---

* ID3 (iterative dichotomiser) was developed by J. Ross Quinlan in the early 1980s. It is the earlier work of decision-tree algorithms.
† IG of a feature is the expected reduction of entropy when portioning the data set using this feature.

CART classifies data by constructing a decision tree. Then, the significance of predictors is ranked according to their contribution to the construction of the decision tree. Furthermore, the ranking indicates the significance of each feature in intrusion detection.

Three steps are included in CART:

Step 1. Tree building
Step 2. Pruning
Step 3. Optimal tree selection

Tree building steps are the same as those presented in Section 2.3.5.1, except that, while splitting a variable at all of its split points, the sample splits into *binary* nodes at each split point.

The optimal tree selection process finds the correct complexity parameter,* so that the information in L is fit, but not overfit. This fit requires an independent set of data. If an independent set of data is not available, we can use CV to pick out the subtree with the lowest estimated misclassification rate.

Application Study 8: Application of CART in Misuse Detection

In Application Study 8, we discuss the application of CART in misuse detection by (Chebrolu et al., 2005). Chebrolu et al. used the KDD cup 1999 intrusion detection data set. The data set includes 5092 cases and 41 variables. Thus, there are 208,772 possible splits in the CART algorithm.

They used the Gini rule for tree splitting. The Gini index evaluates the performance of the rule for splitting the parent node into classes. When the cases in one node are redundant or singular, splitting the node is insignificant or impossible. In such situations, growing nodes in a decision tree can be terminated. Moreover, we can prune branches of the maximal tree by evaluating its subtree. In CART algorithms, the maximal tree is grown without stopping. Then, we can derive a set of subtrees from the maximal tree. Among the subtrees, the best tree is determined with the minimum misclassification error rate. We can obtain the misclassification error rates of all subtrees. We select the best subtree, the subtree, which has the minimum cost. We select features according to their contributions to the construction of the decision tree. The contribution of features can be measured by the role of each input variable in splitting.

Given a CART-tree algorithm, data points are split according to the feature "protocol_type." Once a value for this feature is not available, we have to substitute "service" as a good surrogate, which mimics the action of primary splitting rules. The significance of a feature can be obtained by summing up the improvement-scores across all nodes in the tree when the predictor performs as a primary or

---

* Complexity parameter is a measure of how much additional accuracy a split must add to the entire tree to warrant the additional complexity.

surrogate splitter. For instance, when the predictor acts as the primary splitter, we measure its contribution using I_{ip}. However, when the predictor acts as the nth surrogate, we assign $p^n \cdot I_{ip}$, where $p \in [0, 1]$ denotes "surrogate improvement weight" controlled by users as its significance. We select the significant features for intrusion detection according to their contribution to the construction of decision trees. Features are ranked in terms of percentages.

In Chebrolu et al. (2005), the authors eliminated the features that contributed 0.00% to the ranking. They selected only the primary splitters or surrogates as explained above. Then, the data set was reduced to 12 variables with $C, E, F, L, W,$ $X, Y, AB, AE, AF, AG,$ and AI as variables. Moreover, they trained the CART structure and tested the trained model. They evaluated the performance of the CART algorithm by comparing the learning results from using the full-feature data set and the selected 12-feature data set. The classification accuracy on the normal class was 100%. Furthermore, the classification accuracies of groups U2R and R2L have been increased by using the 12-variable reduced data set. CART classified accurately on smaller data sets.

3.3.6 Bayesian Network

One of the limitations underlining most of the rule-based approaches is that they treat each event as a separate activity without considering the context of the events. A rule relies on the signature of a packet based on a set of elements such as protocol. Because a subset of a packet tracking a malicious user and a signature of a normal user may be matched to activate the rule, rule-based misuse detection systems are known for false alarms. In a false alarm, an alarm may be raised after detecting an activity that may be part of an attack, whereas the activity is actually legitimate network traffic. One way to avoid this problem is to perform inference between rules using BN. This section focuses on BN classification and its application in misuse detection. Section 3.3.6.1 presents the BN model and its application for classification. Section 3.3.6.2 describes the application of BN in misuse detection systems.

3.3.6.1 Bayesian Network Classifier

As discussed in Section 2.1.1.5, BN represents problems in networks, using Bayesian statistics to specify the causal relationships between subsets of variables. We present BN in a directed acyclic graph. Each node represents a random variable. Each arc represents strength of dependence using conditional probability. The starting node and ending node of an arc are called, respectively, the parent or immediate predecessor, and descendant of each other. For example, as shown in Figure 3.5, if a BN has six variables and seven arcs, then, in arc $X_1 \rightarrow X_4$, X_1 is a parent of X_4, and X_4 is a descendant of X_1. For instance, X_1 has no predecessor and three descendants: $X_2, X_3,$ and X_4.

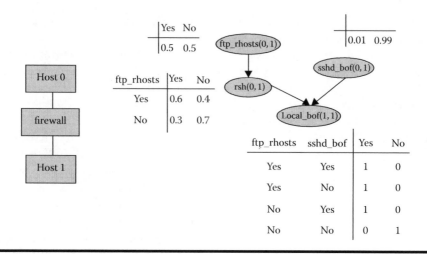

Figure 3.5   Example of BN and CPT.

Along with BN, the conditional probability table (CPT) presents the dependences on the net for each variable/node. For each variable/node, the conditional probability P(variable | *parent* (variable)) is given in CPT for each possible combination of its parents. The advantages of the BN formulation include intuitive notion of anomaly (the theory that anomalousness of an event is directly related to its probability) and relative resilience in the CPT parameterization (the model was apriori parameterized by an expert's best guess).

Given an event with a set of v variables, $X = \{x_1, \ldots, x_i, \ldots, x_v\}$, the pattern distribution of X can be described with the distribution as follows:

$$P(x_1, \ldots, x_v) = \prod_{i=1}^{v} P(x_i \mid Parents(x_i)), \tag{3.14}$$

each value of $P(x_i \mid Parents(x_i))$, $i = 1, \ldots, v$ corresponds to the entries in the CPT for variable x_i. Using the above joint probability generated for any event data X, we can make a classification. Thus, two problems remain in the training or learning of BN model: learning a network structure and training the network once the network structure is known.

Given a training data set $D = \{X_1, \ldots, X_j, \ldots, X_n\}$, where case $X_j = \{x_{j,1}, \ldots, x_{j,i}, \ldots, x_{j,v}\}$, BN algorithms focus on identifying the BN that best represents the posterior probability distribution $P(x_{j,1}, \ldots, x_{j,i}, \ldots, x_{j,v})$. Methods of learning BN structures from data can be categorized into three groups: methods based on linearity and normality assumptions, methods that extensively test independence relations, and Bayesian approaches. For example, we can seek the network BN that maximizes the likelihood of data logarithm. For a more in-depth explanation of this topic, please refer Cooper and Herskovits (1992), Verma and Pearl (1992), and Pearl and

Wermuch (1993). Human experts have knowledge about the direct dependencies between nodes, which can specify conditional probabilities in the network. If the variables are available and some of the variables are hidden, then CPT entries must be computed once the structure of BN is available. Algorithms for training BN are referenced in (Russell and Norvig, 2003).

Application Study 9: Sample BN for Misuse Detection
We demonstrate one application of BN for misuse detection in this section. In Figure 3.5, we have an example of network configuration on the left-hand side and the corresponding BN with CPT on the right-hand side. In this network configuration, a file server, host 1, provides services: file transfer protocol (ftp), security shell (ssh), and remote shell (rsh) services. The firewall allows ftp, ssh, and rsh traffic from a user workstation (host0) to server 1 (host1). The two numbers inside parentheses denote the source destination host. The example addresses four common exploits: sshd buffer overflow (sshd_bof), ftp_rhosts, rsh login (rsh), and local setuid buffer overflow (Local_bof). The attack path can be explained using sequence of nodes. For example, one attack path can be presented as ftp_rhosts $(0, 1) \rightarrow$ rsh$(0, 1) \rightarrow$ Local_bof$(1, 1)$. CPTs are shown for each variable in the network graph. For example, the CPT for the variable Local_bof has a conditional probability for overflow or no overflow in user 1 with the combinational values of its parents: rsh and sshd_bof. We see that

$$P(\text{Local\_bof}(1, 1) = \text{Yes}|\text{rsh}(0, 1) = \text{Yes}, \text{sshd\_bof}(0, 1) = \text{Yes}) = 1,$$

$$P(\text{Local\_bof}(1, 1) = \text{No}|\text{rsh}(0, 1) = \text{No}, \text{sshd\_bof}(0, 1) = \text{No}) = 1.$$

Using BN, human experts can understand the network structure and the underlying relationship in data set attributes easily. Furthermore, they can modify and improve the model.

Application Study 10: Application of BN for Feature Selection in Misuse Detection
Chebrolu et al. (2005) investigated the performance of the feature selection and classification algorithm involving BN. BNs can not only classify data, but can also reduce the data space and improve the performance of misuse detection systems based on the reduced feature space. The strategy for feature selection is to find a minimum subset of the whole feature set that maximizes the performance of a classification algorithm according to a defined performance measure. The Markov blanket (MB) method is used in Chebrolu et al. (2005) to find the significant feature subset, so that all other features are probabilistically independent of this subset. Using a BN classifier on the data, a MB blanket of the class node performs feature selection, and all features outside of the MB are deleted from the BN. In Chebrolu et al. (2005), which used the same data set as noted in Section 2.3.5.4, 17 out of 41 significant features were selected using MB, including *A, B, C, E, G, H, K, L, N,*

Q, V, W, X, Y, Z, AD, and *AF*. Then, the BN model was learned using the training data, and classification was performed on the testing data. There were five types of data: normal, probe, DOS, U2R, and R2L. The feature selection method was more accurate than BN classification using all 41 features for detecting Normal data.

3.3.6.2 Naïve Bayes

The naïve Bayes (NB) classifier makes the assumption of class conditional indepen-dence. Given a data sample, its features are assumed conditionally independent of each other. This assumption is different from the assumption in BN that dependen-cies exist between features. In this sense, NB is a special and simple case of BN. In Schultz et al. (2001), naïve Bayes was used to detect new, previously unseen mali-cious executables accurately and automatically. The method was compared with a traditional signature-based method, and it more than doubled the detection rates for new malicious executables.

3.4 Summary

Rule-based algorithms, such as association rules classifiers, are important in mis-use detection systems. Signatures of attacks can be described accurately by rules. However, rule-based algorithms have difficulties in updating for new attacks. These difficulties constrain their applications. Machine-learning methods, such as fuzzy rules, ANN, SVM, BN, and GP, have been employed and are proven to improve the detection ability for the known and unknown attack types in misuse detection systems. Most machine-learning methods are in the initial stages of research and have not been applied in practical cybersecurity software.

In addition, feature selection before classification is challenging in misuse detec-tion. Detection quality relies on the experience and knowledge of the experts who operate the security programs. It also depends on an exhaustive testing and refining process. Researchers have proposed methods, such as decision trees, to select the significant feature subset to improve the detection accuracy. However, researchers have yet to solve the relationships between different features and between different attacks. To compound the problem, features are, for the most part, unknown.

References

Abraham, A., R. Jain, J. Thomas, and S.Y. Han. DSCIDS: Distributed softcomputing intru-sion detection system. *Journal of Network and Computer Applications* 30 (1) (2007a): 381–398.

Abraham, A., C. Grosan, and C. Martin-Vide. Evolutionary design of intrusion detection programs. *International Journal of Network Security* 4 (3) (2007b): 328–339.

Agrawal, R., T. Imielinski, and A. Swami. Mining Association rules between sets of items in large databases. In: *Proceedings of the 1993 ACM SIGMOD Conference*, Washington, DC, 1993.

Cannady, J. Artificial neural networks for misuse detection. In: *Proceedings of the 1998 National Information Systems Security Conference (NISSC'98)*, Arlington, VA, October 5–8, 1998, pp. 443–456.

Chebrolu, S., A. Abraham, and J.P. Thomas. Feature deduction and ensemble design of intrusion detection systems. *Computers & Security* 24 (2005): 1–13.

Cooper, G.F. and E. Herskovits. A Bayesian method for the induction of probabilistic networks from data. *Machine Learning* 9 (1992): 309–347.

Kruegel, C. and T. Toth. Using decision trees to improve signature-based intrusion detection. In: *Proceedings of the 6th International Workshop on the Recent Advances in Intrusion Detection*, Pittsburgh, PA, 2003, pp. 173–191.

Lee, W.K., S.J. Stolfo, and K.W. Mok. Mining audit data to build intrusion detection models. In: *Proceedings of the 4th International Conference on Knowledge Discovery and Data Mining*, New York, August 1998.

Lee, W.K., S.J. Stolfo, and K.W. Mok. A data mining framework for building intrusion detection models. In: *Proceedings of the IEEE Symposium on Security and Privacy*, Oakland, CA, 1999, pp. 120–132.

Mukkamala, S., G. Janoski, and A.H. Sung. Intrusion detection using support vector machines. In: *Proceedings of Advanced Simulation Technologies Conference*, 2002, pp. 178–183.

Mukkamala, S. and A.H. Sung. A comparative study of techniques for intrusion detection. In: *Proceedings of the 15th IEEE International Conference on Tools with Artificial Intelligence*, Sacramento, CA, 2003, pp. 570–577.

Pearl, J. and N. Wermuch. When can association graphs admit a causal interpretation? In: *Preliminary Papers of the Fourth International Workshop on Artificial Intelligence and Statistics*, Fort Lauderdale, FL, 1993, pp. 141–150.

Russell, S.J. and P. Norvig. *Artificial Intelligence: A Modern Approach*, 2nd edn. Upper Saddle River, NJ: Prentice Hall, 2003, ISBN 0-13-790395-2.

Schultz, M.G., E. Eskin, E. Zadok, and S.J. Stolfo. Data mining methods for detection of new malicious executables. In: *DARPA Information Survivability Conference and Exposition (DISCEX II'01)*, Anaheim, CA, Vol. 1, 2001.

Verma, T. and J. Pearl. An algorithm for deciding if a set of observed independencies has a causal explanation. In: *Proceedings 8th Conference on Uncertainty in AI*, Stanford, CA, 1992, pp. 323–330.

Chapter 4

Machine Learning for Anomaly Detection

Lust for victory will not give you the victory. You must receive the victory from your opponent. He has no choice but to give it to you because he will sense your heart as better or truer. Nature is your friend; it helps you to win. Your enemy will have unnatural movement; therefore you will be able to know what he is going to do before he does it.

Masaaki Hatsumi
Secret Ninjutsu

4.1 Introduction

In this chapter, we briefly describe the problems often encountered and solutions often developed as researchers apply machine-learning methods to anomaly detection. Since anomaly detection comprises a large portion of machine-learning methods, it is important for researchers to understand how this technique works. This chapter contains in-depth studies to aid readers in understanding these concepts. We organize it into the following sections. Section 4.2 contains a description of the difference between anomaly detection and signature detection, and of the key challenges in anomaly detection. Section 4.3 contains a description of an anomaly detection workflow and of the mechanism of machine-learning methods as applied in the workflow. In addition, Section 4.3 contains an analysis of the difficulties, such as non-negligible false alarm rates, that machine-learning methods encounter in application.

85

Section 4.4 contains an explanation of techniques for developing representative machine-learning classifiers and the applications of those classifiers in anomaly detection. The section contains a discussion on supervised machine-learning methods, including rule-based learning, ANN, SVM, KNN, HMM, and Kalman filter, a description of the unsupervised machine-learning methods, including the clustering-based method, random forest, one class SVM, KNN, PCA, and subspace, and a description of other machine-learning methods, including EM, clustering based on probability and information-theoretic learning. This section also includes a discussion on the limitations and difficulties that encumber machine-learning methods in anomaly detection systems. Such problems include an inadequate ability to maintain a high detection rate and a low false-alarm rate (FAR). Finally, Section 4.5 consists of a summary of the achievements and limitations of the present research in anomaly detection, and a guide of emerging research.

4.2 Anomaly Detection

The goal of anomaly detection is to target any event falling outside of a predefined set of normal behaviors. Anomaly detection programs assume that any intrusive event is a subset of anomalous activity. In this aspect, it is different from misuse detection, which first defines the signature of abnormal behavior to indicate attacks. Anomaly detection first defines a profile of normal behaviors, which reflects the health and sensitivity of a cyberinfrastructure. Correspondingly, an anomaly behavior is defined as a pattern in data that does not conform to the expected behaviors, including outliers, abbreviations, contaminants, and surprise, etc., in applications.

When new attacks appear and normal behaviors remain the same, anomaly detection can find the new or unusual attacks and provide an early alarm. Like misuse detection, anomaly detection relies on a clear boundary between normal and anomalous behaviors, where the profile of normal behaviors is defined as different from anomaly events. The profile must fit a set of criteria as outlined below. It must contain robustly characterized normal behavior, such as a host/IP address or VLAN segment and have the ability to track the normal behaviors of the target environment sensitively. Additionally, it should include the following information: occurrence patterns of specific commands in application protocols, association of content types with different fields of application protocols, connectivity patterns between protected servers and the outside world, and rate and burst length distributions for all types of traffic (Gong, 2003). In addition, profiles based on a network must be adaptive and self-learning in complex and challenging network traffic to preserve accuracy and a low FAR.

Anomaly detection should detect malicious behaviors including segmentation of binary code in a user password, stealthy reconnaissance attempts, backdoor service on a well-known standard port, natural failures in the network, new buffer overflow attacks, HTTP traffic on a nonstandard port, intentionally stealthy attacks, variants of existing attacks in new environments, and so on. For example, if a user who usually logs in around 10 am from university dormitory logs in at 5:30 am from an IP address of China, then an anomaly has occurred.

Accurate detection of these malicious behaviors encounters several challenges. The key challenge is that the huge volume of data with high-dimensional feature space is difficult to manually analyze and monitor. Such analysis and monitoring requires highly efficient computational algorithms in data processing and pattern learning. In the huge volume of network data, the same malicious data repeatedly occur while the number of similar malicious data is much smaller than the number of normal data. The imbalanced data distribution of normal and anomaly data induces a high FAR. Much of the data is streaming data, which requires online analysis. It is also difficult to define a representative normal region or the boundary between normal and outlying behavior. The concept of an anomaly/outlier varies among application domains; the labeled anomalies are not available for training/ validation. Training and testing data might contain unknown noises, and normal and anomaly behaviors constantly evolve.

4.3 Machine Learning in Anomaly Detection Systems

As shown in Figure 4.1, a typical anomaly detection system consists of five steps: data collection, data preprocessing, normal behavior learning phase, identification of misbehaviors using dissimilarity detection techniques, and security responses. In data collection, the volume of data is extremely large, and it requires data reduction in data preprocessing. Additionally, most of the data in the network are streaming data, and requires further data reduction. Thus, the data preprocessing step includes feature selection, feature extraction, or a dimensionality reduction technique, and an information-theoretic method.

Machine-learning methods play key roles in building normal profiles and intrusion detection in anomaly detection systems. In anomaly detection, labeled data corresponding to normal behavior are usually available, while labeled data for anomaly behavior are not. Supervised machine-learning methods need attack-free training data. However, this kind of training data is difficult to obtain in real-world network environments. This lack of training data leads to the well-known unbalanced data distribution in machine learning. Moreover, with the changing network environment or services, patterns of normal traffic will change. The differences between training and actual (test) data lead to high false-positive rates (FPRs) of supervised intrusion detection systems (IDSs). Unsupervised anomaly detection can overcome the drawbacks of supervised anomaly detection. Thus, semi-supervised and unsupervised machine-learning methods are employed frequently (Eskin et al., 2002).

These machine-learning algorithms group the normal patterns by following similarity measures between the patterns of input events and predefined normal behaviors, and list the outliers in the abnormal candidate pool. Thus, anomaly detection

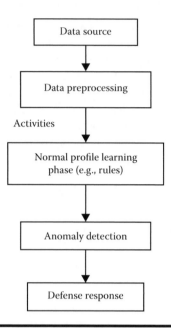

Figure 4.1 Workflow of anomaly detection system.

can detect novel attacks. However, anomaly detection approaches may trigger high rates of false alarm. Because these methods flag any significant deviation from the baseline as an intrusion, it is likely that nonintrusive behavior that falls outside the normal range will also be labeled as an intrusion, resulting in a false positive. Another disadvantage of anomaly detection approaches is that hackers often modify malicious codes or data to make them similar to normal patterns. When such an attack occurs, the intrusive behavior has a high probability of being established as part of the normal profile. When an attack is missed because it is judged to be part of the normal profile, a false negative occurs. In addition, anomaly detection does not differentiate between attacks. The above analysis indicates an attack pattern may not coincide with anomalous activity, and we leave it to the reader to investigate all four possibilities in anomaly detection results according to the confusion matrix in Figure 2.12. The problem we must solve is how to minimize the false negative and false positive rates and to determine what the effects are if we use the suggested methods.

4.4 Machine-Learning Applications in Anomaly Detection

This section contains the examples of machine-learning methods applied in anomaly detection systems in Table 1.3. We introduce the fundamental applications of machine-learning techniques in both host-based and network-based detection systems.

4.4.1 Rule-Based Anomaly Detection (Table 1.3, C.6)

Rules describe the correlation between attribute conditions and class labels. When applied to anomaly detection, the rules become descriptive normal profiles of users, programs, and other resources in cyberinfrastructures. The anomaly detection mechanism identifies a potential attack if users or programs act inconsistently with the established rules. The use of comprehensive rules is critical in the application of expert systems for intrusion detection. This section contains a discussion of associative classification and association rules in anomaly detection and an application study.

Association rules (Table 1.3, C.6) have been applied for constructing anomaly detection models (Lee and Stolfo, 1998; Lee et al., 1999; Apiletti et al., 2008). Constructing anomaly detection models using association rules is performed in two steps. First, system audit data are mined for consistent and useful patterns of program and user behaviors. Then, inductively learned classifiers are trained using the relevant features presented in the patterns to recognize anomalies.

The following contains a description of how to build association rules using audit data. These rules refer to normal user behaviors. By aggregating these rules, we can obtain the normal profile of a network for a specific target.

Lee and Stolfo (1998) introduced frequent episodes (Mannila and Toivonen, 1996) to characterize the audit sequences occurring in normal data by a small set of rules that capture the frequent behaviors in those sequences.* During monitoring, sequences violating those rules are treated as anomalies. Given a set of audit event records in total, T, and each record has a time interval $[t_s, t_e]$, where t_s and t_e are start time and end time. The width of the interval is defined as $w = t_e - t_s$. Given a set of events $X = \{I_1, I_2, \ldots, I_k\}$ (the definition of association rules is presented in Section 2.4.1.1); the minimal occurrence of X is defined as the shortest interval that contains X in the set of audit event records. $support(X)$ is defined as the ratio between the minimal occurrence of X and the total number of records in T. Assuming we have three sets of items, A, B, C, the frequent episode rule is defined as $A, B \rightarrow C, [c, s, w]$, where $s = support (A \cup B \cup C)$ and $s = support (A \cup B \cup C)/support(A \cup B)$ are support and confidence of the rules.

Application Study 1: Application of Association Rules in Audit Data for Anomaly Detection (Table 1.3, C.6)

Lee and Stolfo (1998) detected inside attacks by extracting rules from all audit data. The rules describe the normal behaviors of users in a sequence of events. Thus, the authors' strategy was to learn the most frequent patterns in user audit data. They merged and aggregated the patterns into one normal profile corresponding to each user if two rules had the same functions on the left- and right-hand sides, while their support and confidence values are within 5% of each other, respectively. To measure the similarity between a new pattern and the historical profile patterns

---

* An episode is a collection of events that occur in a specified order. To identify the behavior of a sequence, researchers attempted to discover the frequently occurring episodes in a sequence and describe these episodes as the behavior of the sequence in rules.

Table 4.1   Users' Normal Behaviors in Fifth Week

Sysadm	A system administrator who logs in as root, cats the password file, and runs commands such as top.
Programmer1	A programmer who writes public domain C code using a vi editor, compiles the C code (sometimes successfully), reads and sends mail, and executes Unix commands.
Programmer2	Another programmer with a similar user profile, except that he works afternoons and evenings.
Secretary	A secretary who edits latex files, runs latex, reads mail, and sends mail.
Manager1	A manager who reads and sends mail.
Manager2	A manager who reads mail.

Source: Lee, W. et al., A data mining framework for building intrusion detection models, in: *Proceedings of the IEEE Symposium on Security and Privacy*, Oakland, CA, 1999, pp. 120–132. © [1999] IEEE.

(e.g., Table 4.1), they introduced similarity score, which they defined as m/n, where m is the number of new patterns that match historical normal profile patterns, and n is the number of all new patterns for detection. The higher the similarity score, the more possible the user performs normal behaviors in cyber systems.

As shown in Section 3.4.1.1, the tcpdump data in DARPA were preprocessed with the format presented in Table 4.1. As shown in Table 4.1, the normal working patterns of respective users were summarized, and the authors obtained the frequent episode and frequent sequential patterns from the data of login sessions of the same user. Each user had three profiles for time segments: morning, afternoon, and night. They merged the patterns into each user's profile, using the data from the first 4 weeks. They used the data from the fifth week as training data and recorded the normal range of similarity scores by comparing the patterns from these data to the recorded profiles of the first 4 weeks. The data from the sixth week includes anomaly behaviors that had patterns that were measured with the normal profile, and the resulting similarity score (anomaly) was compared with the normal range (normal) as in Table 4.2. Table 4.2 shows that all of the anomaly behavior has been detected.

This sample uses session-level information that may not be fast enough for real-time detection.

4.4.1.1 Fuzzy Rule-Based (Table 1.3, C.6)

The above rule-based detection techniques use a deterministic value or an interval to quantify rules such that normal and anomaly audit records are split sharply. This split generates difficulties in correctly detecting the normal audit records when

Table 4.2 Normal Similarity Scores and Anomaly Scores

User	Normal	Anomaly
Programer2	(0.58,0.79)	0.00
Secretary	(∞,∞)	0.00
Sysadm	(0.84,0.95)	0.00
Programmer1	(0.31,1.00)	0.04
Secretary	(0.41,0.98)	0.17
Programmer1	(∞,∞)	0.00
Sysadm	(0.64,0.95)	0.00
Manager1	(0.57,1.00)	0.00
Manager2	(1.00,1.00)	0.00

Source: Lee, W. et al., A data mining framework for building intrusion detection models, in: *Proceedings of the IEEE Symposium on Security and Privacy*, Oakland, CA, 1999, pp. 120–132. © [1999] IEEE.

Note: (∞,∞) means that the user did not login during the time segment in the fifth week.

these normal data deviate from the rules in a small range. To solve this problem, we must improve the flexibility of the rule-based techniques using fuzzy logic. Moreover, audit records include many ordinal and categorical features, which bring the fuzziness into rules. For example, a rule may contain the connection duration of a user's process by using the following expression, such as "connection duration = 3 min" or "1 min ≤ connection duration ≤ 4 min."

Following the introduction of frequent episodes at the beginning of Section 4.4.1, we introduce fuzzy frequent episodes. Given the set of event features $F = \{f_1, \ldots, f_d\}$ and the membership degree of x_{ij} in the lth category of feature f_j $m_l(x_{ij})$, $1 \leq l \leq m$, $1 \leq j \leq d$, we have an event (data point) $x_i = (x_{i1}, \ldots, x_{id})$. If f_j is categorical, we have $m_l(x_{ij}) = 0$, or 1. If f_j is fuzzy, we have $0 \leq m_l(x_{ij}) \leq 1$. Then, if any feature x_{ij} is fuzzy, we can normalize its membership function as follows:

$$m(x_{ij}) = \frac{m_l(x_{ij})}{\sum_l m_l(x_{ij})}.$$ (4.1)

For event $x_i = (x_{i1}, \ldots, x_{id})$, the occurrence is calculated as

$$occur(x_i) = \prod_j m(x_{ij}). \qquad (4.2)$$

Furthermore, we obtain the minimum occurrence (*minoccurence*) of an episode by computing the product of its event features. Then, we normalize the occurrence in Equation 4.2 as follows:

$$Occur(x_i) = \frac{occur(x_i)}{\sum_j occur(x_j)}, \quad \text{if } occur(x_i) \geq minoccurence; \text{ else } Occur(x_i) = 0.$$

Here x_j refers to the events, which have the same feature values.

Application Study 2: Application of Fuzzy Rules for Anomaly Detection

Luo and Bridges investigated the fuzzy rule-based anomaly detection using real-world data and simulated data set (Luo and Bridges, 2000). The real-network traffic data were collected by the Department of Computer Science at Mississippi State University by tcpdump (http://www.tcpdump.org/ n.d.). They extracted four features from the data, including SN, FN, RN, and PN.* They divided each feature into three fuzzy sets: LOW, MEDIUM, and HIGH. Then, they derived the fuzzy association rules among the first three features, and fuzzy frequency episode rules for the last feature. They used the traffic data from the afternoon as training data to build these normal pattern fuzzy rules. Next, they used the traffic data from the afternoon, evening, and night, as testing or anomaly detection data. In testing, they introduced a similarity function to compare the normal patterns with the testing patterns. Assuming we obtain a normal rule: $R : X \rightarrow Y$, (c, s), and we have a new rule $R_{new} : X_{new} \rightarrow Y_{new}$, (c_{new}, s_{new}) for similarity testing, then the similarity between these rules were expressed as, $sim(R, R_{new}) = \max(0, 1 - \max(|c - c_{new}|/c, |s - s_{new}|/s))$, if $(X = X_{new}) \cap (Y = Y_{new})$; otherwise, $sim(R, R_{new}) = 0$.

Based on the above equation, we know that the similarity between the normal pattern rule set S_1 and S_2 can be obtained by, $sim(S, S_{new}) = \left(\sum sim(R, R_{new})\right)^2 / |S_1||S_2|$, and $\forall R \in S$, $\forall R_{new} \in S_{new}$.

The results showed that the rules derived from the testing data in the afternoon, evening, and night were very similar, less similar, and at least similar to the rules derived from the training data, respectively. Furthermore, they selected the data in the 3 h of afternoon as training data and nine testing data in 3 h from

---

* SN, FN, and RN denote, respectively, the number of SYN, FIN, and FST flags appearing in TCP packet headers in the last 2 s. PN denote the number of destination ports in the last 2 s.

afternoon, evening, and night as testing data. The experiments showed that the fuzzy rules derived from the testing data in the same time slots as the training data were more similar to the rules generated by the training data than to the rules generated from any other data sets.

The simulated data, including three network traffic data sets, were collected by the Institute for Visualization and Perception Research at University of Massachusetts Lowell. The first data set contained normal patterns, called baselines, and the other two data sets contained IP spoofing intrusions and portscanning intrusions, called network1 and network3, respectively. They extracted the same types of four features as the above experiments. The normal data set was split into training and testing parts. They used the normal training data set to train rule sets and derived testing rule sets on normal testing data on network1 and network3. Then, they derived similarity between these rule sets. The result demonstrated that the fuzzy episode rules could detect anomalies.

4.4.2 ANN (Table 1.3, C.9)

When we apply machine-learning methods to distinguish between normal and anomalous behaviors, two types of profiles can be built: user profiles based on the sequences of individual normal commands and software profiles based on the sequences of system calls. Software profiles abstract the vagaries of users and defeat users who slowly change their behaviors to foil the profiling system. They can also protect user privacy from a surveillance system that monitors user activity.

Using ANN in anomaly detection systems, we hope to generalize from incomplete data and classify online data as a normal anomaly. The back-propagation (BP) ANN, a standard feed-forward ANN, has this ability. First, the ANN structure has to be trained as follows. Input data are fed to the network, and the activations for each level of neurons are cascaded forward. By comparing the desired output and the ground truth, BP ANN structure, e.g., weights in different layers, is updated layer-by-layer in a direction of BP from the output layer to the input layer.

ANN has been applied in cybersecurity by Ghosh et al. (1998, 1999) and Liu et al. (2002). Each of these studies demonstrates ANN's ability to analyze sequences of system calls, which can then be used to deploy an anomaly detection system.

Application Study 3: Application of ANN Approach for Anomaly Detection (Ghosh et al., 1998, 1999; Liu et al., 2002)

Ghosh et al. (1998, 1999) used the BP ANN approach as the anomaly diction model by analyzing program behaviors. They captured system calls using the Sun Microsystem's basic security module (BSM) auditing facility for Solaris. These data showed regular patterns of behavior. They built normal software behavior profiles by capturing the frequencies of system calls to monitor the behavior of programs by noting irregularities in program behavior. The system performed offline intrusion detection in the experiments using the 1998 DARPA intrusion detection evaluation data sets. The experiments showed a 3% FPR (Ghosh et al., 1998) and a 0% FPR (Ghosh et al., 1999), and 77% of attacks were detected.

In Liu et al. (2002), three types ANN methods were investigated: back-propagation (BP), radial basis function (RBF) networks, and self-organizing map (SOM) networks. By using two encoding techniques (binary and decimal representation), the neural networks (NNs) generated high true-positive rates and low false-positive rates. Using binary encoding, the NNs had lower error rates than decimal encoding. However, decimal encoding appears to handle noise well, and the classifiers can be trained with fewer data.

4.4.3 Support Vector Machines (Table 1.3, C.12)

SVM outperforms ANN because it can achieve the global optimum and easily control the overfitting problem by fine tuning support vectors to separate data. Supervised SVM has been employed in anomaly detection by training the SVM structure with both attack data sets and normal data sets. We discuss the application of supervised SVM and ANN on anomaly detection in this section. SVM can also be applied as unsupervised machine learning in this domain.

Application Study 4: Application of SVM Approach for Anomaly Detection

Chen et al. (2005) used BSM audit data from the 1998 DARPA intrusion detection evaluation data sets. As shown in Figure 4.2, they conducted supervised SVM using this data set and compared the results with those obtained using ANN in the same workflow. They collected system call information over processes and extracted frequencies for system calls and processes. They selected the 10 days in which the most attacks appeared in the 7 week training data. Then, they divided the attack data sets into two sets: half for training and half for testing. Next, by replacing "word" and "document" with "system call" and "process," they applied tf×idf-based encoding scheme* to mine the frequency of system calls. Section 4.4.4 contains the detailed description of the encoding scheme. The authors chose Gaussian kernel $k(x, y) = \exp(-(x - y)^2/\delta^2)$ as the kernel function. Then, parameters δ^2 and the margin in the SVM classifier were optimally learned by 10-fold cross validation (CV) using a training data set. Finally, the authors implemented SVM classification over the testing data using the obtained two parameters. They evaluated the detection result

---

* tf×idf method is mostly employed in text mining. It assumes that term frequency (tf, the occurrences of a term in a document) can present the significance of a term in a given document, and the document frequency (df, the occurrences of documents that contain this term) presents the uniqueness of a term in the corpse of documents. Using idf (inverse df), a high weight in a tf×idf scheme is, therefore, reached by a high-term frequency in the given document and a low document frequency of the term in the whole database.

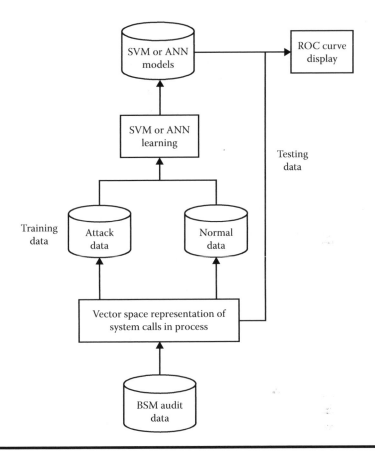

Figure 4.2 Workflow of SVM and ANN testing. (From Chen, W.H. et al., *Comput. Operat. Res.*, 32(10), 2617, 2005. With permission.)

by using ROC with the intrusion detection and FAR. In these experiments, SVM outperformed ANN in simple frequency-based method and tf × idf-based encoding scheme.

In Hu et al. (2003), the performance of robust support vector machines (RSVMs) was compared with that of conventional SVMs and nearest neighbor classifiers in separating normal usage profiles from the intrusive profiles of computer programs. The results indicate the superiority of RSVMs, not only in terms of high intrusion detection accuracy and low false positives, but also in terms of their ability to generalize information in the presence of noise.

4.4.4 Nearest Neighbor-Based Learning (Table 1.3, C.11)

Nearest neighbor-based machine-learning programs assume that the normal pattern of an activity displays a close displacement measured by a distance metric, while anomaly data points lay far from this neighborhood. As described in Section 2.1.2.3, classic KNN employs the voting score among neighborhoods to measure the membership of a given data point. The KNN score is valid only when the size of k exceeds the frequency of any anomaly data type in the data set, and the anomaly data groups are not close to normal data groups. By slightly changing the definition of the nearest neighborhood, variants of nearest neighborhood-based machine-learning methods were proposed in anomaly detection.

We can categorize these methods, based on measure metrics, into two types: distance-based and density-based techniques. Given a set of data points $X = \{x_1, ..., x_m\}$, and a query data point x_{query}, the first method classifies x_{query} as anomaly data if its anomaly score, measured by its distance to its kth nearest neighbor in X, is bigger than a threshold. Different definitions of the anomaly score exist among researchers. For instance, Eskin et al. (2002) measured the anomaly score by the sum of distances between x_{query} and its K nearest neighbors. Ramaswamy et al. (2000) measured the distance between x_{query} and its kth nearest neighbor in X. The distances were measured and ranked for all points. The points at the top of the list, those that have the longest distances, are recognized as anomalies.

The second method assumes normal data lie in higher density areas, while anomaly data have a lower density in the neighborhood. For instance, a local density of the given data point x_{query} can be measured by dividing K by the volume of a hyper-sphere which centers at x_{query}. The volume has to be measured using distance-related techniques. For instance, this sphere can be defined as the smallest sphere centered at x_{query}, which contains K neighbors.

The radius of the sphere is similar to the distance between x_{query}, and its kth nearest neighbor. Subsequently, we can understand density-based methods as an application of inverse distance-based methods. However, the density-based methods encounter challenges when data distribution varies locally by a large amount. As shown in Figure 4.3, p_1 and p_2 are both anomaly points, while C_1 and C_2 are both normal point groups. C_2 is much denser than C_1. The anomaly score based on distance will change significantly due to this distribution, such that a threshold cannot

Figure 4.3   Example of challenges faced by distance-based KNN methods.

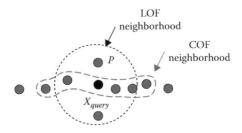

Figure 4.4   Example of neighborhood measures in density-based KNN methods.

be applied easily to identify anomaly data. To solve this problem, density-based methods contribute to local density measures.

As shown in Figure 4.4, the local outlier factor (LOF) and connectivity-based outlier factor (COF) measure the local neighborhood centered at the point X_{query}. In LOF, local density is calculated by dividing K by the volume of the minimum hyper-sphere of the point X_{query}, which is described by the instance above. In COF, the neighborhood of X_{query} grows so that the data point to be included should always hold the minimum distance among all the distances measured between this point and any point in the existing neighborhood. Figure 4.4 shows $k = 6$ and P as detected by LOF. Readers can further discuss what the real differences between distance-based and density-based methods are. What are the advantages and disadvantages of COF and LOF regarding applications?

Application Study 5: Application of KNN Approach for Anomaly Detection

In 2002, Liao and Vemuri used the KNN classifier to classify program behaviors as normal or intrusive. Program behavior, in turn, was represented by the frequency of system calls. Each system call was treated as a word, and the collection of system calls over each program execution was treated as a document. These programs were then classified using the KNN classifier adapted from the document classification method. A short summary of this application follows.

In the project, an array $[A_{ij}]$ was defined to present the occurrence of a system call i in a program j. The tf.idf weighting (see Application Study 4) approach was adapted for calculating the entries of the array,

$$A_{ij} = f_{ij} \times \log\left(\frac{N}{n_i}\right),\tag{4.3}$$

where
  f_{ij} denotes the frequency of the ith system call in program j
  N denotes the total number of programs
  n_i denotes how many times the ith system call is issued

They define a cosine distance metric for the KNN application as follows:

$$dist(X, Y_j) = \frac{\sum_{s_i \in X \cap Y_j} x_i \cdot A_{ij}}{\|X\| \cdot \|Y_j\|}, \tag{4.4}$$

where
   X denotes testing program
   Y_j denotes the jth training program
   s_i denotes a system call occurring in both X and Y_j
   $\|X\|$ and $\|Y_j\|$ denote the norm calculated using Euclidean distance

The experiments were performed using BSM audit data found in the 1998 DARPA intrusion detection evaluation data sets. First, the authors chose 3556 normal programs and 49 distinct system calls in 1 simulation day load for the training phase. Second, they scanned the test audit data for programs to measure the distance using Equation 4.4. Third, the distances were ranked, corresponding to the top K scores for K nearest neighbors for this test audit data. A threshold was applied on the averaged K distances as a cutoff of anomaly detection. Various thresholds and K values were tested in experiments, such that the best performance of the KNN algorithm could be obtained in ROC curves. They reported that the empirical result showed that KNN algorithms detected 100% of the attacks while keeping a FPR at 0.082% with $k = 5$ and threshold = 0.74.

This method seems to offer computational advantages over methods that seek to characterize program behavior with short sequences of system calls and generate individual program profiles.

4.4.5 Hidden Markov Model

HMM considers the transition property of events in cyberinfrastructure. In anomaly detection, HMMs can effectively model temporal variations in program behavior (Warrender et al., 1999; Qiao, 2002; Wang et al., 2006). To apply HMM in anomaly detection, we begin with a normal activity state set S and a normal observable data set of O, $S = \{s_1, ..., s_M\}$, and $O = \{o_1, ..., o_N\}$. Given an observation sequence $Y = (y_1, ..., y_T)$, the objective of HMM is to search for a normal state sequence of $X = (x_1, ..., x_T)$, which has a predicted observation sequence most similar to Y with a probability for this examination. If this probability is less than a predefined threshold, we declare that this observation indicates an anomaly state.

Application Study 6: Application of HMM Approach for Anomaly Detection (Table 1.3, C.8)

In 1999, Warrender et al. performed studies on various publicly available system call data sets from nine programs, such as MIT LPR, and UNM LPR. They suggested that this number roughly corresponded to the number of system calls used by the program. For instance, they implemented 40-state HMMs for many of the programs because 40 system calls composed those programs. The states were fully connected; transitions were allowed from any state to any other state. Transitions and probabilities were initialized randomly, while occasionally, some states were predetermined with knowledge. Then, the Baum-Welch algorithm was applied to build the HMM using training data, and the Viterbi algorithm was implemented on the HMM to find the state sequence of system calls. They assumed that in a good HMM, normal sequences of system calls require only likely transitions and outputs, while anomalous sequences have one or more system calls that require unusual transitions and outputs. Thus, each system call was tested for tracking unusual transitions and outputs. They selected the same threshold, which varied from 0.0000001 to 0.1, for transitions and outputs.

The experiments showed that HMM could detect anomaly data quickly and at a lower mismatch rate. However, HMM training needs multiple passes through the training data, which takes a great deal of time. HMM training also requires extensive memory to store transition probabilities during training, especially for long sequences. We leave the calculation of the required memory size to the reader. Please make further analysis on how to improve the efficiency of HMM in this application.

4.4.6 Kalman Filter

Anomaly detection of network traffic flow is capable of raising an alarm and directing the cyber administrators' attention to the particular original-destination flows. Further analysis and diagnosis can trigger measurements to isolate and stop the anomalies. However, most cybersecurity solutions focus on traffic patterns in one link. Any data flow can transverse multiple links along its path, and anomaly information in the flow may be identified in any route to its destination. Thus, the identification of the data flow in all links in an enterprise information infrastructure will be helpful for the collection of anomaly detection in the network.

A traffic matrix has entries of average workflow from given original nodes to other destination nodes in the given time intervals. These nodes can be computers or routers. As the entries in traffic matrix are dynamic and evolve over time, those entries can be estimated on the recent measurements after a time interval. The entries can be predicted before these recent measurements. The significant difference between the recent estimations and recent predictions will alert a cybersecurity program of an anomalous behavior. Thus, we focus on modeling the dynamic traffic matrix, which consists of all pairs of origin-destination (OD) flows in a cyberinfrastructure. By adapting the notations in Equation 3.14 in Section 3.4.6.1 to the notations in networks, we describe the implementation of Kalman filter in anomaly detection. As no control is involved in cyberinfrastructure, the equation $x_t = A_t x_{t-1} + w_t$, $w_t \sim N(0, Q_t)$ relates network state x_{t-1} to x_t with the state transition matrix A_t and noise process w_t. Equation $y_t = H_t x_t + v_t$, $v_t \sim N(0, R_t)$ correlates y_t, the link counts vector at time t, to x_t, the OD flows. Here, we organize OD flows as a vector account for traffic traversing the link. H_t denotes whether an OD flow (row) traverses a link (column).

As displayed in Figure 2.6, the Kalman filter solves the estimation problem in two steps: prediction and estimation. We do not describe the details of the inference process; interested readers should refer to Soule et al. (2005). If we obtain the prediction $\hat{x}_{t|t-1}$, the error in the prediction of link values is $\varepsilon_t = y_t - H_t \hat{x}_{t|t-1}$. Furthermore, we obtain the residual $\varsigma_t = \hat{x}_{t|t} - \hat{x}_{t|t-1} = K_t \varepsilon_t$, where Kt is the Kalman gain in Figure 2.6. This residual presents the information variation incurred by the new measurement in the network flow. It consists of errors from the network traffic system and anomalies in the infrastructure. Based on this analysis, further anomaly detection schemes can be developed to help network administrators make security decisions.

Application Study 7: Application of Kalman Filter for Anomaly Detection (Table 1.3, C.7) (Soule et al., 2005)

Soule et al. (2005) introduced an approach for anomaly detection for large-scale networks. They attempted to recognize traffic patterns by analyzing the traffic state using a network-wide view. A Kalman filter is used to filter out the "normal" traffic state by comparing the predictions of the traffic state to an inference of the actual traffic state. Then, the residual filtered process is examined for anomalies.

4.4.7 Unsupervised Anomaly Detection

Supervised detection methods use attack-free training data. However, audit data labels are difficult to obtain in real-world network environments. This problem also occurs in signature detection, due to the challenges in manually classifying the small number of attacks in the huge amount of cyber information. Moreover, with the changing network environment or services, patterns of normal traffic will change. The differences between the training and actual data can lead to high FPRs of supervised IDSs.

To address these problems, unsupervised anomaly detection emerges to take unlabeled data as input. Unsupervised anomaly detection aims to find malicious information buried in cyberinfrastructure even without prior knowledge about the data labels and new attacks. Subsequently, unsupervised anomaly detection methods rely on the following assumptions: normal data covers majority while anomaly data are minor in network traffic flow or audit logs; anomaly data points or normal data points are similar in their identity groups while statistically different between groups. We define anomaly detection as an imbalanced learning problem and consider that normal and anomaly data can be clustered. Thus, most of the solutions to unsupervised anomaly detection are clustering-based anomaly/outlier detection techniques. As shown in Figure 4.5, a typical unsupervised anomaly detection

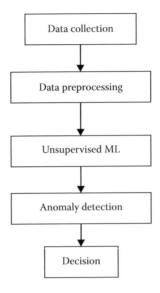

Figure 4.5   Workflow of unsupervised anomaly detection.

system consists of five steps. The first and fifth steps are similar to the other anomaly detection systems. The second, third, and fourth steps contain two assumptions that require the modification and improvement of classic machine-learning methods for cyber anomaly detection. The data processing step will modify the training and testing data so that unsupervised methods can be applied on the valid data based on the above two assumptions. The unsupervised machine-learning methods must be designed for the imbalanced data. The machine-learning results can be used for detection only after labeling the groups, which require intelligent control of some parameters for optimal detection.

4.4.7.1 Clustering-Based Anomaly Detection

Chandola et al. (2006) categorized clustering-based techniques into three groups according to assumptions. Such categorization method is similar to assigning specific patterns or characteristics to the groups of normal and anomalous data. As with KNN, we categorize clustering-based anomaly detection into two groups: distance-based clustering and density-based clustering. The first group includes *k*-means clustering (Portnoy et al., 2001; Jiang et al., 2006), EM (Eskin, 2000; Traore, 2008), and SOM (Sarasamma and Zhu, 2006). The second group includes CLIQUE and MAFIA (Leung and Leckie, 2005). We focus on the first group because, according to our knowledge, the second group has fewer research results, and does not have as good anomaly detection results as the first group. For further information about density-based methods, such as CLIQUE and MAFIA, and their applications, readers should consult Leung and Leckie (2005) and Agrawal et al. (1998) for further reading.

The most deployed distance-based clustering method is adapted from k-means clustering (see Section 2.1.1). Without defining K in these algorithms, the clustering hyper-spheres are constrained by a threshold r. Given data set $X = \{x_1, \dots, x_m\}$ and cluster set $C = \{C_1, \dots, C_K\}$, distance metric $dist(x_i, C_j)$ measures the closeness between data point x_i, $i = 1, \dots, m$, and cluster C_j. To implement distance-based clustering, follow the steps below:

Step 1. Initialize cluster set $C = \{C_1, \dots, C_K\}$.
Step 2. Assign each data point x_i in X to the closest cluster C^*, $C^* \in \{C_1, \dots, C_{K\bar{0}}\}$, if $dist(x_i, C^*) \le r$; or creation of new cluster C' for this data point, and update the cluster set C.
Step 3. Iterate until all data points are assigned to a cluster.

In the above steps, the most employed distance metric is Euclidean distance. If we choose the distance between a data point x_i and cluster C_j to measure $dist(x_i, C_j)$, the above algorithm will be similar to k-means clustering, except we will have an additional constraint r for the clustering threshold. As all training data are unlabeled, we cannot determine which clusters belong to normal or anomaly types. Each cluster may include mixed instances of normal data and different types of attacks. As we assume that normal data over-number anomaly data, generally the clusters that constitute more than a percentage α of the training data set are labeled as "normal" groups. The other clusters are labeled as "attack."

As we implicitly determine abnormal clusters by the size of these classes, some small-sized normal data groups can be misclassified as anomaly clusters especially when we have multi-type normal data. We recommend readers further analyze and explore the solutions to this problem. Meanwhile, threshold r also affects the result of clustering. When r is large, the cluster number will decrease; when r is small, the cluster number will increase. The selection of r is dependent on the knowledge of the normal data distribution. For instance, we know statistically it should be greater than the intra-cluster distance and smaller than the inter-cluster distance. Jiang et al. (2006) selected r by generating the mean and standard deviation of distances between pairs of a sample data points from the training data set.

Once the training data have been clustered and labeled, testing data can be grouped according to their shortest distance to any cluster in the cluster set.

Application Study 8: Application of Clustering for Anomaly Detection

Portnoy et al. (2001) applied the clustering anomaly detection method on the DARPA MIT Knowledge Discovery and Data Mining (KDD) Cup 1999 data set. This data set recorded 4,900,000 data points with 24 attack types and normal activity in the background. Each data point is a vector of extracted feature values from the connection record obtained between IP addresses during simulated intrusions.

The authors performed CV in training and testing. The entire KDD data set was partitioned into 10 subsets. The subsets containing only one type of attacks or full of attacks were removed, such that only four subsets were left for CV. Then, they filtered the training data sets from KDD data for attacks such that the attack data and normal data had a proportion about 1:99 in the resulting training data set.

Before training and testing phases, the authors evaluated the performance using ROC (FP-TP). They ran 10% of the KDD data to measure the performance when choosing the sensitive parameters: threshold r and percentage $1 - \alpha$. They selected $r = 40$ and $\alpha = 0.85$ after balancing between TP and FP in ROC for achieving the higher TP and acceptable FP.

Finally, training and testing were performed several times with different selections of the combinational subsets for training and testing. Clustering with unlabelled data resulted in a lower detection rate for attacks than clustering with supervised learning. However, unlabeled data can potentially detect unknown attacks through an automated or semi-automated process, which will allow cyber administrators to concentrate on the most likely attack data.

4.4.7.2 Random Forests

Random forests have been employed broadly in various applications, including multimedia information retrieval and bioinformatics. The random forests algorithm has better predication accuracy and efficiency on large data sets in high-dimensional feature space. Network traffic flow has such data characteristics such that random forest algorithms are applied (Zhang and Zulkernine, 2006; Zhang, 2008) to detect outliers in data sets of network traffic without attack-free training data. In the framework, the reported results show that the proposed approach is comparable to previously reported unsupervised anomaly detection approaches.

As introduced in Section 2.1.1.9, the accuracy of random forests depends on the strength of the individual tree classifiers and a measure of the dependence between them. The number of randomly selected features at each node is critical for the estimated quality of the above measures.

Consequently, in building the network traffic model, two important parameters must be selected: the number of random features to split the node of trees (N_f), and the number of trees in a forest (N_t). The combinational values of these two variables are selected, corresponding to the optimal prediction accuracy of the random forests.

In the detection process, random forests use proximity measure between the paired data points to find outliers. If a data point has low proximity measures to all the other data points in a given data set, it is likely to be outlier. Given a data set $X = \{x_1, \ldots, x_n\}$, enquiry data point $x_{enquiry} \in X$, and all the other data in class C_j, $x_j \in C_j$, the average proximity between data point $x_{enquiry}$, and all the other data points $x_j \in C_j$ are defined as,

$$\overline{prox}(x_{enquiry}) = \frac{1}{|C_j| - 1} \sum_{x_j \in C_j} prox^2(x_{enquiry}, x_j). \qquad (4.5)$$

The degree of a data point $x_{enquiry}$ to be an outlier of class C_j is represented as

$$\frac{|X|}{\overline{prox(x_{enquiry})}}.$$ (4.6)

We can set a threshold for the above equation so that any $x_{enquiry} \in X$ will be detected as an outlier. In the above, $|C_j|$ and $|X|$ denote the number of data points in class C_j and X, respectively.

The proximity between $x_{enquiry}$ and $x_j \in C_j$, $prox^2(x_{enquiry}, x_j)$, is accumulated by one, when both data points are found in the same leaf of a tree. The final summation result should be divided by the number of trees to normalize the results. Following the above equations, we can obtain proximity, and the degree of an outlier in any class for each data point extracted from a network traffic data set. Moreover, the decision can be made using the threshold.

Application Study 9: Application of Random Forests for Anomaly Detection

Zhang and Zulkernine (2006) applied the random forest algorithm to the DARPA MIT KDD Cup 1999 data set. They selected five services as pattern labels for a random forests algorithm, including ftp, http, pop, smtp, and telnet. Since services appear in any network traffic flow, this labeling process is automatic, and the original labels of attack types or "normal" are removed. Four groups of data sets were generated by combining normal data and attack data at the ratio of 99:1, 98:2, 95:5, and 90:10. A total of 47,426 normal traffic flow data were selected from ftp, pop, telnet, 5% http, and 10% smtp normal services.

The authors evaluated the performance of the system using ROC. They reported a better detection rate while keeping the FP rate lower than in other unsupervised anomaly detection systems presented by Portnoy et al. (2001) and Leung and Leckie (2005). However, they indicated that the detection performance over minority attacks was much lower than that of majority intrusions. They improved the detection system by using random forests in the hybrid system of misuse detection and anomaly detection. We discuss this problem in Chapter 5.

4.4.7.3 Principal Component Analysis/Subspace

As we discussed in Section 3.4.6, anomaly detection in OD flows is challenging due to the high-dimensional features and noisy and large volumes of streaming data. This problem becomes more difficult as Internet links are developed and integrated to more complex and faster networks. Network anomaly detection using dimensionality reduction techniques has received much attention recently. In particular, network-wide anomaly detection based on PCA has emerged as a powerful method for detecting a wide variety of anomalies. PCA has demonstrated its ability in finding correlations across multiple links in network-wide analysis (Lakhina et al., 2004a,b) and detecting a wide variety of anomalies (Lakhina, 2004).

Let matrix Y denote the network traffic data in space $\mathbb{R}^{d \times n}$, where each row presents a data point, e.g., observation at a time point, and each column presents a link in network. As discussed in Section 1.3.2.5, PCA can explore the intrinsic principle dimensionality and present the variance of data along these principle dimensions such that the variability of data can be captured in a lower dimensionality. Meanwhile, traffic on different links is dependent, and link traffic is the superposition of OD flows. Lakhina et al. (2004a,b) showed that, in a 40-link network, three-to-four principal components could capture the majority of variance in the link time-series data.

Using the PCA method described in Section 1.3.2.5, we can project network traffic flow data in matrix Y to any principle component (direction) v_i by $Y \cdot v_i$ (eigenvalue). The value of $Y \cdot v_i$ indicates the significance of network flows captured in the ith principal component. Given observations in matrix Y are time-series network flow, principal component v_i presents the ith strongest temporal trend in the whole network flows. As normal data dominate network traffic, we can assign the top principal flow in normal group, and the remaining flows as anomalies.

Let S denote the space spanned by the first p principal components and $\tilde{S}$ denote the remaining principal components. Then, each traffic flow y can be decomposed into two subspaces: normal traffic vector $\bar{y}$ and anomaly traffic vector $\tilde{y}$. Using the top p principal components as columns, we obtain a matrix $Q = [v_1, ..., v_p]$. Next, we project data Y onto normal space S and anomaly space $\tilde{S}$ by $\bar{y} = QQ^T y$, and $\tilde{y} = (1 - QQ^T)y \cdot \tilde{y}$ can measure the sudden anomaly behavior in network OD flow. Moreover, we can use this decomposition to detect the time of the anomaly flow, identify the anomaly source and destination, and quantify the size of the anomaly.

Assuming the network-traffic flow data follows multivariate Gaussian distribution, a threshold ε_β^2 can be obtained using statistical estimation. If $\|\tilde{y}\|^2 \leq \varepsilon_\beta^2$, we say this network traffic flow y is normal at the $1 - \beta$ confidence level. Lakhina et al. (2004a,b) applied the Q-statistic test using the results from Jackson and Mudholkar (1979).

PCA-based subspace methods have been explored in a number of research reports (Lakhina, 2004; Lakhina et al., 2004a,b, 2005; Li, 2006; Ringberg et al., 2007) because of their effective ability to diagnose network traffic anomalies in an entire cyber system. However, it has also been found that tuning PCA to operate effectively is difficult and requires more robust techniques than have been presented thus far.

The Ringberg et al. (2007) study identified and evaluated four challenges associated with using PCA to detect traffic anomalies; e.g., sufficient large anomalies can contaminate the normal subspace. Robust statistical methods are developed to solve the sensitivity problems. Moreover, Li et al. (2006) showed how to use random aggregations of IP flows (i.e., sketches) for a more precise identification of the underlying causes of anomalies. They presented a subspace method to combine traffic sketches to detect anomalies with a high accuracy rate and to identify the IP flows(s) that are responsible for the anomaly.

Table 4.3   Data Sets Used in Lakhina et al. (2004a)

Networks	Definition	#PoPs	#Links
Sprint-Europe 1 (Jul. 07–Jul. 13)	European backbone of a US tier-1 ISP carrying commercial traffic for companies, local ISPs, etc.	13	49
Sprint-Europe 2 (Aug. 11–Aug. 17)			
Abilene (Apr. 07–Apr. 13)	Internet2 backbone and carrying academia and research traffic for major universities in the continental United States.	11	41

Source: Lakhina, A. et al., Characterization of network-wide anomalies in traffic flows, in: *Proceedings of the 4th ACM SIGCOMM Conference on Internet Measurement*, Taormina, Sicily, Italy, 2004a, pp. 201–206. With permission.

Application Study 10: Application of PCA/Subspace for Anomaly Detection (Table 1.3, C.4 and C.11)

Lakhina et al. (2004a,b) collected three network-traffic data sets from two backbone networks: Sprint-Europe and Abilene. As shown in Table 4.3, the authors aggregated packets into flows and aggregated traffic-flow byte counts, which they then divided into bins of 10 min to sample both Sprint and Abilene data sets.

Because the true anomalies have to be identified in data sets before the quality of the estimated anomalies of the proposed PCA-based subspace method can be determined, the authors employed an exponential weighted moving average and Fourier scheme on the OD flow level to capture the volume anomalies. Then, they evaluated the PCA-based subspace method in diagnosing the above networks using the detection rate (TP) and false-alarm rate (FP), and the diagnosis effectiveness in the event that the time and location of anomalies varied. The results showed that PCA-based subspace consistently diagnoses the largest volume anomalies with a higher detection rate and a lower FAR.

4.4.7.4 One-Class Supervised Vector Machine

As shown in Section 3.4.3, a standard SVM is a supervised machine-learning method, which requires labeled data for training the classification model. SVM has been adapted into an unsupervised machine-learning method in Jackson and Mudholkar (1979). The one-class SVM attempts to separate the data from the origin with a maximum margin by solving the following quadratic optimization:

$$\min_{w \in F, \xi_i \in R, \rho \in R} \frac{1}{2}\|w\|^2 + \frac{1}{vl}\sum_{i}^{l} \xi_i - \rho, \tag{4.7}$$

$$\text{s.t. } (w \cdot \phi(x_i)) \ge \rho - \xi_i, \quad \xi_i \ge 0. \tag{4.8}$$

In the above, ρ is the origin, $v \in (0, 1]$ denotes a parameter, which balances the maximum margin and contains most of the data in the separated region. In anomaly detection, v corresponds to the ratio of detected anomalies in the entire data set. ξ_i presents slack variables. Nonzero ξ_i are penalized in objective function. F denotes the l dimensional feature space of the given data set X. $\phi(x)$ is a feature map from data point $x \in X$ to the point $\phi(x)$ in feature space F. Parameters w and ρ are weights and solve the hyper-plane. Using the optimization result, we obtain the following decision function:

$$f(x) = \text{sgn}((w \cdot \phi(x)) - \rho). \tag{4.9}$$

By introducing a Lagrangian with its multipliers α_i, we reformulate the optimization problem as a dual problem as follows:

$$\min_{\alpha} \sum_{ij} \alpha_i \alpha_j K_{\phi}(x_i, x_j), \tag{4.10}$$

and

$$\text{s.t. } \alpha_i \in \left[0, \frac{1}{vl}\right], \quad \sum_{i} \alpha_i = 1, \tag{4.11}$$

corresponding to the decision function,

$$f(x) = \text{sgn}\left(\sum_{i} \alpha_i K_{\phi}(x_i, x) - \sum_{j} \alpha_j K_{\phi}(x_i, x_j)\right). \tag{4.12}$$

Application Study 11: Application of One Class SVM/KNN/Cluster-Based Estimation for Anomaly Detection (Table 1.3, C.4 and C11)

Eskin et al. (2002) presented algorithms to process unlabeled data by mapping data points to a feature space. Anomalies were detected by finding the data points in the sparse regions of the feature space. They presented two feature-mapping methods for network connection records and system call sequences: data-dependent normalization feature mapping, and spectrum kernel. They also implemented three algorithms and assembled them with the two feature-mapping methods.

The motivation of feature mapping rose from the assumption that some probability distribution generated data in high-dimensional feature space, and anomalies lie in the low-density region of the probability distribution. To avoid the difficulties of finding this probability distribution, anomalies were located in the sparse region of a feature space. Given two data points in the input data set x_1 and x_2, instead of using $d(x_1, x_2) = \|x_1 - x_2\|$ to calculate the distance between these two data points we obtained the distance $d_{\phi}(x_1, x_2) = \|\phi(x_1) - \phi(x_2)\|$ by using feature mapping $\phi()$. They used kernel function $K_\phi(x_1, x_2)$ in computing $d_\phi(x_1, x_2) = \|\phi(x_1) - \phi(x_2)\|$ to simplify computation. They applied radial basis kernel $K_\phi(x_1, x_2) = \exp(-(\|x_1 - x_2\|^2/\sigma^2))$ in the applications. Using the above kernel function and the mapped distance function, they applied fixed-width clustering method (as discussed in Section 4.4.7.1 and application study) to compute how many data points were within a fix width of the enquiry data point in the feature space section. For instance, given data points x_1 and x_2 and a fixed width w, these two data points are considered to be within one cluster if $d_\phi(x_1, x_2) \leq w$. The data points falling in the small clusters were labeled as anomalous.

Next, they applied KNN (as discussed in Section 4.4.4) by using the sum of distances between the enquiry data and the k nearest neighbors as a score. Their algorithm is based on inequalities of triangles. Given the clustering result above, they obtain a cluster set C for data set X. For example, in Figure 4.6, using fixed width w, we obtain two clusters centered at $c(x)$ and $c(y)$. We obtain,

$$d(x, x_1) \leq 2w, \tag{4.13}$$

and

$$\left\| d(x, x_1) - d(c(x), x_1) \right\| \leq d(c(x), x) \leq w. \tag{4.14}$$

Then, given data point x, we can find a lower bound for the data points in the nearest neighborhood of x as follows:

$$d_{\min} = \min_{c \in C} d_\phi(x, c(x)) - w. \tag{4.15}$$

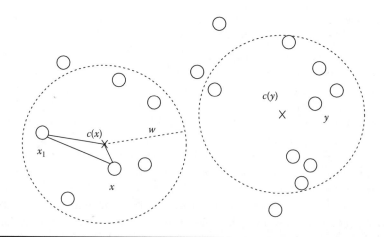

Figure 4.6 Analysis of distance inequalities in KNN and clustering.

Here, $\min_{c \in C} dist(x, c(x))$ calculates the minimum distance between data point x and its cluster center $c(x)$. Then, the data points $\{x_i\}$ in this nearest cluster are evaluated by the distance $dist(x, x_i)$ between x_i and x. If $dist(x, x_i) < d_{min}$, then data point x_i belongs to the same cluster in KNN. The algorithm will terminate for data point x until k data points, which meet this criteria, are found. If the clusters in C do not have enough candidate data points for KNN, try the second nearest cluster for data point x and update d_{min} using Equation 4.15.

Once they had performed the equation that we have applied above, the authors applied one-class SVM using the sequential minimal optimization algorithm to solve for optimization (Platt, 1999). To examine the proposed methods, they used MIT DARPA for system call data and KDD CUP 99 data as network data. They filtered many of the attacks in KDD data, so that there was 1%–1.5% malicious data in the data set. They used 3 weeks of data from the BSM portion of the DARPA set, including two programs: ps and eject. The data sets were split for training and testing purposes. They varied detection threshold and evaluated the system performance using ROC curves with detection rate (TP) and false-alarm rate (FP). The unsupervised machine learning and detection results were compared against the ground truth. They obtained the empirical parameter settings as below (Tables 4.4 through 4.6).

Experimental results showed the algorithms performed perfectly on the system calls. The authors explained that the spectrum kernel contained all coordinates for all possible subsequences for feature mapping; a large number of the same subsequences

Table 4.4 Parameter Settings for Clustering-Based Methods

Clustering-Based Methods	Network Traffic Data	Eject	ps
Width	40	5	10

Table 4.5 Parameter Settings for KNN

KNN	Network Traffic Data	Eject	ps
K	10,000	2	15

Table 4.6 Parameter Settings for SVM

One Class SVM	Network Traffic Data	System Calls
v	0.01	0.05
σ^2	12	1

in system calls led to similar process traces. The normal processes clumped in the feature space while many subsequences that occurred in malicious processes did not appear in the normal processes.

The three algorithms performed similarly over the KDD network data: all three obtained lower detection rates than were obtained for misuse and signature detection. They attributed the lower detection rate to the inaccessibility of the clean training data, the same feature region used by both attacks and normal data.

4.4.8 Information Theoretic (Table 1.3, C.5)

As shown in Sections 4.4.4 and 4.4.7.3, the deviations in traffic volume (number of bytes or packets) can be used as signals for detecting anomalies. Although volume-based detection techniques can find significant traffic deviations, many anomalous behaviors do not cause large changes in traffic volume. Moreover, most research in anomaly detection and identification is limited in point solutions for specific types of anomalies, e.g., portscan. Thus, researchers exert efforts to extract the associative relationship between traffic features in network flows, such that the corresponding anomaly detection techniques can detect the small anomalies in network-wide traffic. Entropy can be used to summarize and analyze feature distributions.

Lakhina et al. (2005) showed that entropy enables the highly sensitive detection of a wide range of anomalies by capturing unusual changes in network flow and feature distributions. This work provides additional information for the exploration of raw network flow in the classification of anomalies via unsupervised learning. Feinstein et al. (2003) computed the entropy of packet header fields to identify DDoS attacks. They developed anomaly detection techniques based on the observation that that entropy values for networks under attack have a wider range than entropy values for networks that are not under attack. Lee and Xiang (2001) used several entropy-based measures to characterize an audit data set. These measures included conditional entropy, relative conditional entropy, information gain, and information cost. The experiments showed the efficiency of using these measures in machine-learning modeling and evaluation for anomaly detection.

4.4.9 Other Machine-Learning Methods Applied in Anomaly Detection (Table 1.3, C.2)

Machine-learning methods have been proposed to learn the probability distribution of data and to apply statistical tests to detect outliers. Eskin (2000) presented a mixture probability model of normal and anomalous data based on EM algorithms. The probability distribution can be estimated using machine-learning techniques. He used bootstrap for anomaly detection. Other statistical machine-learning methods have been investigated in anomaly detection applications, such as mean and variance (Cannady, 1998; Soule et al., 2005), Hotelling's T^2 test and chi-square test

(Ye et al., 2002; Feinstein et al., 2003), Helinger score (Yamanishi and Takeuchi, 2001), histogram density (Yamanishi et al., 2000), Bayesian law (Mahoney and Chan, 2002), cumulative summation (CUSUM), and statistical test (Soule et al., 2005). Ye et al. (2001) used a series of probabilistic techniques of anomaly detection, including decision tree, Hotelling's T^2 test, Chi-square multivariate test, and Markov chain in an information system for detecting intrusions. These techniques were applied to the same training set and the same testing set of computer audit data to investigate the frequency and order of computer audit data.

4.5 Summary

In this chapter, we have described supervised machine-learning and unsupervised machine-learning methods. Extensive techniques have been studied in the past few years. While a large number of problems have not been solved, such as how to reduce false alarms while retaining a high detection rate, anomaly detection machine-learning techniques have been advantageous over misuse detection techniques in detecting new or unknown attacks efficiently. Unsupervised machine-learning methods outperform supervised machine-learning methods in updating rules intelligently while the detection rates downgrade.

In real-world applications, it is difficult to find sufficient attack data and normal data for training or testing. Most attacks will remain unknown. Meanwhile, online anomaly detection methods for streaming networks are being developed for future machine-learning methods. Subsequently, the design and application of unsupervised machine-learning methods for anomaly detection will be important in developing better cybersecurity software in the future.

We do not include semi-supervised machine-learning methods in this chapter, although they have been applied on both labeled and unlabeled training data so that a small amount of labeled training data can improve the clustering result. Readers should refer to Chandola (2006) and Sugato et al. (2004) for further information on the subject.

Abnormal detection depends predominantly on accurately profiling normal behaviors among users or programs. In this chapter, we have discussed a number of techniques for accurate profiling, such as rule-based, KNN, PCA, and subspace clustering methods. We find many challenges in dealing with the huge amounts of dynamic network flows. One solution is to find the dominant trends or characteristics for profiling cyber information so that we can simplify data sets of the cyber-infrastructure into groups or lower dimension. We will further discuss profiling in Chapter 6.

As we discussed in Chapter 3 and in this chapter, misuse detection systems have a high accuracy rate for detection, but are not able to detect new or unknown attacks. Anomaly detection systems can potentially find new attacks, but they generally have a lower accuracy rate for detection and a higher FAR. Hybrid systems have been developed to integrate misuse and anomaly detection techniques so that the abilities of these techniques can be combined. These hybrid systems achieve better detection accuracy than misuse or anomaly detection techniques do when used alone. We describe machine-learning applications in hybrid detection systems in Chapter 5.

References

Agrawal, R., J. Gehrke, D. Gunopulos, and P. Raghavan. Automatic subspace clustering of high dimensional data for data mining applications. In: *Proceedings of the ACM SIGMOD International Conference on Management of Data*, Seattle, WA, 1998, pp. 94–105.

Apiletti, D., E. Baralis, T. Cerquitelli, and V. D'Elia. Characterizing network traffic by means of the NetMine framework. *Computer Networks* 53 (6) (2008): 774–789.

Cannady, J. Artificial neural networks for misuse detection. In: *Proceedings of the 1998 National Information Systems Security Conference* (*NISSC'98*), Arlington, VA, 1998, pp. 443–456.

Chandola, V., E. Banerjee et al. Data mining for cyber security. In: *Data Warehousing and Data Mining Techniques For Computer Security*, edited by A. Singhal, Springer, New York, 2006.

Chen, W.H., S.H. Hsu, and H.P. Shen. Application of SVM and ANN for intrusion detection. *Computers & Operations Research* 32 (10) (2005): 2617–2634.

Eskin, E. Anomaly detection over noisy data using learned probability distributions. In: *Proceedings of the International Conference on Machine Learning* (*ICML*), Palo Alto, CA, 2000.

Eskin, E., A. Arnold, M. Prerau, L. Portnoy, and S. Stolfo. A geometric framework for unsupervised anomaly detection: Detecting intrusions in unlabeled data. In: *Applications of Data Mining in Computer Security*, edited by S. Jajodia and D. Barbara. Dordrecht: Kluwer, 2002, Chap. 4.

Feinstein, L., D. Schnackenberg, R. Balupari, and D. Kindred. Statistical approaches to DDoS attack detection and response. In: *Proceedings of DARPA Information Survivability Conference and Exposition*, Washington, DC, 2003, pp. 303–314.

Ghosh, A.K., J. Wanken, and F. Charron. Detecting anomalous and unknown intrusions against programs. In: *Proceedings of the 1998 Annual Computer Security Applications Conference* (*ACSAC*), Phoenix, AZ, 1998.

Ghosh, A.K., A. Schwartzbard, and M. Schatz. Learning program behavior profiles for intrusion detection USENIX Association. In: *Proceedings of the 1st USENIX Workshop on Intrusion Detection and Network Monitoring*, Santa Clara, CA, 1999.

Gong, F. Deciphering detection techniques: Part II. Anomaly-based intrusion detection. white paper, Mcafee Network Security Technologies Group, 2003.

Luis MartinGarcia, Tcpdump/Libpcap public repository, http://www.tcpdump.org/, Accessed on January 31, 2011.

Hu, W.J., Y.H. Liao, and V.R. Vemuri. Robust support vector machines for anomaly detection in computer security. In: *Proceedings of the International Conference on Machine Learning*, Las Vegas, NV, 2003, pp. 282–289.

Jackson, J.E. and G.S. Mudholkar. Control procedures for residuals associated with principal component analysis. *Technometrics* 21 (3) (1979): 341–349.

Jiang, S., X. Song, H. Wang, J. Han, and Q. Li. A clustering-based method for unsupervised intrusion detections. *Pattern Recognition Letters* 27 (7) (2006): 802–810.

Lakhina, A., M. Crovella, and C. Diot. Characterization of network-wide anomalies in traffic flows. In: *Proceedings of the 4th ACM SIGCOMM Conference on Internet Measurement*, Taormina, Sicily, Italy, 2004a, pp. 201–206.

Lakhina, A., M. Crovella, and C. Diot. Diagnosing network-wide traffic anomalies. In: *Proceedings of the 2004 Conference on Applications, Technologies, Architectures, and Protocols for Computer Communications*, Portland, OR, 2004b, pp. 219–230.

Lakhina, A., M. Crovella, and C. Diot. Mining anomalies using traffic feature distributions. In: *Proceedings of the 2005 Conference on Applications, Technologies, Architectures, and Protocols for Computer Communications*, Philadelphia, PA, 2005.

Lee, W. and S.J. Stolfo. Data mining approaches for intrusion detection. In: *Proceedings of the 7th USENIX Security Symposium*, San Antonio, TX, 1998.

Lee, W. and Xiang, D. Information-theoretic measures for anomaly detection. In: *IEEE Symposium on Security and Privacy*, Oakland, CA, 2001.

Lee, W., S.J. Stolfo, and K.W. Mok. A data mining framework for building intrusion detection models. In: *Proceedings of the IEEE Symposium on Security and Privacy*, Oakland, CA, 1999, pp. 120–132.

Leung, K. and C. Leckie. Unsupervised anomaly detection in network intrusion detection using clusters. In: *Proceedings of the Twenty-Eighth Australasian Conference on Computer Science*, Newcastle, Australia, 2005, pp. 333–342.

Li, X., F. Bian, M. Crovella, C. Diot, R. Govindan, G. Iannaccone, and A. Lakhina. Detection and identification of network anomalies using sketch subspaces. In: *Proceedings of the 6th ACM SIGCOMM Conference on Internet Measurement*, New York, 2006, pp. 147–152.

Liao, Y.H. and V.R. Vemuri. Use of *k*-nearest neighbor classifier for intrusion detection. *Computers & Security* 21 (5) (2002): 439–448.

Liu, Z., G. Florez, S.M. Bridges. A comparison of input representations in neural networks: a case study in intrusion detection. In: *Proceedings of the 2002 International Joint Conference on Neural Networks*, Honolulu, HI, 2002.

Luo, J. and S.M. Bridges. Mining fuzzy association rules and fuzzy frequency episodes for intrusion detection. *International Journal of Intelligent Systems* 15 (8) (2000): 687–703.

Mahoney, M.V. and P.K. Chan. Learning nonstationary models of normal network traffic for detecting novel attacks. In: *Proceedings of the eighth ACM SIGKDD International Conference on Knowledge Discovery and Data Mining*, Edmonton, Canada, 2002, pp. 376–386.

Mannila, H. and H. Toivonen. Discovering generalized episodes using minimal occurrences. In: *Proceedings of the 2nd International Conference on Knowledge Discovery in Databases and Data Mining*, Portland, OR, 1996.

Platt, J. Fast training support vector machines using sequential minimal optimization. In: *Advanced in Kernel Methods-Support Vector Learning*, edited by B. Scholkopf, C.J.C. Burges, and A.J. Smola, pp. 185–208. Cambridge, MA: MIT Press, 1999.

Portnoy, L., E. Eskin, and S. Stolfo. Intrusion detection with unlabeled data using clustering. In: *Proceedings of ACM CSS Workshop on Data Mining Applied to Security (DMSA)*, Philadelphia, PA, 2001.

Qiao, Y., X.W. Xin, Y. Bin, and S. Ge. Anomaly intrusion detection method based on HMM. *Electronics Letters* 38 (13) (2002): 663–664.

Ramaswamy, S., R. Rastogi, and K. Shim. Efficient algorithms for mining outliers from large data sets. In: *Proceedings of the 2000 ACM SIGMOD International Conference on Management of Data*, New York, 2000, pp. 427–438.

Ringberg, H., A. Soule, J. Rexford, and C. Diot. Sensitivity of PCA for traffic anomaly detection. *ACM SIGMETRICS Performance Evaluation Review* 35 (1) (2007): 109–120.

Sarasamma, S.T. and Q.A. Zhu. Min-max hyperellipsoidal clustering for anomaly detection in network security. *IEEE Transactions on Systems, Man, and Cybernetics, Part B: Cybernetics* 36 (4) (2006): 887–901.

Soule, A., K. Salamatian, and N. Taft. Combining filtering and statistical methods for anomaly detection. In: *Proceedings of the 5th ACM SIGCOMM Conference on Internet Measurement*, Berkeley, CA, 2005.

Sugato, B., B. Mikhail, and R.J. Mooney. A probabilistic framework for semi-supervised clustering. In: *Proceedings of the Tenth ACM SIGKDD International Conference on Knowledge Discovery and Data Mining*, Seattle, WA, 2004.

Traore, I. and W. Lu. Unsupervised anomaly detection using an evolutionary extension of k-means algorithm. *International Journal of Information and Computer Security* 2 (2) (2008): 107–139.

Wang, W., X. Guan, X. Zhang, and L. Yang. Profiling program behavior for anomaly intrusion detection based on the transition and frequency property of computer audit data. *Computers & Security* 25 (7) (2006): 539–550.

Warrender, C., S. Forrrest, and B. Pearlmutter. Detecting intrusions using system calls: Alternative data models. *IEEE Symposium on Security and Privacy*, Oakland, CA, 1999, pp. 133–145.

Yamanishi, K. and J.I. Takeuchi. Discovering outlier filtering rules from unlabeled data: Combining a supervised learner with an unsupervised learner. In: *Proceedings of the Seventh ACM SIGKDD International Conference on Knowledge Discovery and Data Mining*, Edmonton, Canada, 2001, pp. 389–394.

Yamanishi, K., J.I. Takeuchi, G. Williams, and P. Milne. On-line unsupervised outlier detection using finite mixtures with discounting learning algorithms. In: *Proceedings of the Sixth ACM SIGKDD International Conference on Knowledge Discovery and Data Mining*, Boston, MA, 2000, pp. 320–324.

Ye, N., X.Y. Li, Q. Chen, S.M. Emran, and M.M. Xu. Probabilistic techniques for intrusion detection based on computer audit data. *IEEE Transactions on Systems, Man, and Cybernetics—Part A: Systems and Humans* 31 (4) (2001): 266–274.

Ye, N., S.M. Emran, Q. Chen, and S. Vilbert. Multivariate statistical analysis of audit trails for host-based intrusion detection. *IEEE Transactions on Computers* 51 (2002): 810–820.

Zhang, J. and M. Zulkernine. Anomaly based network intrusion detection with unsupervised outlier detection. In: *IEEE International Conference on Communications*, Istanbul, Turkey, 2006.

Zhang, J., M. Zulkernine, and A. Haque. Random-forest-based network intrusion detection systems. *IEEE Transactions on Systems, Man, and Cybernetics, Part C: Applications and Reviews* 38 (5) (2008): 649–659.

Chapter 5

Machine Learning for Hybrid Detection

> Coming together is a beginning. Keeping together is progress. Working together is success.
>
> **Henry Ford**
> *Teams and Team Work*

In this chapter, we address hybrid intrusion detection techniques, which we categorize into three groups based on different combinational methods. We then analyze the ability of the hybrid methods to guide the design and development of these systems using results obtained by previous researchers. Furthermore, we investigate how to design and employ hybrid systems to raise the detection rate for known intrusions and decrease the false-positive rate for unknown attacks. Several intrusion detection system/machine-learning hybrids are demonstrated, and their abilities for intrusion detection are analyzed. The techniques we explore in this chapter are artificial neural network, association rules, random forest classifiers, and other machine-learning algorithms. As hybrid systems are normally generated based on the existing anomaly and misuse detection systems, we do not analyze the mechanism of machine-learning methods and their applications in intrusion detection. For that information, please refer to Chapters 3 and 4.

First, we introduce the fundamental background for hybrid detection systems. We describe the difference between anomaly detection and signature detection and explain the key challenges in anomaly detection. Second, we introduce a hybrid detection workflow and describe the mechanism of hybrid methods as applied in the workflow. In addition, we analyze the difficulties that intrusion detection systems face in cybersecurity applications. Such difficulties include locating suspicious events and lowering non-negligible false-alarm rates. Third, we present the basic techniques and applications of several representative hybrid systems in detail.

We discuss misuse–anomaly sequence detection systems, anomaly–misuse sequence detection systems, parallel detection systems, and complicated detection systems. We analyze the application of machine-learning methods in these systems in application studies. Then, we briefly introduce several other hybrid systems and the respective machine-learning methods in this domain. We analyze the improvements made by hybrid systems over the fundamental misuse and anomaly detection systems in the intrusion detection rate and the false-alarm rate. Fourth, we summarize the achievements and limitations of the present research results in anomaly detection and guide readers in the emerging research directions.

5.1 Hybrid Detection

Since we discussed misuse/signature detection techniques in Chapter 3, we know that misuse detection methods are designed to build signatures for malicious data so that attacks matching the malicious patterns will be detected. Most misuse detection systems have a high detection rate and a low false-alarm rate, are easy to implement, and perform detection quickly. However, misuse detection techniques suffer from the difficulties of detecting unknown attacks. In Chapter 4, we explain that anomaly detection techniques aim to build normal patterns in a cyberinfrastructure, such that they can capture the patterns that deviate significantly from the normal model. As attacks or other malicious data generally perform abnormal behaviors, anomaly detection methods can capture new attacks. However, if normal data shows the same patterns as malicious data, the number of false alarms rises. Building a profile for normal patterns must ensure that both the detection rate and the false-alarm rate are acceptable. A wide profile can cause a low detection rate, and few attacks can be detected. A narrow profile can cause a high rate of false alarms. As misuse detection methods and anomaly detection methods have compensational functions and abilities, hybrid techniques have been proposed to integrate the flexibility and intelligence of anomaly detection methods and the accuracy and reliability of misuse detection methods.

A simple assembly of any misuse detection system and another anomaly detection system may not improve detection accuracy over either system. For optimal performance, we bring the systems together and keep them together. However, running the systems together will not ensure that the hybrid system works successfully.

We must explore the hybrid system to achieve positive interactions and good performance between the two systems. Achieving such an interaction will be the key topic of discussion in this chapter.

In brief, designing a good hybrid detection system requires us to consider two critical issues before implementation. First, we have to determine the best candidates of misuse or anomaly detection systems for the integration and the good pairs of the misuse or anomaly detection systems for the hybrid system. This determination can be difficult to make from among so many misuse and anomaly detection systems. Second, we need to consider the optimal or suboptimal way to integrate the given detection systems based on the different fundamental techniques, so that we can achieve the best balance between the detection and false-alarm rates and maintain the ability to detect new intrusions.

The selection of misuse and anomaly detection systems for combination is an application-specific problem. We provide a detailed discussion of the problem in the application studies. We broadly present several available integration method frameworks and categorize the existing hybrid detection methods into these frameworks. On the basis of the combinational approaches (Zhang and Zulkernine, 2006a; Zhang et al., 2008), we classify the available integration methods into four groups: anomaly–misuse sequence detection (Figure 5.1a),

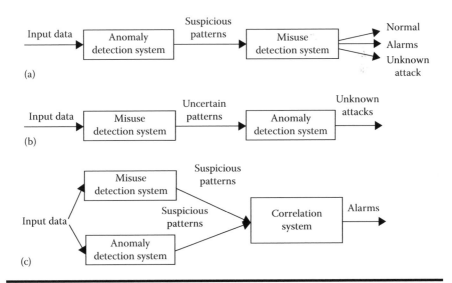

Figure 5.1 Three types of hybrid detection systems. (a) Anomaly–misuse sequence detection system. (b) Misuse–anomaly sequence detection system. (c) Parallel detection system. (Adapted from Zhang, J., Zulkernine, M., and Haque, A., Random-forest-based network intrusion detection systems, *IEEE Trans. Syst. Man Cybernet. C Appl. Rev.*, © 2008 IEEE.)

misuse–anomaly sequence detection (Figure 5.1b), parallel detection (Figure 5.1c), and complex mixture detection systems. The complex mixture model is application specific and is difficult to illustrate in a simple framework. Therefore, we will not attempt to explain it here, but will present a thorough explanation in the application studies.

We analyze these mechanisms of combination. Anomaly–misuse sequence detection systems, such as audit data analysis and mining (ADAM) (Barbarra et al., 2001), are designed to reduce the false-alarm rate by excluding suspicious patterns that are not classified as alarms by the misuse detection system. Misuse–anomaly sequence detection systems are designed to improve the ability of detecting new intrusions missed by misuse detection systems. Such systems include the hybrid system using the random forests algorithms in Zhang and Zulkernine (2006) and Zhang et al. (2008). Parallel intrusion detection systems, such as the next-generation intrusion detection expert system (NIDES) (Anderson et al., 1995), are used to correlate misuse and anomaly detection results to provide a stronger detection decision. In complex mixture detection systems, such as intrusion detection using the AdaBoost algorithm (Agrawal et al., 1998), normal and anomalous data are applied to train an intrusion detection system at the same time. The detection results also include both groups. We group the systems, which do not have a clear structure falling into sequence or parallel hybrid architectures, in the complex mixture detection systems section.

5.2 Machine Learning in Hybrid Intrusion Detection Systems

In hybrid intrusion detection systems, misuse and anomaly detection subsystems have a similar workflow to what we studied in Chapters 3 and 4. Both methods include five steps: data collection, data preprocessing, normal/anomalous behavior learning, identification of malicious/normal behaviors using detection techniques, and decisions. Hence, similar procedures are included in data collection and preprocessing, such as data reduction and feature selection. Machine-learning methods also play key roles in building normal/anomalous profiles and intrusion detections. Hybrid systems are used for intrusion detection, because a decision about one suspicious event will be made by the combined intrusion detection subsystems rather than a single intrusion detection subsystem. The objective for using hybrid systems is to detect the new intrusions missed by the misuse detection subsystem, while increasing the detection ability of its anomaly subsystem on true intrusions and false alarms. A simple hybrid system cannot guarantee a better performance than a single intrusion detection subsystem because of the different viewings of intrusions by different intrusion detection subsystems. The efficient hybrid system depends on the effective incorporation of these subsystems.

5.3 Machine-Learning Applications in Hybrid Intrusion Detection

In Section 5.3, we introduce hybrid intrusion detection systems. We analyze several typical frameworks of hybrid intrusion detection systems and explore the strengths and weaknesses in each framework. We describe the applications of these systems to help readers understand the design and workflow of the methods. Meanwhile, the benchmark of the applications will also help readers learn how to improve the intrusion detection systems using hybrid techniques. Examples for hybrid detection are listed in Table 1.4.

5.3.1 Anomaly–Misuse Sequence Detection System

The anomaly–misuse sequence has been analyzed well in Tombini et al. (2004). We summarize the framework briefly to demonstrate the underlying theory and the results of combining the systems. Given a set of cyber audit data X as input, the anomaly detection system outputs two data sets A_u and A_n, as shown in Figure 5.2.

In this example, A_u and A_n denote the subsets of audit data X detected as unknown and normal by the anomaly detection system. We obtain the following property of the sets: $A_u \cup A_n = X$, $A_u \cap A_n = \phi$. The unknown audit data in A_u will be input to the misuse detection system to detect the malicious data set. If M_i and M_u denote the subsets of audit data set X, detected as intrusive and unknown by the misuse detection system, then the output of the misuse system consists of $A_u \cap M_i$ and $A_u \cap M_u$. We also have the following property for the misuse detection system: $M_i \cup M_u = X$ and $M_i \cap M_u = \phi$.

To analyze the errors occurring in anomaly and misuse detection as well as the combinational system, the ground truth of the audit data X is introduced with its subsets X_i and X_n to denote intrusive and normal data subsets, respectively. We have $X_i \cup X_n = X$ and $X_i \cap X_n = \phi$. Then, the anomaly detection results of data set X can be presented by four subsets: $A_u \cap E_i$, $A_u \cap E_n$, $A_n \cap E_i$, and $A_n \cap E_n$, which correspond to the subsets of A^{TP}, A^{FP}, A^{FN}, and A^{TN}. Similarly, misuse detection results of data

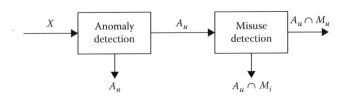

Figure 5.2 The workflow of anomaly–misuse sequence detection system. (Tombini, E., Debar, H., Me, L., and Ducasse, M., A serial combination of anomaly and misuse IDSes applied to HTTP traffic, in: *Proceedings of Twentieth Annual Computer Security Applications Conference*, Tucson, AZ, © 2004 IEEE.)

set X consist of four subsets: $M_i \cap E_i$, $M_i \cap E_n$, $M_u \cap E_i$, and $M_u \cap E_n$, corresponding to M^{TP}, M^{FP}, M^{FN}, and M^{TN}. Furthermore, we have the following properties for these subsets: $A^{FP} \cup A^{TP} = A_u$, $A^{FP} \cap A^{TP} = \phi$, $A^{FN} \cup A^{TN} = A_n$, $A^{FN} \cap A^{TN} = \phi$, $M^{FP} \cup M^{TP} = M_i$, $M^{FP} \cap M^{TP} = \phi$, $M^{FN} \cup M^{TN} = M_u$, and $M^{FN} \cap M^{TN} = \phi$. Using these notations, we can obtain the useful correct subsets: $A^{TP} \cap M^{TP}$ and $A^{TN} \cap M^{TN}$. Similarly, we have incorrect subsets: $A^{FP} \cap M^{FP}$ and $A^{FN} \cap M^{FN}$. The other subsets either have suspicious data between anomaly detection and misuse detection or are empty. For example, conflict occurs in $A^{FN} \cap M^{TP}$ when the anomaly detection system declares the event normal, and the misuse detection system declares it malicious. In this case, the anomaly detection system is wrong. These suspicious data can be explained further according to the sequence of anomaly detection and misuse detection.

In the framework, as shown in Figure 5.2, the following three subsets are the output of the system: A_n, $A_u \cap M_i$ and $A_u \cap M_u$. In this system, A_n is not sent to the misuse detection system while it has the error $A^{FN} \cap M^{TP}$. To ensure the framework obtains a high degree of accuracy, subset $A^{FN} \cap M^{TP}$ must be negligible, as explained in the paragraph above.

$A_u \cap M_u$ consists of $A^{TP} \cap M^{FN}$ and $A^{FP} \cap M^{TN}$. The events in both subsets need an administrator to analyze the results because of the uncertainty for classifying them into the normal and anomalous groups. $A_u \cap M_i$ consists of $A^{TP} \cap M^{FP}$ and $A^{FP} \cap M^{TP}$. The first subset is empty. The second subset, together with $A^{FP} \cap M^{TN}$, filters out the malicious events and normal events to reduce false alarms. On the basis of the above analysis, we conclude that the high detection accuracy of the anomaly–misuse sequence detection system depends on the high detection rate of the anomaly detection system and the high detection rate of false alarms using misuse detection.

5.3.2 Association Rules in Audit Data Analysis and Mining (Table 1.4, D.4)

The ADAM (Barbarra et al., 2001) is an online network-based intrusion detection system (IDS) that uses an association rules algorithm to detect intrusions. As shown in Figures 5.3 and 5.4, ADAM consists of both a training and a testing phase. In the offline training phase (as shown in Figure 5.3), data that do not contain any attacks are input into the association rules mining algorithm to extract the rules for normal behavior. Next, training data, which include attacks, are input into an online association rules algorithm to determine which itemsets maintain a high support rate within a given timeframe. These itemsets are compared to those in the normal profile for a related period. We then determine the value of support for any itemset that has not appeared in the profile. If the support value surpasses the predefined threshold, we assign the itemset to the group of suspicious hot patterns. Given features selected for itemsets and the known labels for training the data set, we input these suspicious itemsets as false alarms or attacks into a decision-tree

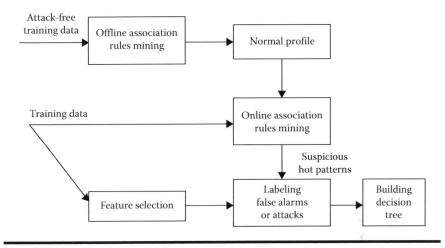

Figure 5.3 Framework of training phase in ADAM. (Barbarra, D., Couto, J., Jajodia, S., Popyack, L., and Wu, N., ADAM: Detecting intrusions by data mining, in: *Proceedings of the 2001 IEEE, Workshop on Information Assurance and Security*, West Point, NY, © 2001 IEEE.)

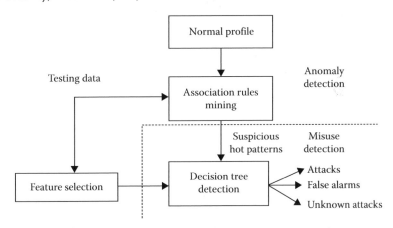

Figure 5.4 Framework of testing phase in ADAM. (Barbarra, D., Couto, J., Jajodia, S., Popyack, L., and Wu, N., ADAM: Detecting intrusions by data mining, in: *Proceedings of the 2001 IEEE, Workshop on Information Assurance and Security*, West Point, NY, © 2001 IEEE.)

classifier for training. This decision-tree classifier works as a misuse detector in the testing phase. The final decision-tree classifier consists of rules that classify itemsets into three groups: known attacks, false alarms, and unknown attacks.

In the testing phase (as shown in Figure 5.4), testing data is input into the online association rules mining algorithm to find the suspicious patterns. Using the selected feature set of these suspicious itemsets, we obtain input for the decision-tree classifier. This framework constitutes an anomaly detection system. Finally, the rules in the decision-tree classifier can classify suspicious data into three categories: attacks, false alarms, and unknown attacks. The itemsets in the group of unknown attacks are reported to a security officer for further analysis.

Application Study 1: ADAM Using Rule-Based Machine Learning and Decision Trees in Network Intrusion Detection

Barbarra et al. (2001) tested the ADAM hybrid detection system on the 1999 DARPA intrusion data. They used an itemset that had been collected from the raw packet data of the audit trail. The features of the itemsets include the IP addresses of the source and destination, the source and destination ports, the starting time of the connection, and the status of the TCP connection.

They evaluated the performance of ADAM by comparing it with a number of famous misuse detection and anomaly detection systems, such as the University of California Santa Barbara's state transition analysis tool (STAT) (Ilgun et al., 1995) and SRI International's event monitoring enabling responses to anomalous live disturbances (EMERALD) (Porras and Neumann, 1997). The experimental results showed that ADAM ranked in the top three for accurate detection of the attacks of DoS and PROBE. Only STAT and EMERALD ranked higher in detecting attacks, while the ADM detection accuracy was almost the same as that of EMERALD, which had the best accuracy. ADAM most missed attacks that were carried out on a single connection and were detected well by the misuse detection systems.

Lee et al. (1999) introduced the mining audit data for automated models for intrusion detection (MADAM) ID framework. MADAM performed data mining on system audit data to determine the activity patterns of users. Once the patterns were determined, predictive features were mined from them. Machine-learning algorithms were then applied to the audit records, which were processed using the predefined feature definitions. Once the audit records were obtained, MADAM generated intrusion detection rules.

5.3.3 Misuse–Anomaly Sequence Detection System

A workflow of the misuse–anomaly sequence detection system is shown in Figure 5.5. Notations in the figure match those presented in Section 5.3.1. The audit data X are input into a misuse detection system, and the known malicious patterns are detected by matching the signatures of attacks. The detected attacks are filtered out in subset M_j, while the unknown audit data in subset M_u are input into the descendent anomaly detection system. We obtain two subsets in the anomaly detection system: $M_u \cap A_n$ and $M_u \cap A_u$. Hence, we have three outputs in this system: M_j, $M_u \cap A_n$, and $M_u \cap A_u$. The subset $M_u \cap A_u$ has been analyzed in Section 5.3.1, and we focus on the other two subsets in this section.

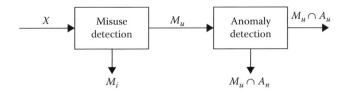

Figure 5.5 A representation of the workflow of misuse–anomaly sequence detection system that was developed by Zhang et al. (2008). (Zhang, J., Zulkernine, M., and Haque, A., Random-forest-based network intrusion detection systems, *IEEE Trans. Syst. Man Cybernet. C Appl. Rev.*, © 2008 IEEE.)

In this system, M_i is not sent to an anomaly detection system as long as it contains the error $M^{FP} \cap A^{TN}$. To ensure the framework obtains a high accuracy rate, subset $M^{FP} \cap A^{TN}$ must be negligible. A misuse detection system can improve the accuracy of the framework, because most misuse detection systems produce a high detection rate and low false-positive rate. Thus, this framework takes advantage of this quality of misuse detection systems.

Another subset $M_u \cap A_n$ includes suspicious subsets $M^{FN} \cap A^{TN}$ and $M^{TN} \cap A^{FN}$. The events in both subsets require the analysis of an administrator because of the uncertainty in classifying them into normal and anomalous groups. A^{FN} can be ensured low in building an accurate profile of normal behaviors. To have a low M^{FN}, the rules in the misuse detection system must have a good coverage of malicious data.

In brief, the objective of using a misuse–anomaly sequence detection system is to obtain a low false-positive rate. Obtaining this low rate requires that the anomaly detection system ensures a low false-positive rate, or the combined system will result in a high false-alarm rate.

Application Study 2: Using Random Forest in Network Intrusion Detection (Table 1.4, D.6)

Zhang and Zulkernine (2006a,b) and Zhang et al. (2008) presented a misuse–anomaly sequence detection framework. They employed the random forests algorithms in both misuse and anomaly detection components. We have discussed the random forests algorithm in Section 2.3.1.7 and its application in anomaly detection in Section 4.4.7.2. Refer to Zhang and Zulkernine (2006a,b) and Zhang et al. (2008) for details. In this section, we focus on the description of the framework of misuse–anomaly sequence detection with random forests.

As shown in Figure 5.6, the hybrid system detection method consists of offline and online phases. The anomaly detection and misuse-pattern building processes are offline while the misuse detection process is online. Random forests algorithms build intrusion and service patterns and detect outliers. First, the labeled training data are input into the random forests algorithm to train the intrusion pattern

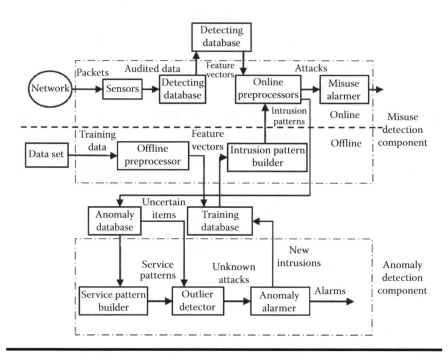

Figure 5.6 **The workflow of misuse–anomaly detection system in Zhang et al. (2008). (Zhang, J., Zulkernine, M., and Haque, A., Random-forest-based network intrusion detection systems,** *IEEE Trans. Syst. Man Cybernet. C Appl. Rev.,* **© 2008 IEEE.)**

builder module for misuse detection. Second, the online misuse detector splits the network traffic data into two groups: malicious data and unknown data. Malicious data will match intrusion patterns and will raise alarms. Unknown data cannot match any pattern in this builder and are sent to anomaly databases for offline anomaly detection. Third, the data from the anomaly database are input into the random forests algorithm to train the service pattern builder and outlier detector. Fourth, the outlier detector detects anomalous data among the anomaly database and raises alarms. After a cyber administer confirms the alarms, the new intrusions are feedback to the training database of misuse detection system to update the intrusion pattern builder.

Zhang et al. conducted experiments on 1999 KDD of DARPA data set. Five types of connections were selected: ftp, http, pop, smtp, and telnet. The researchers labeled data as one of two types: intrusion or normal. They generated a training data set to build a misuse detection system, which consists of 16,919 connections. They also generated a testing data set for a hybrid detection system, which consists of 49,838 connections.

Zhang et al. selected the 34 most important intrusion pattern features. They also optimized the primary tuning parameter (Mtry) and the number of trees for random forests algorithms in both misuse and anomaly detection systems. The misuse detection system resulted in a 94.2% detection rate and a 1.1% false-positive rate, while the hybrid detection system resulted in a 94.7% detection rate and a 2% false-positive rate. Their method demonstrated that the proposed parallel detection system using random forests could improve the performance of misuse detection by detecting new intrusions while maintaining a low false-positive rate. Meanwhile, the proposed anomaly detection system is limited in detecting intrusions, which have lower outliers than normal data.

Application Study 3: Using Weighted Signature Generation over Anomalous Internet Episodes in Network Intrusion Detection

Hwang et al. (2007) designed a hybrid detection system combining SNORT and an anomaly detection system through automated signature generation from Internet episodes. As shown in Figure 5.7, they used SNORT to detect attack signatures, and then the corresponding traffic flows were removed. The remaining traffic data,

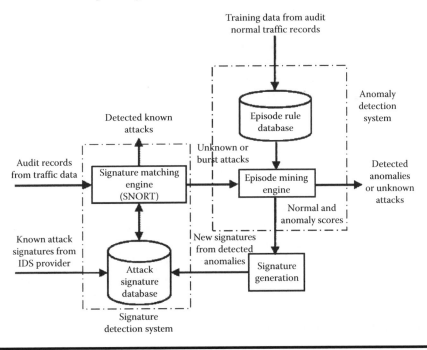

Figure 5.7 The workflow of the hybrid system designed in Hwang et al. (2007). (Hwang, K., Cai, M., Chen, Y., and Qin, M., Hybrid intrusion detection with weighted signature generation over anomalous internet episodes, *IEEE Trans. Dependable Secure Comput.*, © 2007 IEEE.)

including suspicious items (unknown attacks), were input into the episode mining engine. Using the incoming suspicious traffic connections, the episode mining engine generated frequent episode rules that were compared to the episode rules built on normal traffic records. The mismatched episodes were labeled as anomalous and fed into an attack signature database to generate attack signatures and update SNORT. We first introduce the key components in the episode mining engine and signature generation and signature generation framework. The episode mining engine includes episode rules mining and pruning. Please refer to Section 4.4.1 for background on episode rules mining.

Hwang et al. (2007) defined a frequent episode rule as $A,B \rightarrow C,[c,s,w,f]$, where f is the minimum number of occurrences needed to establish the rule. They defined the other parameters as have already been explained in Section 4.4.1. Hwang et al. lowered the support threshold using a so-called minimum support base value of an episode as the threshold to filter frequent episode rules, so that more anomalous network connections were employed in the generation of episode rules. Given items $X = \{A, B, C\}$, the support base of item X was defined as support value of the axis itemset, denoted by $support_b(X)$, e.g., $support(A,B)$, when A and B are common services in the network. Then, the minimum support base value could be presented as $min(support_b(X))$. Given a threshold f_r, they defined base-support fraction by $f(X) = support(X)/support_b(X)$. If $f(X) \geq f_r$, then an episode rule set X was generated. In addition, episodes were pruned, if they were rarely used to detect anomalies to reduce the false-positive rate and improve the search efficiency. For example, long rules might introduce redundant information, and replacing the long rules with shorter ones in normal profiles can reduce the false-alarm rate. Please refer to Hwang et al. (2007) and Qin and Hwang (2004) for detailed analyses of these pruning techniques.

In the signature generation module, the anomaly score was assigned to a given connection through a comparison of its frequent episode rules with the normal profile.* Furthermore, the anomaly score of a pattern was obtained by summing the anomaly scores of all connections matching a pattern. Signatures were generated when the patterns had high anomaly scores. As shown in Figure 5.8, the signature generation module included four steps.

The clustering analysis unit was designed to classify the attacks into respective groups using density-based clustering, which classified the items falling into the low-density regions as noises. The unit of weighted frequent itemsets (WFIs) mining followed the principle that if a connection contains set X, it should contain all subsets of X. If the support of an itemset X is bigger than a threshold *min_sup*, this

---

* An anomaly score is defined as the deviation degree of a connection from normal traffic; normality score denotes the degree of matching between a connection and normal traffic. Qin and Hwang (2004) used both. These two definitions compensate for each other, and one is necessary to describe the matching process. In this chapter, we only use an anomaly score to simplify a description.

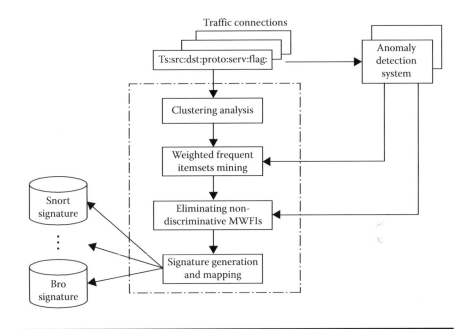

Figure 5.8 **The workflow in the signature generation module designed in Hwang et al. (2007). (Hwang, K., Cai, M., Chen, Y., and Qin, M., Hybrid intrusion detection with weighted signature generation over anomalous internet episodes, *IEEE Trans. Dependable Secure Comput.*, © 2007 IEEE.)**

threshold should support all subsets of X. Given w_i, the weight of connection C_i obtained from its anomaly score or normality score, the weighted support of item set X was defined as $sup_w(X) = \sum_{i, X \in C_i} w_i \big/ \sum_i w_i$, with i denoting the index of connections. Using a threshold of the minimum weight support, the significant WFI sets, which have a larger weighted support than the threshold, were obtained. In the unit of signature generation and mapping, WFIs were represented by maximal weighted frequent itemsets (MWFIs). MWFIs were WFI sets that contained supersets that had a support bigger than their minimum weight support. Then, the item numbers of the MWFIs were extracted and decoded into the format of the signatures of the detected anomalies. Hwang et al. (2007) further considered the MWFIs with a high support rate as nondiscriminative and deleted these itemsets after recalculating the weighted support of MWFIs using normality scores.

They mixed the real network traffic data set, collected by the University of Southern California, with ten days of data from the DARPA 1999 data set to evaluate the performance of the proposed scheme. They used SNORT 2.1 to mine more than 2,000 signatures installed, and 24,619 alerts occurred for the detected incidents. Since the anomaly detection system generated 37,223 traffic episode rules, Hwang et al. used the intrusion detection rate, the false-alarm rate, and the ROC to evaluate the performance of the propose hybrid intrusion detection system. The experimental results showed that the proposed system increased the detection rate from the 30% that SNORT detected alone to 60%, while keeping less than a 3% false-alarm rate. The hybrid intrusion detection system also automatically upgraded the SNORT signature set by 33%.

5.3.4 Parallel Detection System

Using the notations from Section 5.3.1, we introduce the parallel detection system as shown in Figure 5.9.

Given a set of audit data X as input, the anomaly detection system and the misuse detection system perform intrusive detection independently and in parallel. The output of anomaly detection system consists of two subsets A_u and A_n, and the output of the misuse detection system also consists of two subsets M_u and M_i. An intelligent correlation system, called resolver, is designed to analyze these subsets and report the detection results. The combination of these subsets composes the final results of the parallel detection system, including $A_n \cap M_i$, $A_n \cap M_u$, $A_u \cap M_i$, and $A_u \cap M_u$. Among these four subsets of detection results, $A_n \cap M_u$ and $A_u \cap M_i$ improve the detection rate of normal and intrusive patterns, respectively. The other two subsets denote the suspicious data between misuse and anomaly detection systems and need further analysis. The subset $A_n \cap M_i$ implies that a set of malicious behaviors defined by intrusive signatures in the misuse detection system fall into the normal profile defined in the anomaly detection system. Hence, both or either of these signatures and profiles may need to be updated. The subset $A_u \cap M_u$ presents the unknown data for both misuse and anomaly systems. Uncertainty exists such that further investigation is needed. Thus, in parallel detection systems, a correlation system plays a key role. However, at this point, details about its design have not been published. The parallel system analyzes the detection results from both misuse and anomaly detection systems.

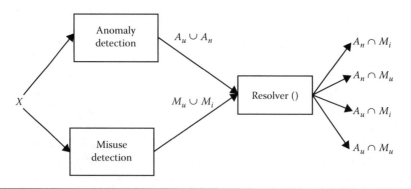

Figure 5.9 Workflow of parallel detection system.

Given prior knowledge about intrusive or normal data, the parallel detection system can reduce the chances of missing intrusions among suspicious data and the false-alarm rate. The NIDES, developed by SRI, is an example for such parallel detection systems (Anderson et al., 1995).

Application Study 4: NIDES Using Rule-Based and Other Machine-Learning Methods in Network Intrusion Detection

The NIDES is an early, historical example of hybrid intrusion detection (Anderson et al., 1995). NIDES was designed to examine the real-time audit data of a group of hosts to detect intrusions. NIDES is a host-based IDS and not primarily a network IDS. NIDES consists of an expert rule-based system that will encode known intrusive behaviors, and innovative statistical algorithms that will alert administrators to the presence of malicious data. As shown in Figure 5.10, real-time NIDES includes the following key components: agen, Arpool, an anomaly detection system (statistical analysis), a misuse detection system (rule-based analysis), and a resolver. The NIDES workflow is as follows: the agen program collects audit data in each target host system, Targethost 1, ..., Targethost *N*, and delivers the NIDES formatted audit data to the Arpool process. The Arpool program collects audit data from all target hosts and feeds the data set to the descendant detection systems. In anomaly detection systems, statistical machine-learning methods maintain historical profiles of each user and detect the deviation of the current behavior of the user. This system updates the user profiles regularly. The interesting and unusual events that could threaten cybersecurity are reported to administrators for analysis. The rule-based misuse system flags any observed event that exhibits the defined suspicious or malicious patterns. New rules can be defined and combined with the existing rules to update the current expert system. Resolver, the correlation system, filters the alarms generated by the antecedent detection systems by eliminating the redundant alarms. As a single user's action may generate a large number of alarms in an anomaly detection system when he or she performs an abnormal behavior, the resolver significantly reduces the workload of the cyber administrator.

In the above, we introduce NIDES, a hybrid intrusion detection system that monitors user behavior and detects malicious behavior in real time. NIDES can also perform periodic analysis of user profiles in batch mode. For a detailed explanation of NIDES, please read Anderson et al. (1995).

Application Study 5: Combining the Results of Anomaly and Misuse Detection Models to Improve the Overall Rate of Detection (Table 1.4, D.2 and D.3)

Endler (1998) used the audit trails provided by the Solaris SHIELD basic security module (BSM) in the anomaly and misuse detection approaches. In this project, the researchers combated the drawbacks of both systems by combining them into one system that can detect threats to cybersecurity in real time. Both models used

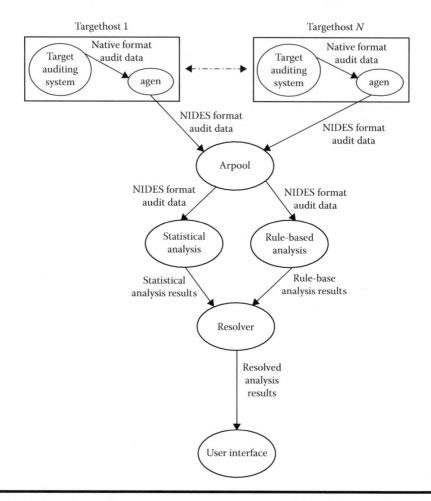

Figure 5.10 Workflow of real-time NIDES. (From Anderson, D., Frivold, T., and Valdes, A., Next-generation intrusion detection expert system (NIDES)—A summary, Technical Report SRI-CSL-95-07, SRI, 1995. With permission.)

the same BSM audit data to detect intrusions in the form of a UNIX buffer to overrun attacks that obtain root access. The anomaly detection is built with a histogram-based analysis of system calls, and the misuse detection consists of ANN that has been trained on system calls clusters.

Over a 6-week period, the author used the data from four simulated users to generate BSM audit data on the system. Each user had a distinct profile of system usage. The author trained a multilayer perceptron ANN using 362 labeled normal events and buffer overrun attack records in the misuse detection system. The testing data included all user actions and all 569 system events, in sequences of signals of 50 min. Combinations of two attacks were used in the training process to test

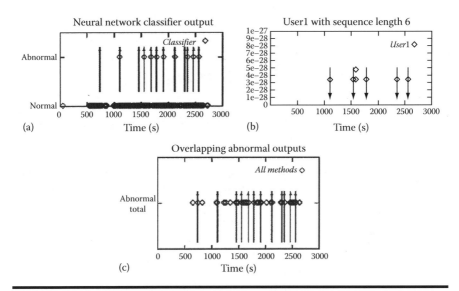

Figure 5.11 **(a) Misuse detection result, (b) example of histogram plot for user1 test data results, and (c) the overlapping by combining and merging the testing results of both misuse and anomaly detection systems. (From Endler, D., Intrusion detection: Applying machine learning to Solaris audit data, in:** *Proceedings of the 1998 Annual Computer Security Applications Conference (ACSAC),* **Los Alamitos, CA, 1998. With permission.)**

the ability of the system to determine the extrapolation accuracies of the system in detecting new attacks. As shown in Figure 5.11a, the best classification result was obtained by combining attacks 2 and 5 in the training data. In Figure 5.11, arrows denote true attacks, and diamonds denote detected attacks.

The author also used a statistical histogram to describe the distribution of normal and anomalous data sets in the anomaly detection system. By selecting a threshold empirically, he distinguished the attacks from the normal data set. He collected 22,444 signals for training and 25,457 signals for testing. The sequences of these signals were converted into sequences of patterns by a sliding window. In the training process, the researchers used the histogram function as a classifier to describe the normal user profiles for each user. Then, he detected anomalous data among the testing data set using an empirical threshold on the obtained histogram. He obtained four histograms over frequency-time for four users. For example, as shown in Figure 5.11, the detected attack occurred in 50 min time intervals. He selected a threshold of $6e$–28 and isolated the instances as buffer-overrun instances when they fell below this threshold.

Combining the histograms of both misuse detection and anomaly detection, as described above, the author focused on the overlapping area. He proposed to reduce the false-positive alarm rate by only mining regions consisting of 30 or 60 s at one time and not mining any regions that contained less than three detected attacks. However, we could not find experimental results for this proposed method.

5.3.5 Complex Mixture Detection System

This system has no clear boundary between the misuse and anomaly detection subsystems. We apply the AdaBoost algorithm as a typical example of intrusion detection.

AdaBoost is widely used in supervised machine learning. It performs weight-based classification on a number of weak classifiers according to a function of classification errors. As discussed in Section 2.2.1.7, the AdaBoost algorithm is simple and efficient in implementation, given simple weak classifiers. Compared with other machine-learning methods, the AdaBoost algorithm is less susceptible to overfitting. AdaBoost tends to resist overfitting in practice, while it sensitive to outliers. Since AdaBoost algorithms must be trained using both attack and normal labeled data, we categorize it as a hybrid detection method.

Given the labeled data of networks, as shown in Figure 5.12, we can train the weak classifiers and improve strong classifiers using AdaBoost algorithms. Then, we can employ the trained, strong classifiers to classify new data into normal

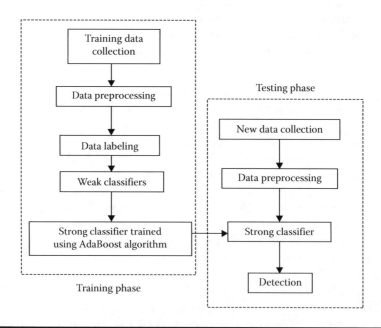

Figure 5.12 Workflow of hybrid detection system using the AdaBoost algorithm. (Adapted from Hu, W.M., Hu, W., and Maybank, S., AdaBoost-based algorithm for network intrusion detection, *IEEE Trans. Syst. Man Cybernet. B Cybernet.*, © 2008 IEEE.)

and anomaly types. Given an AdaBoost algorithm, we can select weak classifiers among ANN, KNN, SVM, decision trees, etc. The computational complexities of such an action depend on the training of the classifiers. The computational complexity of a strong classifier depends mostly on the computational complexity of a weak classifier. Thus, we prefer to choose simply structured machine-learning methods for weak classifiers.

Application Study 6: AdaBoost-Based Machine Learning for Network Intrusion Detection

Hu et al. (2008) proposed a fast network intrusion detection system using an AdaBoost-based machine-learning algorithm. In this framework, they used decision stumps as a weak classifier. Decision stumps is a decision-tree classifier, with only one root node and a categorical or numeric class label. Given a numeric feature, decision stumps searched all possible thresholds and selected the one with the minimum false classification rates for both normal and attack samples.

The resulting weak classifier made decisions based on a simple threshold for a single feature: if the feature value was above the obtained threshold, the output was set to +1; otherwise, the output was set to –1. Given a categorical feature x_{ij}, $j = 1, \ldots, d$, of a data sample $x_i \in X$ (referring to notations in Section 2.2.1.7), decision stumps divided feature j into two subsets S_{1j} and S_{2j}. The resulting weak classifier made decisions for feature j based on the belongings of x_{ij} between these two subsets. As with numeric data, decision stumps selected the optimal subsets with the minimum false classification rates summarized for both normal and attack samples.

Hu et al. used the KDD CUP 1999 data set to test the algorithm. They labeled each TCP/IP connection data as attack or normal data manually. As shown in Table 5.1, they used a large number of data labeled as "others" in testing. "Others" was the label for unknown attack data used in the training phase. When preparing data, they followed the framework and methods that were presented in Lee et al. (1999) and selected three groups of features: basic features of TCP and connections, content features suggested by domain knowledge, and traffic features computed using a 2 s window.

Hu et al. (2007) proposed adjustable initial weights to reduce the false-alarm rate. The severe imbalance of data in intrusion detection and the equal weight settings for samples in classical classification methods leads to a high false-alarm rate. These methods consider the overall accuracy and miss capturing the minority-class classification accuracy. The initial weights were defined as

$$
w_1(i) = \begin{cases} \dfrac{r}{n^+}, & y_i = +1 \\[2ex] \dfrac{1-r}{n^{-1}}, & y_i = -1 \end{cases}, \quad i = 1, \ldots, m. \tag{5.1}
$$

Table 5.1 The Number of Training and Testing Data Types

Normal	Attack			Total	
	DOS	U2R	R2L	PROBE	
	391458	52	1126	4107	
Training data types					
97278	396743			494021	

Normal	Attack					Total
	DOS	U2R	R2L	PROBE	Others	
	223298	39	5993	2377	18729	
Testing data types						
60593	250436					311029

Source: Hu, W.M., Hu, W., and Maybank, S., AdaBoost-based algorithm for network intrusion detection, *IEEE Trans. Syst. Man Cybernet. B Cybernet.*, © 2008 IEEE.

Here, r controls the panel on the false-alarm rate. "+1" refers to attack, and "–1" refers to normal data. n^+ and n^- are the numbers of normal and attack samples in the training data set, respectively. This weight setting is designed to reduce the false-alarm rate by enlarging the scale factor r. Hu et al. (2007) expected to correct the imbalance between the detection and false-alarm rates by selecting a suitable value for r. For example, it was shown that when r was changed from 0.5 to 0.7, the false-alarm rate decreased from 0.665% to 0.307%, while the detection rate simultaneously decreased from 90.77% to 90.04%. They also compared these two rates with the results of the other anomaly detection algorithms including genetic clustering, SVM, hierarchical SOM, RSS-DSS, and bagged C5. They concluded that the AdaBoost-based algorithm caused a low false-alarm rate, but maintained a high detection rate and a fast computation speed.

The proposed method is limited in incremental online learning. It is not adaptive to changing network environments and does not automatically label the updated sample data. This drawback limits its online applications in the presence of streaming data. The authors also suggested testing the new weak machine-learning model.

5.3.6 Other Hybrid Intrusion Systems

Ghosh and Schwartzbard (1999) used ANN models in both the anomaly detection and the misuse detection systems to test the ability of the systems to detect both novel attacks and variations of known attacks. Seleznyov and Puuronen (2000) presented a hybrid architecture to discover the temporal aspects of user behavior.

The anomaly detection system was designed to catch, encode, and update variations of user behavior through online learning. The misuse detection system that performs efficient and accurate detection of misuse actions that had been exposed in the past. Bashah et al. (2005) proposed to integrate fuzzy association rules and ANN in a hybrid intelligent intrusion system.

In addition, the authors proposed several alert correlation techniques (shown in Table 1.4), which they argue will aid in the analysis of intrusion alerts. These techniques include approaches based on alert attribute similarity (Dain and Cunningham, 2001a), previously known (or partially known) attack scenarios (Dain and Cunningham, 2001b), and prerequisites and consequences of known attacks (Cuppens and Miège, 2002). The alert correlation is limited to the abilities of the IDSs, and these techniques perform poorly when the IDSs miss critical attacks. Ning et al. (2004) presented an integration of two alert correlation methods: (1) alert similarity attributes and (2) the prerequisites and consequences of attacks.

5.4 Summary

In this chapter, we analyze the existing hybrid intrusion detection systems theoretically and empirically. Theoretically, the hybrid structures can be divided into four groups although the detailed machine-learning methods and incorporation techniques have significant influences on the intrusion detection results. Except for the common difficulties faced by misuse and anomaly detection techniques, such as the huge volume of streaming data source, which we discussed in the previous chapters, hybrid detection systems have a unique challenge in how to incorporate the different detection techniques into the most effective and powerful system.

Although researchers from various institutes and universities have spent much time and effort investigating the hybrid systems with machine-learning methods, most of them focused only on specific machine-learning techniques or combinations of particular misuse and anomaly detection systems. Studies on hybrid detection systems, especially those that study fundamental hybrid techniques, as presented by Tombini et al. (2004), are based on the studies in misuse and anomaly detection systems. The premise of these systems is that the misuse intrusion detection systems have a high detection rate and a lower false-alarm rate for known attacks, while anomaly detection systems can detect novel attacks as well as low false-positive rates. Hence, the combination of these two systems should improve the performance of either of the detection systems. Most but not all of the hybrid intrusion detection systems outperformed the respective individual misuse and anomaly detection systems as can be seen from experimental results. Future directions of the research are suggested below.

Emerging research on the fusion and correlation of intrusion techniques in hybrid systems may provide better cybersecurity in the future and reduce the false-alarm rate by using other data-mining or machine-learning methods. Furthermore, no literature is available on how to embed and combine different types of machine-learning methods in hybrid detection systems fundamentally and systematically. Because we have not found any literature that focuses on evaluating these hybrid intrusion detection systems comparatively, we can only guess that these improvements will increase cybersecurity in the near future.

References

Agrawal, R., J. Gehrke, D. Gunopulos, and P. Raghavan. Automatic subspace clustering of high dimensional data for data mining applications. In: *Proceedings of SIGMOD*, Seattle, WA, 1998, pp. 94–105.

Anderson, D., T. Frivold, and A. Valdes. Next-generation intrusion detection expert system (NIDES)—A summary. Technical Report SRI-CSL-95-07, SRI, 1995.

Barbarra, D., J. Couto, S. Jajodia, L. Popyack, and N. Wu. ADAM: Detecting intrusions by data mining. In: *Proceedings of the 2001 IEEE, Workshop on Information Assurance and Security*, West Point, NY, 2001, pp. 11–16.

Bashah, N., I.B. Shannugam, and A.M. Ahmed. Hybrid intelligent intrusion detection system. *World Academy of Science, Engineering and Technology*, 11 (2005): 23–26.

Cuppens, F. and A. Miège. Alert correlation in a cooperative intrusion detection framework. In: *IEEE Symposium on Research in Security and Privacy*, Oakland, CA, 2002.

Dain, O. and R. Cunningham. Building scenarios from a heterogeneous alert stream. In: *Proceedings of the 2001 IEEE Workshop on Information Assurance and Security*, West Point, NY, 2001a, pp. 231–235.

Dain, O. and R. Cunningham. Fusing a heterogeneous alert stream into scenarios. In: *Proceedings of the 2001, ACM Workshop on Data Mining for Security Applications*, Philidelphia, PA, 2001b, pp. 1–13.

Endler, D. Intrusion detection: Applying machine learning to Solaris audit data. In: *Proceedings of the 1998 Annual Computer Security Applications Conference (ACSAC)*, Los Alamitos, CA, 1998, pp. 268–279.

Ghosh, A.K. and A. Schwartzbard. A study in using neural networks for anomaly and misuse detection. In: *Proceedings of the Eighth USENIX Security Symposium*, Washington, DC, 1999, pp. 141–152.

Hu, W.M., W. Hu, and S. Maybank. AdaBoost-based algorithm for network intrusion detection. *IEEE Transactions on Systems, Man, and Cybernetics—Part B: Cybernetics* 38 (2) (2008): 577–583.

Hwang, K., M. Cai, Y. Chen, and M. Qin. Hybrid intrusion detection with weighted signature generation over anomalous internet episodes. *IEEE Transactions on Dependable and Secure Computing* 4 (1) (2007): 41–55.

Ilgun, K., R.A. Kemmerer, and P.A. Porras. State transition analysis: A rule-based intrusion detection approach. *IEEE Transactions on Software Engineering* 21 (3) (1995): 181–199.

Lee, W., S.J. Stolfo, and K.W. Mok. A data mining framework for building intrusion detection models. In: *Proceedings of the IEEE Symposium on Security and Privacy*, Oakland, CA, 1999, pp. 120–132.

Ning, P., D. Xu, C. Healey, and R.S. Amant. Building attack scenarios through integration of complementary alert correlation method. In: *Proceedings of the 11th Annual Network and Distributed System Security Symposium*, San Diego, CA, 2004.

Porras, P.A. and P.G. Neumann. EMERALD: Event monitoring enabling responses to anomalous live disturbances. In: *Proceedings of the Nineteenth National Computer Security*, Baltimore, MD, 1997, pp. 353–365.

Qin, M. and K. Hwang. Frequent episode rules for internet traffic analysis and anomaly detection. In: *Proceedings of IEEE Network Computing and Applications (NAC)*, Cambridge, MA, 2004.

Seleznyov, A. and S. Puuronen, HIDSUR: A hybrid intrusion detection system based on real-time user recognition. In: *Proceedings of 11th International Workshop on Database and Expert Systems Applications*, Greenwich, U.K., 2000, pp. 41–45.

Tombini, E., H. Debar, L. Me, and M. Ducasse. A serial combination of anomaly and misuse IDSes applied to HTTP traffic. In: *Proceedings of Twentieth Annual Computer Security Applications Conference*, Tucson, AZ, 2004, pp. 428–437.

Zhang, J. and M. Zulkernine. A hybrid network intrusion detection technique using random forests. In: *Proceedings of the First International Conference on Availability, Reliability and Security*, Vienna, Austria, 2006a, pp. 262–269.

Zhang, J. and M. Zulkernine. Anomaly based network intrusion detection with unsupervised outlier detection. In: *IEEE International Conference on Communications*, Istanbul, Turkey, 2006b.

Zhang, J., M. Zulkernine, and A. Haque. Random-forest-based network intrusion detection systems. *IEEE Transactions on Systems, Man, and Cybernetics, Part C: Applications and Reviews* 38 (5) (2008): 649–659.

Chapter 6

Machine Learning for Scan Detection

Our military imperative is no longer just to hit the enemy; today, we and the rest of the joint team, can kill whatever we find. Our greatest challenge today is to identify and understand the enemy we need to affect, preferably before it has a chance to strike.

To maintain the initiative, we cannot wait until enemies announce themselves. Before they strike, we must know: who are they; where are they; and, what they want. With this knowledge we can strip emerging enemies of their anonymity.

Lt. Gen. David A. Deptula
Lead Turning the Future: The 2008 Strategy for United States Air Force Intelligence, Surveillance, and Reconnaissance.

In this chapter, we address scan detection techniques. In Chapters 3 and 4, we have discussed a "scan" attack in some intrusion detection systems (IDSs). Strictly speaking, a scan is not a real attack but is the precursor to an attack. Scans find vulnerabilities in cyberinfrastructures that they can use to infiltrate systems easily and successfully. Thus, we consider scan detection a preventive process that is different from the classical IDSs that are designed to detect malicious patterns demonstrated during cyber attacks. In this chapter, we introduce and describe scan detection technologies. Scans can be regarded as intrusions and can be detected using intrusion detection techniques. For instance, a number of IDSs have been applied to detect scans and other attacks among the attacks in the famous MIT DARPA intrusion detection data sets.

As the precursors of attacks, scans have noticeable characteristics, and the detections require a variety of techniques to combat the special challenges. Such techniques include evasive approaches and exploitation of huge amounts of streaming traffic between the combinational hosts and services. Scan detection encounters the same problems as intrusion detection techniques. Its problems are very similar to those encountered using anomaly detection, in that it is difficult to identify scans with a high detection rate and with a low false-alarm rate (FAR). As the final task of scan detection is to prevent attacks to the cyberinfrastructure, further investigation of scan sources is necessary after correct scan detection. In all of these scan detection and accessory analysis techniques, data-mining and machine-learning methods have roles similar to those in IDSs.

Chapters 2 through 5 contain discussions on the fundamental machine-learning methods and implementations. In this chapter, we focus on solutions to scan detection problems in applications. We also describe the machine-learning techniques designed for specific applications, such as the associative memory mapping, and visualization modules that have been designed for such purposes. We introduce scan techniques and scan detection. We categorize scan techniques into three groups: horizontal scan techniques, vertical scan techniques, and coordinated scan techniques. We describe the highest number of possible patterns that the scans can have. Then, we explain how researchers can discover scan patterns and detect scans based on the knowledge we have obtained regarding the scans.

We analyze the cause of the low detection rate and the high FAR to provide the possible machine-learning solutions. Next, we study several scan detection systems in detail. We discuss their feasibility for detecting different scan groups, such as horizontal scans. We also analyze the applications of machine-learning methods in these systems in application studies. Then, we briefly summarize other scan detection methodologies and the respective machine-learning methods. Finally, we summarize the achievements and limitations of the present research results in scan detection, and guide readers in the directions of emerging research.

6.1 Scan and Scan Detection

As we have explained previously, IDSs detect and identify attacks on cyberinfrastructures. As in physical battle, reconnaissance is a precursor to battle in cybersecurity. Hackers and other malicious users explore the vulnerabilities and resource information of targeted cyberinfrastructures by running scans on these systems before launching real attacks. For defenders, the protection against the reconnaissance is often more valuable than fighting real attacks, due to the time and effort that is saved by preventing hackers from receiving intelligence about a system.

In cybersecurity, reconnaissance missions, or scans, normally target multiple destinations, e.g., several host IP addresses or services on various ports. In literature, we find scans that have several applications. First, cyber administrators audit networks by scanning the infrastructure. Second, peers look for previous collaborators via p2p services. Third, malicious users detect the vulnerabilities of cyberinfrastructures to prepare attacks. We only focus on the malicious uses of scan techniques in this chapter.

In scanning cyberinfrastructures, attackers attempt to collect sufficient intelligence of the computer network systems to prepare for breaking into the systems via detecting vulnerable sites. Initially, attackers can infer the profile, also called a footprint, of the targeted cyberinfrastructure using the collected information, such as mail servers, IP address range, billing contacts, and so on. Meanwhile, attackers will search for the paths to alive and accessible resources in the system via scanning techniques. In scanning, attackers generally send a series of messages to the targeted system, and learn the services and the weakness in the structures of the infrastructure through the feedback from these messages.

For instance, attackers send messages to the ports of a computer system to check the accessibility of these ports, which is indicated by the responses of the ports. From these responses, attackers can infer the information of the accessible IP addresses of the system and the system architecture. Ping sweep, also called ICMP ECHO requests, is the typical example to query multiple hosts using the message of ICMP ECHO request packets. In a ping sweep, attackers can receive a reply from the targeted system if the system is alive, otherwise they cannot receive a reply.

This process includes scanning a target at each port of a given infrastructure, a network of IPs, or the combinational set of IPs and ports. Hence, it is also called a portscan. During a portscan, attackers try to find ports or services that are alive and running on the targeted system by connecting to the TCP or UDP ports of the system. Then, attackers can steal infrastructure information, such as user names and system banners, by illegally logging into the system or maliciously using the services through the running ports. Holes or security flaws of the operational system or the wrong configuration of services can cause these vulnerabilities.

In the above scanning procedure, attackers are interested in investigating the footprints of particular combinational IPs and ports.* As a footprint can characterize the targeted computer system distinctively, it represents the ground information that attackers attempt to obtain. Based on the footprint pattern, scans can be categorized into three types (Staniford et al., 2002a; Yegneswaran et al., 2003): vertical scan, horizontal scan, and coordinated scan. A horizontal scan attempts to

---

* In Staniford et al. (2002a), a footprint refers to the set of port/IP combinations, which the attacker is interested in characterizing.

find a particular service/port running in any host among networks. It is launched on a single port of interest in a listed IP address. As pointed out in an investigation by Yegneswaran et al. (2003), horizontal scans have been the main sources of recent scan attacks.

A vertical scan attempts to find particular services in a range of ports on a single host. This scan is launched on a single IP address of interest to characterize the services on the host. A coordinated scan, also called a distributed scan, attempts to scan an interested portion of ports among a range of IP addresses. It is launched and controlled by a single attacker, but distributed on multiple resources that target desired ports and hosts. Braynov and Jadliwala (2004) further clustered the cooperation between scanners into two groups: action correlation and task correlation. In the action correlation, one scanner correlates his/her collaborators though an action, while in task correlation, scan correlations are grouped according to the malicious aims of the tasks.

Most scan detection techniques are not developed to detect a particular group of scans but are used for generic approaches. However, exceptions to this methodology do exist. Scan detection techniques are mostly classified into two groups: single source portscan detection and distributed source portscan detection. These groups correspond to whether researchers would like to investigate a single IP or multiple IPs. To investigate a single IP, detection techniques focus on finding the single source of the IP address that launched scans. Threshold hold detection is the most employed single-source scan detection method to detect a fixed number of IP addresses or ports, across a Y-sized time window, such as SNORT (Roesch, 1999) and BRO (Paxson, 1998).

To investigate multiple IPs, clustered hosts that require the collection of network traffic data are targeted in scan detection. The network traffic data include connection information such as source IPs, the durations of the connections, and the starting and ending time of connections. The scan detection technique searches for similar and anomaly patterns among traffic data. One of the typical examples is the stealthy probing and intrusion correlation engine (SPICE) and statistical packet anomaly detection engine (SPADE) (Staniford et al., 2002).

According to the input data, we can also classify scan detection methods into packet-level-based and flow-level-based detection. Packet-level-based detection analyzes the packet payloads, while the flow-level-based detection uses the aggregated traffic information obtained by network tools, e.g., Cisco NetFlow (Cisco IOS NetFlow—Cisco Systems, 1992–2010).

6.2 Machine Learning in Scan Detection

Subsystems in scan detection systems have a workflow similar to the one that we studied for anomaly detection in Chapter 4. As shown in Figure 6.1, the workflow includes five steps: data collection, data preprocessing, scan pattern learning, scan detection, and report and analysis.

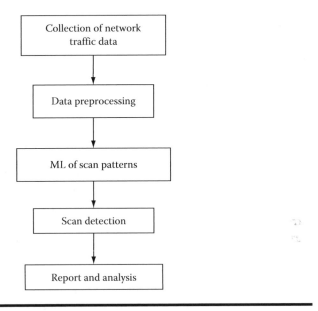

Figure 6.1   Workflow of scan detection.

The collection of network traffic data should be real time for the purpose of scan detection. Because of the huge streaming network flows, practical implementation requires scan techniques that are able to deal with network traffic data in batches or streams. This data collection needs a scalable scan detection technique to work accurately. Expert knowledge is critical for accurate feature extraction and selection in data preprocessing.

Machine-learning methods generally need a representative feature set to present knowledge concisely and accurately. Both supervised machine-learning and clustering methods are used in scan pattern learning, and most of these techniques are application specific. These techniques are designed differently from the classical machine-learning methods, due to the dynamic properties found in scans. Thus, when classical machine-learning methods are applied in scan detection, the detection results cannot support a decision in a straightforward way, because most detection techniques cannot provide detailed information about source information. Cyber administrators need tools to comprehend and analyze the scans based on the detection report. Visualization and supervised machine-learning and clustering methods facilitate further investigation of attack sources (Muelder et al., 2007).

6.3 Machine-Learning Applications in Scan Detection

In this section, we introduce scan detection techniques through application studies. We analyze several typical frameworks of scan detection systems and explore the strengths and weaknesses of each framework. We describe the applications of these systems to help readers understand the design and workflow of different methods. The benchmark of the applications will also help readers learn how to improve scan detection systems. Examples for scan detection are listed in Table 1.5.

Application Study 1: SPICE and SPADE Using Cluster and Correlation Methods in Stealthy Scan Detection (Table 1.5, E.1)

Staniford et al. (2002a,b) presented an SPICE and an SPADE to detect stealthy portscans. Stealthy portscans refer to the varieties of scan techniques that can elude traditional IDS systems. Examples of these techniques include randomizing the scanning order of IP addresses and port sequences, randomizing the scanning lull, slowing down the scanning frequencies, and randomizing attack resource IPs and ports. Traditional IDS systems, such as SNORT, graph-based intrusion detection system (GrIDS), and BRO, use the occurrence of connections on resource IPs within time windows. Due to the limitations of time windows, the traditional IDS techniques are not capable of detecting a slow randomized stealth scan.

For SPICE, Staniford et al. designed an anomaly score to estimate the total information of a scan footprint based on the conditional probability distribution of normal traffic packets. They collected the traffic packets, including source and destination addresses and ports, over days or weeks. Next, they reported the anomalous events with significant anomaly scores to the event correlation engine. The above processes are also involved in SPADE. SPADE is the preprocessor plug-in of SNORT. In the correlation engine, the authors applied a simulated annealing algorithm to cluster the sufficiently anomalous packets and sent out reports of unusual activity (e.g., portscans).

Given a combination of a destination's IP and port x in a packet, the probability that this port is targeted for a scan is $P(x)$. The anomaly score for this combination is defined as

$$A(x) = -\log(P(x)). \tag{6.1}$$

Given the combination set X and $x \in X$, which include all possible destination pairs of IPs and ports for a scan, we can obtain the anomaly score for this scan as

$$A(X) = \sum_{x \in X} A(x). \tag{6.2}$$

This design maintains the records of event likelihood, from which the anomalousness of a given packet is approximated. The packets with anomaly scores above a threshold will be sent to a correlation engine. It is not feasible to measure the full joint probability distribution of events based on packet features, such as IP addresses and ports. BN can estimate the joint probabilities based on the conditional probability of the packet features (see Section 2.1.1.5 for a full description of BN). We leave it to readers to derive the joint probabilities of a destination IP and ports and a source IP and ports, given the probability of a destination port and a source IP, given by conditional probabilities of P (source port | destination port) and P (destination IP | source IP, destination port) respectively.

A correlation engine groups events and the heuristics between events into the architecture of a correlation graph. In correlation graphs, nodes (packets) denote an event and an undirected edge denotes the correlation strength between nodes. The correlation strength between events can be calculated using heuristic functions. Only the nodes that have bond strengths above a threshold can be kept in a group (Figure 6.2). To add a new event to the graph, random initial bonds are assigned to this event first. After the random initial bonds are assigned to the first event, a simulated annealing algorithm can be implemented to find the cluster composed of strong bonds. When the cluster obtains an anomaly score bigger than a threshold, it will be detected as a scan attack. In SPICE, packets are kept longer if they are more anomalous. The lengthy scanning of the packets should make it possible to detect all scans used by current techniques.

In experiments, Staniford et al. used a 3 week observation of 1,258,251 TCP syn packets on a small company network. Among these data, they manually identified 28 horizontal scans, including 1,245 packets and 4 nmap network scans that contained 107,026 packets. They evaluated the performance of SPICE and SPADE in terms of efficiency and effectiveness. Efficiency was defined as the ratio of the number of true positives over all positives. Effectiveness was defined as the ratio of true positives over all true ground truths.

The authors conducted experiments with different configurations of the anomaly score threshold using SPADE, and found that the efficiency was above 85% and the effectiveness was above 99.7%. In the implementation of correlator, they found that SPICE was able to detect randomized scans that extended as long as 90 min. The FPR was reported as low.

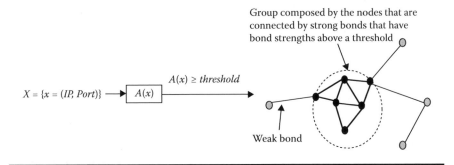

Figure 6.2   Workflow of SPADE.

Application Study 2: GrDIS Using Rule-Based Machine Learning in Coordinated Scan Detection (Table 1.5, E.2)

Staniford-Chen et al. (1996) presented the GrIDS to detect and identify large-scale scans, based on the topography of the networks using packet-level information. In GrIDS, activity graphs can represent the traffic patterns in both individual hosts and in aggregated hierarchical architecture. As shown in Figure 6.3, a typical GrIDS system consists of four important modules in standardized structure: software manager, graph engine, data sources, and module controller process. Each host has a module controller to start or stop two specific modules: software manager and engine for a department. A software manager can rearrange the distribution of graph hierarchy and dynamically manage the states of modules. A graph engine obtains information from a data source to aggregate a subgraph into an upper level graph with a parent engine. Each host has a data source that monitors the activities on the host and networks, and reports the collected information to a graph engine.

In a graph engine, nodes denote hosts or departments, while edges denote network traffic between nodes. Connected nodes and directed edges compose a graph containing its global information. To build a graph, a user must build rule sets from reports. These rules are independent of each other, and are combined to determine the attributes of the combined graphs. Figure 6.4 shows the workflow for how to combine rule sets and propagate graphs into a hierarchical architecture. In this way, upper-level graphs can deduce information about the infrastructure. A central organizational server (OHS) is responsible for the topology of the infrastructure and the maintenance of a consistent topographic architecture during transactions. These transactions include moving departments or hosts, changing a graph engine, and so on.

GrIDS aggregates information in individual hosts into the whole network system using hierarchical graphs, which can reveal the causal relationship between

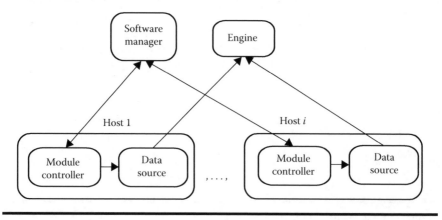

Figure 6.3 Architecture of a GrIDS system for a department.

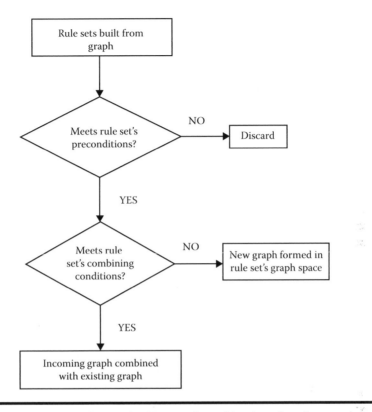

Figure 6.4   Workflow of graph building and combination via rule sets.

host activities. Thus, users can build GrIDS to detect large-scale automated or coordinated scans in near real time. For instance, when one IP address is connected to multiple IP addresses because of a scan, the topography of the graphs shows a fan structure. GrIDS does not use the probability for packets; therefore, it is limited in case of stealthy scans. Staniford et al. did not demonstrate experimental results.

Application Study 3: Using Threshold Random Walk in Horizontal Scan Detection (Table 1.5, E.3)

Jung et al. (2004) developed a threshold random walk (TRW), an online detection algorithm, based on sequential hypothesis testing to detect malicious remote scanners while maintaining promptness and high accuracy. This method is based on the observation that benign remote sources have more precise knowledge about the targeted hosts and services than scanners, such that their successful connection rate is higher than the scan rate. They used detection rate TP and FAR in the framework.

Here, TP refers to the conditional probability describing the cases in which the connection is really launched by scanners and the sequential hypothesis is correct. FP refers to the conditional probability, which denotes the cases in which benign users launch the connection but the hypothesis is that scanners launched the connection. We prefer to specify thresholds α and β to both TP and FP, such that

$$TP \geq \alpha \quad \text{and} \quad FP \leq \beta. \tag{6.3}$$

Given observation $S = \{S_1, \ldots, S_n\}$ including n connection attempts, the likelihood ratio is calculated as follows:

$$\Lambda(S) = \prod_{i=1}^{n} \frac{P_{i1}}{P_{i0}}, \tag{6.4}$$

where P_{i1} denotes the discrete probability distribution of connection to host S_i when the hypothesis is that a scanner launched the connection, and P_{i0} is the corresponding conditional probability distribution when hypothesis is benign. This ratio was assigned an upper bound η_1 and lower bound η_0 to accept the hypotheses that a given remote source is either a scanner or benign. They were expressed as $\eta_0 \leq \Lambda(Y) \leq \eta_1$. Using statistical test equations in Equation 6.3, Jung et al. deduced the approximate solutions to these two bounds as

$$\eta_1 = \frac{\beta}{\alpha} \quad \text{and} \quad \eta_0 = \frac{1-\beta}{1-\alpha}. \tag{6.5}$$

Readers can refer to Jung et al. (2004) for more information regarding the deduction process.

Using the above bounds solution, the real-time scan detection algorithm consists of the following steps:

Step 1. Collect sample data and update sample data set S.
Step 2. Calculate $\Lambda(S)$ using Equation 6.4.
Step 3. If $\Lambda(S) \geq \eta_1$, classify the observed event S as a scanner; if $\Lambda(S) \leq \eta_0$, classify the observed event S as benign. Otherwise, return to Step 1.

In the above steps, a detect decision corresponds to a random walk with regard to the two thresholds. In Step 1, only the sample data that has a new destination will be added to update the sample data set.

Using an analysis of traces from two qualitatively different sites, it is shown that TRW requires a much smaller number of connection attempts (four or five) to detect malicious activity than previous schemes, while also providing theoretical bounds on the low (and configurable) probabilities of missed detections and false alarms.

Table 6.1 Testing Data Set Information

		LBL	*ICSI*
1	Total inbound connections	15,614,500	161,122
2	Size of local address space	131,836	512
3	Active hosts	5,906	217
4	Total unique remote hosts	190,928	29,528
5	Scanners detected by Bro	122	7
6	HTTP worms	37	69
7	other_bad	74,383	15
8	Remainder	116,386	29,437

Source: Jung, J., Paxson, V., Berger, A.W. and Balakrishnan, H., Fast portscan detection using sequential hypothesis testing, in *IEEE Symposium on Security and Privacy*, Oakland, CA, © 2004 IEEE.

The authors conducted experiments on two groups of network traffic data sets, collected by the Lawrence Berkeley National Laboratory (LBL) and the International Computer Science Institute (ICSI) at the University of California, Berkeley. The LBL data set is sparser than the ICSI data set (as shown in Table 6.1). Both data sets had entries of TCP connection logs labeled as "successful," "rejected," and "unanswered." The remaining entries were of undetected scanners. The TP and FP rates obtained from TRW were compared with those obtained from SNORT and BRO. The authors selected $\alpha = 0.99$ and $\beta = 0.01$ in the experiments. TRW showed the highest TP detection rate, while maintaining a lower FPR. In this experiment, the significant advantage of TRW was speed. It required only four or five connection attempts to detect scans. However, attackers sometimes used this method to deny the legitimate source connectivity by deceiving scanning behavior.

Application Study 4: Using Expert Knowledge-Rule-Based Data-Mining Method in Scan Detection (Table 1.5, E.4)

Simon et al. (2006) formulated scan detection as a data-mining problem. They attempted to apply data-mining approaches to build machine-learning classifiers based on the labeled training data set and proportional feature selection. Then, they employed the learned machine-learning model to detect scanners.

Given a set of network traffic traces, they extracted each trace as a pair of source IP and destination port, SIDP or <source IP, destination Port>. They classified normal users and scan attackers who used the same destination ports but accessed them from

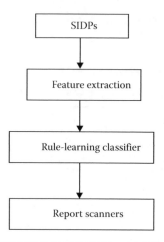

Figure 6.5   Workflow of scan detection using data mining in Simon et al. (2006). (From Simon, G. et al., Scan detection: A data mining approach, in: *Proceedings of the Sixth SIAM International Conference on Data Mining (SDM)*, Bethesda, MD, pp. 118–129, 2006. With permission.)

different source IPs. As shown in Figure 6.5, the designed scan detection method followed the workflow of traditional data-mining methods. In feature extraction, they introduced four sets of features to integrate expert knowledge. Among these feature sets, three sets were useful for the classification of SIDPs.

The first set included four statistical features of a destination IP and port, e.g., the averaged number of distinct destination IPs over all destination ports that source IP had attempted to connect. The second set included six statistical features of source IPs, which described the role and behaviors of the source IPs, e.g., the ratio of distinct destination IPs that attempted to connect by the source IP that did not provide any service on destination ports to any source. The third set included four statistical features of individual destination ports, e.g., the ratio of a distinct destination IP that attempted to connect by the source IP that did not provide any service on destination ports to any source. Readers should refer to Simon et al. (2006) to learn the definition of features in the three extracted feature sets of the network traces.

Simon et al. (2006) selected a rule-based learning classification algorithm, RIPPER (proposed by Cohen [1995]), as their classifier because of the efficiency and effectiveness of RIPPER in dealing with imbalanced and nonlinear data. RIPPER elicits classification results in the form of rules.

In their experiments, Simon et al. collected network traffic traces for 2 days from an infrastructure at the University of Minnesota consisting of five networks and a number of subnetworks. They constructed one sample set every 3 h and finally obtained 13 sample sets. They used the first sample set as a training set and the other 12 sample sets as testing sets. The length of observation adapted to the sufficient and necessary classification of SIDPs. Simon et al. labeled all SIDPs in five groups: scan, p2p, noise, normal, and unknown. They evaluated the proposed data-mining method by measures: precision, recall, and F-score (see their definition in Chapter 1). The scan detection results were compared to those obtained using TRW. The authors selected multiple thresholds to find the most competitive performance of TRW.

The experimental results showed that the proposed method outperformed TRW in all three measures. The proposed method also showed consistent performance among all 12 testing data sets. The F-score was maintained above 90% corresponding to a high precision rate and a low FPR. They attributed the success of the proposed method to its ability to correlate one source IP address with multiple destination IP addresses. The correlation allowed the rule-based learning method to detect scanners earlier. In addition, they found that the proposed method could detect scans in a short time, based on the trained model using training data obtained over a long time. In experiments, Simon et al. tested the collected data set that was collected in 3 days, in a 20 min time window.

These experiments showed that data-mining models can integrate expert knowledge in rules to create an adaptable algorithm that could substantially outperform the state-of-the-art methods, such as TRW, for scan detection in both coverage and precision.

Application Study 5: Using Logistic Regression in Horizontal and Vertical Scan Detection on Large Networks

Gates et al. (2006) developed logistic regression modeling for scan detection in large cyberinfrastructures that have the following characteristics: huge volume flow-level traffic data, multiple routers for data collection, multiple geographic and administrative domains, and unidirectional traffic flow.

Given a set of network traffic traces, Gates et al. extracted events from the traffic traces of each single source IP, which were bounded by quiescent periods. They sorted the traffic traces in each event according to destination IP and ports. They extracted 21 statistical features for scan detection, e.g., ratio of unique source ports to number of traffic traces. Based on the statistical analysis of the contribution of each feature to the scan detection, they selected the most significant six features for each event. These six features include the percentage of traces that appear to have a payload, the percentage of flows with fewer than three packets, the ratio of flag combinations with an ACK flag set to all flows, the average number of source ports per destination IP address, the ratio of the number of unique destination IP addresses to the number of traces, and the ratio of traces with a backscatter-related flag combination such as SYN-ACK to all traces. They used these six features as input in logistic regression model to calculate the probability of an event containing a scan,

$$P(\text{outcome is scan}) = \frac{\exp\left(\alpha_0 + \sum_{i=1}^{n} \alpha_i f_i\right)}{\left(1 + \exp\left(\alpha_0 + \sum_{i=1}^{n} \alpha_i f_i\right)\right)}. \tag{6.6}$$

In the above equation, f_i denotes the selected features for logistic regression calculation, and $n = 6$. $\alpha_0, \ldots, \alpha_n$ are coefficients determined by both experts and the training data set.

In the experiment, Gates et al. split data sets into three groups: elicitation, training, and testing. They collected elicitation traffic traces, which included 129,191 events, for 1 h (Muelder et al., 2007). They collected training traffic trace sets in the subsequent hour and included 130,062 events. Then, they collected 127,873 testing events in the following hour after collecting and training the data set. They randomly selected three groups of data with respect to the three data sets: elicitation, training, and testing. These three groups consisted of 100, 200, and 300 sample data, respectively.

The expert manually labeled each of the events as containing a scan or not containing a scan. The same expert was involved in labeling events as scanned or not scanned. The elicitation group included 30 randomly selected observations and the 70 observations with the largest variances. Using the values of the 21 features, the expert estimated the probability of an event containing a scan. They used the estimated probabilities to determine the coefficients' prior values in Equation 6.6. Combined with the training data set, they estimated the posterior feature coefficients using the Bayesian approach. Furthermore, they selected the six most significant features and their corresponding coefficients in the regression model using the Akaike Information Criterion (AIC).*

Then, they input the 300 testing data into the learned regression model to generate an estimated probability for each event. If the probability was greater than 0.5, the event was classified as a containing scan; otherwise, it was classified as normal. Using the ground truth labeled by the expert, the authors obtained the detection rate and FAR at 95.5% and 0.4%, correspondingly. They also conducted performance compassion between the proposed method and TRW ($\alpha = 0.01$ and $\beta = 0.99$) on the same training and testing data set, and found that the proposed method obtained as high detection accuracy as the TRW did. However, this proposed scan detection method cannot be implemented in real-time applications

---

* AIK measures the fitness of a regression model for a given data set. AIK is mostly employed for model selection. Generally, the selected model corresponds to the lowest AIC for the given data set. The commonly used equation for calculating AIC is $AIC = 2k - 2\ln(L)$, where k denotes the number of coefficients in the regression model and L denotes the maximized likelihood of the estimated model.

due to its requirement of the collection of sufficient flow-level traffic flows for a single source IP.

Application Study 6: Using Bidirectional Associative Memory and ScanVis in Scan Detection and Characterization (Table 1.5, E.5)

Muelder et al. (2007) presented a study on how to use associative memory-learning techniques to compare network scans and create a classification that can be used by itself or in conjunction with visualization techniques to better characterize the sources of these scans. These scans produced an integrated system of visual and intelligent analysis, which is applicable to real-world data.

As shown in Figure 6.6, the proposed method consists of four steps in scan detection and characterization: the collection and labeling of network traffic data, the training of bidirectional associative memory (BAM) using the controlled scan data, the classification of network unknown traffic scan data using the learned BAM model, and the visualization and characterization of scan patterns. Controlled scan data are the set of scan data of which we know the properties, such as the source IP and ports, source hardwire and software, and so on.

The first three steps focus on scan classification, as with the other supervised machine-learning methodologies that we have discussed in the previous sections. The fourth step is an additional contribution to the in-depth analysis of scan patterns that enables cyber administrators to perform respective controls over the detected scans. Muelder et al. (2007) assumed scan detection was performed using the existing data-mining techniques, and controlled data were available for classification. Thus, the focus of the research was in the BAM classification process, and the application of ScanVis (Muelder et al., 2005) was in scan characterization.

BAM maps from one pattern space, e.g., layer X, to another pattern space, e.g., layer Y, by using a two-layer associative memory, as shown in Figure 6.7.

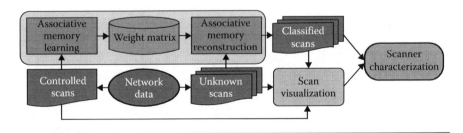

Figure 6.6 Workflow of scan characterization in Muelder et al. (2007). (With kind permission from Springer Science+Business Media: *Proceedings of the Workshop on Visualization for Computer Security*, Sacramento, CA, Intelligent classification and visualization of network scans, 2007, Muelder, C., Chen, L., Thomason, R., Ma, K.L., and Bartoletti, T., Copyright 2007.)

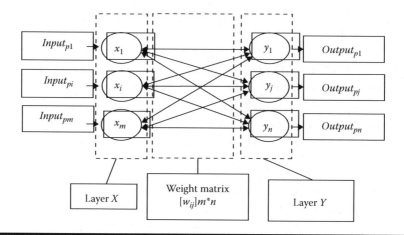

Figure 6.7 Structure of BAM.

The associative memory consists of a weight matrix $\left[w_{ij}\right]_{m^*n}$, and the weight w_{ij} corresponds to the mapping from input neuron x_i to y_j with $w_{ij} = \sum_{p=1}^{P} Input_{p,i} \cdot Output_{p,j}$, where p is the index of patterns, $i = 1, \ldots, m$ and $j = 1, \ldots, n$. Given detected scans and their corresponding patterns, we can generate the weight matrix as a classifier for the scans in the similar patterns. The mapping between the pair x_i and y_j can be performed as follows: if $Input_{pi} \cdot w_{ij} > 0$ ($w_{ij} \cdot Output_{pj} > 0$), $Output_{(p+1)i} = 1$ ($Input_{(p+1)i} = 1$), $Input_{pi} \cdot w_{ij} < 0$ ($Output_{pj} \cdot w_{ij} < 0$) $Output_{(p+1)i} = -1$ ($Input_{(p+1)i} = 1$), or $Output_{(p+1)i} = Output_{pi}$ ($Output_{(p+1)j} = Output_{pj}$). Here, "1" and "–1" indicate whether the corresponding neurons are activated.

ScanVis (Muelder et al., 2005) was designed to facilitate the profiling of the detected scans and discover the real scan sources underlining advanced hiding techniques. Combined with machine-learning methods, ScanVis can also solve the difficulties of classifying the normal traffic flows and scan attacks, such as the existence of WebCrawler and a scanner on the same port. As shown in Figure 6.8, ScanVis consists of four components. The first two of these components, collection of traffic flows and scan detection, are performed in BAM, such that the principle work locates in the global and local view. These two parts provide the overview of comparisons between scans and a detailed comparison in locals between scans. A feedback from local viewing can be input by users to fine tune the global comprehension of the scans, while users can easily look into details in local region.

Scan fingerprints reduce the observed data size. Thus, they can be compared visually. The operation of a global view using scan fingerprints includes the following components: metrics derivation, paired comparison, and quantitative evaluation of scan match. Metrics are selected to present data more concisely and comprehensively, e.g., the number of visits per unique address. In paired

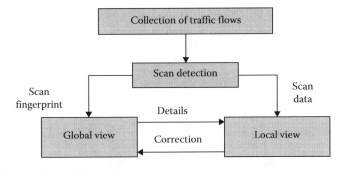

Figure 6.8 Structure of ScanVis. (Adapted from Muelder, C. et al., A visualization methodology for characterization of network scans, in *IEEE Workshops on Visualization for Computer Security*, Minneapolis, MN, pp. 29–38, 2005. With permission.)

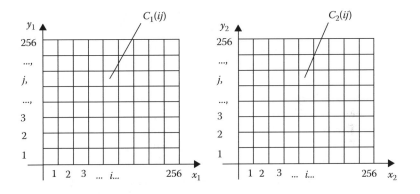

Figure 6.9 Paired comparison of scan patterns.

comparison, each of the two neighboring scans is displayed in a 256-by-256 grid-based color panel, in which coordinates x and y correspond to the third and fourth bytes of the destination IP addresses in a class B network. As shown in Figure 6.9, using the extracted fingerprints $c(i,j)$ and $c'(i,j)$ for each grid in the paired scans, we can obtain the similarity between them. To quantitatively compare paired scans, Muelder et al. (2005) proposed three wavelet scalograms for each scan, $D_k = (d_{k,1}, \ldots, d_{k,2^{n-k}})$, $S_k = (s_{k,1}, \ldots, s_{k,2^{n-k}})$, and $\sigma_k = \left(\sum S_k / 2^{n-k} \right)$, for the given scan data series $D_0 = (d_{0,1}, \ldots, d_{0,2^n})$ and $0 < k < n$. They also recommended several functions for the calculation of $d_{k,1}$ and $s_{k,1}$, e.g., $d_{k,i} = |d_{k-1,i} + d_{k-1,i+1}| / 2$ and $s_{k,i} = |d_{k-1,i} - d_{k-1,i+1}| / 2$. Furthermore, the wavelet similarity between scans can be measured using distance functions, such as Euclidean distance. Based on the scalogram similarity between paired scans, scan clusters can be generated in an overview graph (Figure 6.9). The clustered scans can aid cyber administrators to investigate attack sources through the local analysis of an individual scan in the same cluster.

In experiments, Muelder et al. collected real-world scan data from the cyberinfrastructure at Lawrence Livermore National Lab (LLNL). Each scan data contained time information and the destination address. They showed a number of clustering results for visualization. However, no performance evaluation has been provided for recognition accuracy and speed. In addition, the recognition is performed by human visualization, and automatic scan comparisons have not been investigated.

6.4 Other Scan Techniques with Machine-Learning Methods

As we explained in Study Application 3, SNORT and BRO used rule-based threshold techniques in scan detection. These techniques have low effectiveness and efficiency. Leckie and Kotagiri (2002) built a probabilistic system based on the Bayesian model. Using conditional probability, they estimated the likelihood of source IPs scanning the destination services on targets.

Robertson et al. (2003) assigned a score to each source IP according to the account of its failed connection with the destinations. If the score was greater than a given threshold, the source IP was detected as a scanner. They also developed a peer-center surveillance detection system to strengthen the scan detection ability even if they received no response in scanning. Yegneswaran et al. (2003) investigated the daily activities of source IPs in coordinated scans and found that there was no locality among the scanning activities across the source IPs. They also applied the information-theoretic approach to investigate the possibility of using the traffic information between networks to detect attackers. Conti and Abdullah (2004) developed a visualization method to detect coordinated scans and attack tools in normal traffic flows. Although they had not provided a clear visualization, results show that this method detected the distribution of coordinated scans.

6.5 Summary

In this chapter, we have investigated popular scan and scan detection techniques. Normally, scans represent the characteristics of attackers and scans can lead to potential attacks in similar scanned destinations across networks. Thus, scan detection can help users protect cyberinfrastructures from attacks.

Traditional scan detection methods use rule-based thresholding. These techniques normally result in a low detection rate and an unacceptable FAR, the same problem as occurs in most of the anomaly detection systems. The GrIDS approach constructs a hierarchical network graph, which can be helpful for cyber administrators to investigate the causal relations between network activities, especially in large-scale networks. The aggregation of information in networks facilitates scan detection in multiple hosts or in groups of hosts, and consolidates its scalability to recognize the global scan patterns.

SPICE and SPADE detect stealth scans, especially when scans are evasive and in small-sized time windows normally used in traditional methods such as SNORT, BRO, and GrIDS. Using BN and clustering methods, SPICE and SPADE can detect slow scans at a high-detection rate and a low FAR. The TRW approach is used to detect scans quickly while solving effectiveness and efficiency problems in SNORT and BRO. This approach works as the gold standard for many innovative scan detection approaches. In comparison with TRW, it was found that SPICE needs days or weeks to collect packets and find clusters and correlations. The running time is longer, and the computation is more complex than with TRW. Simon et al. have demonstrated that expert rule-based data-mining techniques can outperform TRW in scan detection in terms of accuracy and coverage. Other machine-learning methods can be introduced into the workflow to improve the scan detection results. Gates et al. integrated logistic regression and feature extraction and selection into one module and found the hybrid scan detection result was similar to TRW.

To the best of our knowledge, most of the clustering and classic machine-learning methods have not been explored in scan detections. This lack of exploration can be because the dynamic and huge-scale network flows require an effective, real-time responsive learning ability in detection systems. Besides accuracy, scan detection needs sufficient coverage and scalability in large-scale cyberinfrastructures. As shown in Application Study 6, machine-learning classification and clustering methods can be integrated in both the global and local viewing of scan patterns in networks. This global and local viewing of scan patterns can potentially solve coverage and scalability problems. Meanwhile, the research could potentially extend to the further analysis of scan patterns, which will aid cyber administrators in launching preventive measures for potential attacks.

References

Braynov, S. and M. Jadliwala. Detecting malicious groups of agents. In: *Proceedings of the First IEEE Symposium on Multi-Agent Security and Survivability*, Philadelphia, PA, 2004.

Cohen, W.W. Fast effective rule induction. In: *Proceedings of the 12th International Conference on Machine Learning*, San Mateo, CA, 1995.

Conti, G. and K. Abdullah. Passive visual fingerprinting of network attack tools. In: *Proceedings of 2004 CCS Workshop on Visualization and Data Mining for Computer Security*, Washington, DC, 2004, pp. 45–54.

Gates, C., J.J. McNutt, J.B. Kadane, and M.I. Kellner. Scan detection on very large networks using logistic regression modeling. In: *Proceedings of the 11th IEEE Symposium on Computers and Communications (ISCC)*, Cagliari, Sardin, 2006.

Jung, J., V. Paxson, A.W. Berger, and H. Balakrishnan. Fast portscan detection using sequential hypothesis testing. In: *IEEE Symposium on Security and Privacy*, Oakland, CA, 2004.

Leckie, C. and Kotagiri, R. A probabilistic approach to detecting network scans. In: *Proceedings of the 2002 IEEE Network Operations and Management Symposium*, Florence, Italy, 2002, pp. 359–372.

Muelder, C., L. Chen, R. Thomason, K.L. Ma, and T. Bartoletti. Intelligent classification and visualization of network scans. In: *Proceedings of the Workshop on Visualization for Computer Security*, Sacramento, CA, 2007.

Muelder, C., K.L. Ma, and T. Bartoletti. A visualization methodology for characterization of network scans. In: *IEEE Workshops on Visualization for Computer Security*, Minneapolis, MN, 2005, pp. 29–38.

Paxson, V. Bro: A system for detecting network intruders in real-time. In *Proceedings of the Seventh USENIX Security Symposium*, San Antonio, TX, 1998.

Robertson, S., E.V. Siegel, M. Miller, and S.J. Stolfo. Surveillance detection in high bandwidth environments. In: *Proceedings of the 2003 DARPA DISCEX III Conference*, Washington, DC, 2003, pp. 130–139.

Roesch, M. Snort-lightweight intrusion detection for networks. In: *Proceedings of the 13th USENIX Conference on System Administration*, Seattle, WA, 1999, pp. 229–238.

Simon, G., H. Xiong, E. Eilertson, and V. Kumar. Scan detection: A data mining approach. In: *Proceedings of the Sixth SIAM International Conference on Data Mining (SDM)*, Bethesda, MD, 2006, pp. 118–129.

Staniford, S., J.A. Hoagland, and J.M. McAlerney. Practical automated detection of stealthy portscans. In: *Proceedings of the Seventh ACM Conference on Computer and Communications Security*, Athens, Greece, 2002a.

Staniford, S., J.A. Hoagland, and J.M. McAlerney. Practical automated detection of stealthy portscans. *Journal of Computer Security* 10, 105–136 (2002b).

Staniford-Chen, S., S. Cheung, R. Crawford, M. Dilger, J. Frank, J. Hoagland, K. Levitt, C. Wee, R. Yip, and D. Zerkle. GrIDS: A graph-based intrusion detection system for large networks. In: *The 19th National Information Systems Security Conference*, Baltimore, MD, 1996.

Yegneswaran, V., P. Barford, and J. Ullrich. Internet intrusions: Global characteristics and prevalence. In: *Proceedings of the 2003 ACM Joint International Conference on Measurement and Modeling of Computer Systems*, San Diego, CA, 2003, pp. 138–147.

Chapter 7

Machine Learning for Profiling Network Traffic

Character is that which reveals moral purpose, exposing the class of things a man chooses and avoids.

Aristotle

7.1 Introduction

In this chapter, we address techniques for profiling network traffic. We investigate a large number of methods for profiling normal or anomalous behaviors in cyberinfrastructures, such that we can detect the anomalous patterns accurately and efficiently. By using misuse detection systems, we extract rules or signatures from prior knowledge to characterize anomalous behaviors or intrusions. By using anomaly detection systems, we attempt to learn normal behaviors such that we can recognize both the known and unknown anomalous patterns among the remaining rules. Using hybrid intrusion systems, we combine both the normal and anomalous profiling processes to improve the detection rate and decrease the false-alarm rate. For the above three types of IDSs, it is essential to profile either normal or anomalous behaviors before launching detection procedures. In this chapter, we focus on the components of networks that involve prior interesting events.

Network administrators monitor a huge amount of network traffic flows to identify hidden problems, such as attacks or misuse of services, analyze the network traffic, and identify significant patterns in the traffic flows. For such monitoring

159

to be successful, we must provide a tool that can generalize and elucidate the significant characteristics or signatures of network traffic in the report, such that the network administrators reading the report will understand the dominant behaviors in the network, such as the communities of hosts, the provider/server of services, and malicious flows.

In Chapter 6, we discussed scan detection and introduced several methods of scan characterization, such as BAM and ScanVis. The philosophy of profiling network traffic is similar to scan characterization, and we can regard scan characterization as a specific application for this chapter. Scan, or portscan, is a malicious behavior in network traffic and its characterization, including clustering and visualization, can facilitate the network administrators to detect scan attacks. Similarly, profiling will facilitate the detection of broader dominant events in networks.

In this chapter, we introduce profiling techniques and data-mining and machine-learning applications in the profiling systems. First, we define network traffic profiling and introduce related knowledge in the network traffic. Then, we categorize profiling methods according to the pattern types of interest in the network, such as applications. We expose the challenges in network profiling. Second, we introduce the data-mining and machine-learning solutions to the difficulties in network traffic profiling. We outline the workflow of profiling and concentrate on the roles of data-mining and machine-learning methods in the pattern learning and recognition phases.

Third, we study several network profiling systems in detail. We present the fundamental data-mining and machine-learning techniques in the systems, including supervised classification and clustering methods. Then, we illustrate the implementation processes and performances of these techniques in application studies. In addition, we briefly summarize other network traffic profiling methodologies and corresponding applications. Finally, we summarize the development of the network traffic profiling systems and introduce several research directions, as presented in literature.

7.2 Network Traffic Profiling and Related Network Traffic Knowledge

Profiling modules perform clustering algorithms or other data-mining and machine-learning methods to group similar network connections and search for dominant behaviors. We distinguish profiling from the term "profile" used for anomaly detection in Chapter 3. Using anomaly detection, we aim to group similar normal data and build a normal model so that we can identify outliers. However, in profiling modules, we focus on grouping similar network behaviors and finding the trends that these behaviors follow.

As with the scan detection introduced in Chapter 6, network profiling methods have been developed for other specific applications, such as heavy hitters, gaming, chatting, p2p, and suspicious traffic in FTP, HTTP, and SMTP. Such profiling applications require access to a system capable of capturing interactions between hosts through empirical signatures or statistical analysis.

Currently, researchers are interested in profiling common behaviors in network traffic. Such behaviors include the communications between hosts and the performance of the hosts. The communication between hosts can be patterned using entropy, traffic volume, feature distributions, and so on. The host performances appear in their port utilization to provide service or other interactions. The host IP addresses and the associated port numbers are used for profiling, to investigate the traffic flows.

Researchers are attempting to solve two of the largest problems in network profiling: the huge amount of network traffic flows and the difficulties in detecting patterns in the traffic data and in the learned patterns. For example, even if we extract the association rules to describe the correlation between traffic flows, the huge number of rules still hampers profiling analysis and pattern recognition. In this case, clustering methods along with data-mining techniques need to extract the dominant patterns efficiently and effectively. Furthermore, visualization ability can strengthen the role of network traffic profiling in cyber administration.

7.3 Machine Learning and Network Traffic Profiling

In this chapter, we focus on network traffic profiling but specifically not on the pattern detection process. Hence, the workflow in Figure 7.1 includes four steps: data collection, data preprocessing, network traffic profiling, and reporting.

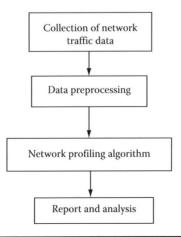

Figure 7.1 Workflow of network traffic profiling.

The network traffic data can be collected online or offline. Most of the profiling techniques work on online data, but only offline data have been used in the applications. Offline profiling is sufficient for some applications, such as traffic classification at the application level using graphlets (Karagiannis et al., 2005). In data preprocessing, features are selected according to a profiling objective or analysis afterward. A network profiling algorithm can be signature-based classification, a data-mining or machine-learning clustering method, or IP blacklist filtering.

We focus on data-mining and machine-learning clustering methods and only briefly introduce the other methods in the latter applications. Both supervised machine-learning and clustering methods are used in the network traffic profiling or pattern learning process. These techniques include common clustering methods, such as association rules mining and classification, *k*-means clustering, DBSCAN, AutoClass and shared nearest neighbor (SNN), and application-specific algorithms, such as cluster miner in AutoFocus (Estan et al., 2003). Profiling results can be further simplified and abstracted to aid the cyber administrator in analyzing profiling reports. Visualization tools can aid in this process.

7.4 Data-Mining and Machine-Learning Applications in Network Profiling

In Application Study 1, we examine the NETMINE framework, which demonstrates how to aggregate and classify association rules from traffic flows, and generalize association rules to guide analysis. In Application Study 2, AutoFocus displays methods for aggregating traffic flows into clusters over the resource consumption, along a single feature and joint features. Application Study 3 contains an example of how to extract significant clusters of behaviors, classify behaviors, and characterize the dominant interactions between dimensions using data mining and entropy, to profile the communication patterns between end users and services. In Application Study 4, we introduce how to use the SNN profiling module in the Minnesota Intrusion Detection System (MINDS) and discover unexpected patterns in network traffic. Application Study 5 demonstrates the traffic pattern classification using *k*-means, DBSCAN, and AutoClass over traffic statistical features. Examples of data mining and machine learning for network profiling are categorized in Table 1.6.

Application Study 1: NETMINE Using Association Rules Mining and Classification for Network Traffic Profiling

Apiletti et al. (2008) designed the NETMINE framework to characterize the network communications. The objective of NETMINE was to extract the principal association rules in network communities to facilitate the exploration and

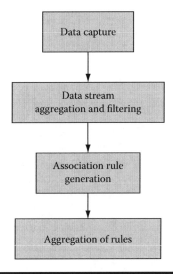

Figure 7.2   Workflow of NETMINE.

recognition of significant traffic patterns for cyber administrators or domain experts. As shown in Figure 7.2, NETMINE consists of four components: data capturing, data stream aggregation and filtering, association rule mining, and association rules aggregation.

Apiletti et al. used the available data collection tools to capture network traces. They concurrently preprocessed the captured traces and packets to reduce the sample data size. In these queries, they aggregated similar traffic packets over a continuous sliding time window and filtered out those less-correlated packets for pattern extraction. Given a set of protocol features $F = \{f_1, \ldots, f_n\}$, such as source IP address, each packet is a subset of F, and the associations of these features can be presented using association rules. The sliding windows are associated with two parameters: window size and moving step of the window, both measured by a time unit (e.g., second). The window size measures the coverage of the aggregating and filtering rules in continuous enquiries.

The aggregating function groups the packets that share similar features, such as source IP address. Then, the filtering function removes the packets that account for less than a threshold of the aggregated traffic flows in the sliding window. The preprocessed streaming packets include a large number of infrequent flows, which convey relevant information. To extract those seemingly trivial rules, a feasible solution was proposed to aggregate or generalize the feature values or association rules in a hierarchical taxonomy. For example, Apiletti et al. aggregated IP addresses into subnets and port numbers into three categorical levels for TCP ports, as shown in Figure 7.3.

The items in lower levels aggregated only when their generated rules were below the minimum support value. Itemsets were generated from lower-level $k-1$ to higher-level k in iteration k. Only the itemsets above the support level were used for apriori

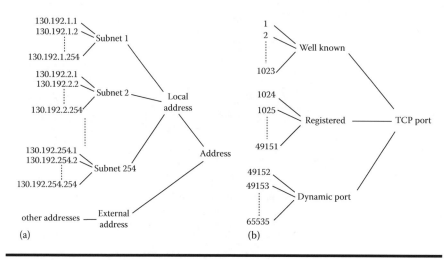

Figure 7.3 Examples of hierarchical taxonomy in generalizing association rules. (a) Taxonomy for address. (b) Taxonomy for ports. (Reprinted from *Comput. Netw.*, 53, Apiletti, D., Baralis, E., Cerquitelli, T., and D'Elia, V., Characterizing network traffic by means of the NetMine framework, 774–789, Copyright (2008), with permission from Elsevier.)

rules generation. Then, the generalized rules were classified into groups according to the basic features in network traffic. For example, traffic flows can be semantically presented by rules: {*source IP*} ⇒ {*destination IP*} and {*destination IP*} ⇒ {*source IP*} with respective rule deduction direction. Services can be presented by the following rules: {*destination address*} ⇒ {*destination port*} and {*destination port*} ⇒ {*destination address*}, and service usage can be presented by the following rules: {*destination port*} ⇒ {*source address*} and {*source address*} ⇒ {*destination port*}. The combination of these rules can generate three other basic groups, e.g., traffic flow and service: {*destination address*} ⇒ {*destination port, source address*} and {*destination port, source address*} ⇒ {*destination address*}.

Apiletti et al. evaluated the proposed methods on two data sets. The data sets were captured on the backbone network at the Politecnico di Torino. The selected features included source address/port, destination address/port, and flow size. To facilitate the selection of the generalized rules, they used the lift quality index of rule $X \Rightarrow Y$ as follows:

$$lift(X, Y) = \frac{support(X \Rightarrow Y)}{support(X)support(Y)}. \tag{7.1}$$

In the above equation, X and Y are two itemsets, and $support(X)$, $support(X)$, and $support(X \Rightarrow Y)$ are the supports of X, Y and the rule $X \Rightarrow Y$, respectively. Lift value 1 indicates that the two itemsets are independent of one another; a lift value being greater (less) than 1 indicates a positive (negative) correlation. Experimental results showed that generalized rules were extracted. These generalized rules contained lower frequent itemsets that were insufficient to meet the minimum support level if considered individual rules. The generalized rules were a higher percentage of the total rules when the support threshold was increased.

This method extracts generalized association rules, which provide a high-level abstraction of the network traffic and allows the discovery of unexpected and more interesting traffic rules. The proposed technique exploits taxonomies to drive the pruning phase of the extraction process. Extracted correlations are automatically aggregated in more general association rules according to a frequency threshold. Eventually, extracted rules are classified into groups according to their semantic meaning, thus allowing a domain expert to focus on the most relevant patterns.

Application Study 2: AutoFocus for Clustering Multidimensional Traffic

Aggregation on one feature or on few features can generalize the network flows, e.g., using association rule generalization in NETMINE. This method can result in the selection of the wrong dimensions for aggregation without any prior knowledge, which can lead the administrator to insignificant features. Thus, identifying the significant features among the traffic streams is necessary. To obtain meaningful aggregation, clustering methods have been proposed in network traffic profiling (Ertöz et al., 2003; Estan et al., 2003; Chandola et al., 2006; Xu et al., 2008).

Estan et al. (2003) proposed a method, called AutoFocus, to automatically characterize and cluster network traffic based on resource consumption along dimensions. The resource consumption was defined as the coverage of traffic volume in the clusters of a network, e.g., using a number of packets to calculate the traffic volume. AutoFocus compressed, combined, and prioritized the clustering results into an easily comprehensive report. Five features were included in this research: source IP/port, destination IP/port, and protocol. The traffic cluster included sets of possible values of these features. As shown in Figure 7.4, AutoFocus consists of three steps: data collection, cluster mining, and report formatting. Data collection, also called traffic parser, accepts packet traces and other raw network data. Cluster miner composes the principal element of AutoFocus by four main components in its clustering algorithm: computing clusters, compressing traffic clusters, computing traffic changes, and prioritizing clusters in a report. In a report, users can recognize traffic categories and clusters, which are presented graphically after aggregation and ranking.

The input data included seven attributes: the five features listed above, and the packet and byte counters. The packet counter reports the number of matched packets in terms of the five features, while the byte counter accounts for the number of bytes in the packets. The "estimate" counter can be computed as the sum of the "estimates" of its children. First, for a single feature, source IP addresses are listed as leaves with subnets as nodes and roots in the hierarchical tree architecture.

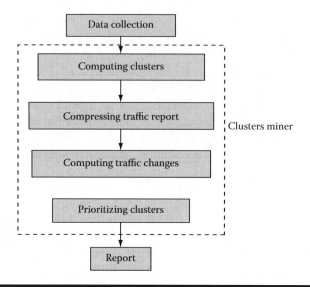

Figure 7.4   Workflow of AutoFocus.

Each node, including the leaves and roots, has a counter. A counter value above the predefined threshold value indicates the corresponding cluster. Once these clusters are found, multiple one-dimensional hierarchies are combined into a dimension-overlapping structure. Each node in the structure has a parent from each dimension. Clusters are generated when their counters are above the threshold. Optimization methods help to prune the clustering space by focusing on clusters that have one-dimensional ancestors above the threshold, and batching clusters.

Second, the compression algorithm traverses all clusters in the order of a specific measure. Each cluster has an "estimate" counter that accounts for the maximum "estimate" among all dimensions (here we have five features). For each dimension, the maximum "estimate" of a cluster corresponds to the sum of the "estimates" of its children. A cluster is reported when the deviation between its "estimate" and real traffic data is above the threshold, or when the "estimate" is replaced by real traffic data.

Third, in a measurement time interval of the actual change of each reported cluster from the previous step is compared to the estimated change of that cluster. A cluster is reported when the difference between the actual change and estimated change is greater than the threshold. Fourth, clusters are ranked using a measure called an unexpectedness score. Assuming features (dimensions) are independent from each other, an unexpected score is defined as the deviation from a uniform model. Given a cluster with a real percentage of volume $X\%$ and its features having an independent real percentage of volume $\{Y_1\%, \ldots, Y_d\%\}$, the unexpectedness of the cluster is $X\% / \prod Y_i\%$, where d is the dimension size of the cluster and $i = 1, \ldots, d$. This score measures the anomaly behavior among dimensions.

Estan et al. evaluated AutoFocus using the three collected traces on three cyberinfrastructures. The first trace was collected from 31 days of data on a small network exchange point in San Diego; the second trace was collected over 39 days of connections in a large research institute. The third trace was composed of an 8 h trace from an OC-48 backbone link. The investigation showed that AutoFocus recognized unexpected patterns in network traffic, such as a weekly pattern, a temporary network outage, a worm epidemic, and p2p applications.

Application Study 3: Using Information-Theoretic Techniques in Network Traffic Profiling (Table 1.6, F.5)

Xu et al. (2008) developed a general methodology to automatically discover and elucidate significant behavior profiles from Internet backbone traffic, using entropy-based data-mining techniques. The authors focused on profiling the communication patterns of the network traffic in an abstraction to facilitate network administrators to understand and identify the anomalous events easily. Four end-host and service features were included in this research: source IP/port and destination IP/port. Along each feature dimension, traffic flows, which had the same feature value in this dimension, aggregated into a cluster. Hence, clusters were generated in all four dimensions. In each dimension, the significance of clusters was measured using entropy. As shown in Figure 7.5, the proposed method consisted of three steps: data collection, traffic profiling, and reporting. Data collection accepted packet-header traces in networks.

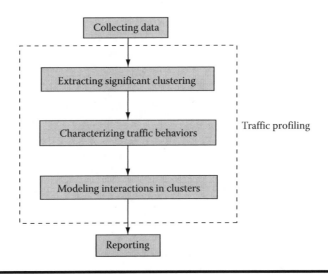

Figure 7.5 Workflow of network traffic profiling as proposed in Xu et al. (2008). (Xu, K., Zhang, X.L., and Bhattachayya, S., Internet traffic behavior profiling for network security monitoring, *IEEE/ACM Trans. Netw.* © 2008 IEEE.)

Traffic profiling for this method consisted of three components: significant cluster extraction, automatic behavior classification, and structural modeling for interpretative analysis. In the report, which is generated from the information, users can identify unwanted or anomaly traffic easily.

To profile traffic flow, significant clusters were generated for each feature dimension. They defined significance by relative uncertainty (RU) as follows:

$$RU(X) = \frac{H(X)}{H_{max}(X)} = \frac{-\sum_{x_i \in X} p(x_i) \log p(x_i)}{\log \min\{N_x, m\}} \tag{7.2}$$

where

$p(x_i)$ is the estimated probability of random variable X taking the value x_i
X takes N_x discrete values and m observations
$H_{max}(X)$ is the maximum entropy of X

RU measures the observational randomness or uniqueness without regard to sample or observation size. The higher RU values indicate more observations of X.

The first step in traffic profiling is to extract significant clusters along the single dimensional feature. Given a set of distinctive observed values, $A = \{a_1, ..., a_n\}$, in one feature dimension, the most significant cluster S of A was defined on two conditions: any feature value in S holds greater probability than any of the values in the remaining subset of A, $A-S$, and the feature values in S are more distinct than those in subset $A-S$. The second condition measures the uniformity of values using $RU(X|A - S) > \beta$, where β is a predefined threshold. The bigger threshold β (near 1) introduces a uniform subset $A-S$. Another threshold α, which can be optimized using the following steps, can measure the first condition:

Step 1. Initialize α, β, $k = 0$, $\theta = RU(X|A - S)$
Step 2. If $\theta > \beta$, stop and report S; if not, $\alpha = \alpha \times 2^{-k}$ and $k = k + 1$
Step 3. Assign all feature values that have a probability greater than threshold α to S and all the others to $A-S$
Step 4. Calculate $\theta = RU(X|A - S)$ and return to Step 2

Xu et al. (2008) showed that a single feature dimension is not sufficient for finding significant clusters based on fixed thresholds.

The second step in traffic profiling is to group the obtained clusters into distinctive behavior classes. As four feature dimensions have been involved in any traffic flow, three other feature dimensions and *RU*s, called *RU* vectors, are associated with each cluster defined by a single feature dimension. Each dimension is partitioned into categories, and the whole *RU* vector space is split into a number of nonoverlapping cell tubes, called behavior classes (BCs). In an observation time slot, we calculate the number of clusters in each BC. Then, we obtain the average number of clusters over these time slots.

Furthermore, we can predict the occurrences of clusters in each BC over time. Based on these three measures of all BCs, we can evaluate the temporal performance of the BCs. On the same networks and over two time lengths, we can collect two data sets and extract the respective clusters and BC performance associated with the RUs for each data point. Using this method, the time transition for each data point can be investigated and analyzed. For example, Manhattan distance and Hamming distance are used to describe the behavior transition for RUs in different dimensions.

In the third step, feature interactions are modeled in clusters using the so-called dominant state analysis. The dominant states refer to the subsets of the three associated feature values for a cluster, which induces the approximation of the original probability distribution of the data set. Given three-dimensional feature sets A, B, and C for a cluster in the order of RUs, $RU(A) > RU(B) > RU(C)$, the dominant state analysis includes the following three steps (as shown in Figure 7.6). First, label feature value $a_i \in A$ as substantial, if $p(a_i) \geq \delta$; second, label feature value $c_k \in B$ as substantial if $p(b_j|a_i) \geq \delta$, given substantial $a_i \in A$. Third, label a feature value as substantial if $p(c_k|a_i,b_j) \geq \delta$, given substantial $a_i \in A$ and $b_j \in B$. Using these three steps, the dominant flows are captured in the extraction like $a_i \rightarrow \{*,*\}$, $(a_i \rightarrow b_j) \rightarrow \{*\}$, and $a_i \rightarrow b_j \rightarrow c_k$.

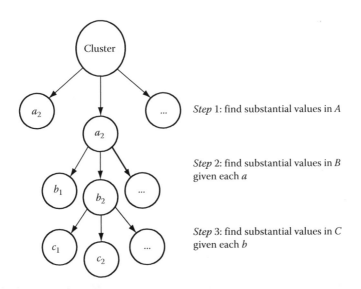

Figure 7.6 Procedures of dominant state analysis. (Xu, K., Zhang, X.L., and Bhattachayya, S., Internet traffic behavior profiling for network security monitoring, *IEEE/ACM Trans. Netw.* © 2008 IEEE.)

Xu et al. evaluated the proposed method using packet-head traces collected from five links in a large-scale backbone ISP network. They aggregated traffic flows using traces every 5 min, and reported that three principal groups of profiles were found in the traffic flows: sever/service behaviors, heavy-hitter hosts, and scan/exploit profiles. They also demonstrated that the further investigation of the clustering results can identify anomaly flows even if these flows appear rarely.

Application Study 4: Using Shared Nearest Neighbor Clustering in Network Traffic Profiling (Table 1.6, F.2)

SNN uses the shared nearest neighbors to define the similarity between data points. For example, data points A and B have neighbor sets NN(A) and NN(B). In SNN, the similarity of A and B is defined as

$$similarity(A, B) = \left| NN(A) \cap NN(B) \right|, \tag{7.3}$$

where $|.|$ refers to the cardinality of the given data set. The neighborhood of a data point can be defined using k-nearest neighbor or specified-radius area.

SNN maintains local connections in relatively uniform regions, while it breaks links in transition regions. With this property, SNN is able to prevent the distances between data points becoming uniform such that these clustering methods cannot classify data points correctly when dimensionality increases. Given a set of data points, the SNN algorithm includes the following steps:

Step 1. Compute the similarities between the data points and construct a similarity matrix, which describes the links between data points by the similarity values.

Step 2. Retain only the predefined number of the most nearest neighbors in the matrix, and link the shared data points into clusters.

Step 3. Obtain the size of the SNN neighborhood at each data point, and remove all data points except those that are in an SNN neighborhood with a greater size than the predefined threshold; these data points are called core data points.

Step 4. Group the core data points within a predefined window in the same cluster; discard the noncore data points outside of the windows of any core data point, and assign the remaining data points to the nearest clusters.

Since SNN is insensitive to variants of the shapes, sizes, and densities of clusters in a noisy data set, especially in high-dimension feature space, it has been selected for network intrusion detection (Ertöz et al., 2003) and network traffic profiling (Chandola et al., 2006) for MINDS. Chandola et al. implemented the SNN clustering algorithm in profiling network communications and detected the dominant behaviors. They collected two data sets: one set consisting of 850,000

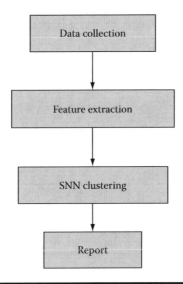

Figure 7.7   Profiling procedure in MINDS.

connections from 1 h of data at a U.S. Army fort, and one set consisting of 7500 traffic flows from the University of Minnesota network. As shown in Figure 7.7, the features, including start time, flow duration, source/destination IP address, source/destination port, protocol type, number of packets, and flow volume, were extracted. Chandola et al. ran the SNN clustering algorithm on the two data sets and obtained a number of interesting clusters for each set. Reader should refer Chandola et al. (2006) for a detailed analysis. Based on the clustering results, the report facilitated analyzation and identification of the anomaly or unexpected profiling of behaviors in cyberinfrastructures.

Application Study 5: Using *k*-Means, Density-Based Spatial Clustering of Applications with Noise, and Probability-Based Clustering in Network Traffic Classification (Table 1.6, F.4)

Erman et al. (2006) used *k*-means, density-based spatial clustering of applications with noise (DBSCAN), and AutoClass clustering algorithms to classify network traffic. The AutoClass method aims to find the probability distribution of a data set to cluster the data points (Cheeseman and Strutz, 1996). The AutoClass algorithm, based on Bayesian model, uses EM to build the most probabilistic model and its estimated parameters. Mixture models, including intercluster mixture probability and intra-cluster probability distribution functions, were estimated so that intra-cluster similarity and interclass similarity could be calculated. These similarities determined the best set of parameters used for the mixture model. Refer to Cheeseman and Strutz (1996) for details.

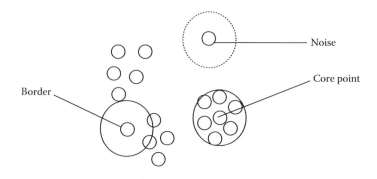

Figure 7.8 Example of the concepts in DBSCAN.

The DBSCAN (Ester et al., 1996) algorithm groups data points into clusters that have a higher density than a threshold number (MinPts) within a window of a specified size defined by the distance to the data point (Eps). As shown in Figure 7.8, given the specified N_{th} = 5 and Eps, the radius of the clustering window Eps = 1, data points are classified into three types of clusters according to the local density around them: core points, border points, and noises. Core point clusters have more than MinPts neighboring data points within Eps distance, while a border point is located in the neighborhood of a core point but has less neighboring data points within the Eps distance. Noises include all the other data points except for core points and border points. Given a core point p, any data point q of the other data points within the Eps distance from p is within the density range of p. Any data point q is within the density range of core point p, if q is within Eps distance from any other data points, which are directly density reachable or density reachable from p. Two data points are density connected, if they share at least one common density-reachable data point. DBSCAN algorithm attempts to group the core points within a specified Eps and MinPts into one cluster, group the border points within a specified neighborhood of a core point in the same cluster, and discard noises.

The DBSCAN algorithm includes the following steps:

Step 1. Find all of the data points that are density-reachable from a data point of interest p.

Step 2. Group the detected data points in a cluster, if p is a core points; if, p is a noise, move to another data point of interest and return to Step 1.

The above steps continue until all data points have been clustered.

Erman et al. evaluated the application of these three clustering algorithms in traffic classification in (2006). They used two empirical packet traces: the publicly available Auckland IV trace from the University of Auckland and the collected traffic trace from the University of Calgary. The first data set consisted of TCP/IP headers of traffic connections for three days, linking the campus network to the Internet. The second data set included a full payload of packets collected from 1 h of activity on the University of Calgary's Internet link. Erman et al. used port numbers to determine the true classes of the connections for the first data set, and known applications, such as http, p2p, smtp, and pop3, to classify the second data set. In the data sets, they considered features, such as the number of packets, average packet size, average payload size, number of bytes, and average interval of packets. To combat the imbalanced distribution of data across the classes, e.g., http dominated the data sets, they selected 1000 (2000) random samples from each class of the first (second) data set as clustering data. They repeated the selection 10 times for both of the data sets to generate 20 data sets for the clustering evaluation. They evaluated the algorithm effectiveness defined by the following accuracy measure:

$$Accuracy = \frac{\#TP \ of \ all \ clusters}{\# \ connections}. \tag{7.4}$$

Then, they measured the significance of the clustering results by ranking the ratios of the percentage of connections to the percentage of clusters.

Erman et al. reported that the AutoClass algorithm obtained the best accuracy among the three methods, with 92.4% for Auckland IV and 88.7% for the Calgary data set. However, the DBSCAN algorithm recognized 50% of the connections in the five largest clusters (total 190 clusters) and 75.4% of the important connections with 97.6% accuracy. This second result is valuable for predicting a single category of network traffic.

7.4.1 Other Profiling Methods and Applications

Karagiannis et al. (2005) presented a multilevel classification, the BLIND Classification (BLINC), for network traffic profiling. This classification method is signature-based. Karagiannis et al. focused on classifying network connections based on host behaviors associated with applications. They analyzed the host patterns in three levels: social, functional, and application. At the first level, they investigated the number of hosts communicating with the targeted host, and the community among these hosts. At the second level, they investigated the functional roles of a host in providing service and usage. At the third level, they generated graphlets to characterize the types of applications, so that a host can be classified according to the degree of matching between the graphlets and the host behavior. They then used the traffic header packet features to conduct experiments on two data sets collected in universities. They found that BLINC resulted in more than 90% accuracy and covered more than 80% of the traffic flows.

Lakhina et al. (2004) implemented the proposed subspace method (refer to Section 4.4.7.3) over a large-scale academic network. The authors conducted experiments on the three types of extracted data, including the number of bytes, the number of packets, and the number of IP flows over a variant series time. They demonstrated that each traffic type attracts interest to a variant set of anomalies due to the use of the proposed subspace method. These anomalies included abnormal host behavior, anomalous activity, and network failures.

In Lakhina et al. (2005), the researchers extended their work, and used entropy to summarize and analyze the packet feature distribution in the network traffic. They focused on OD flows and displayed that the entropy-based subspace methods strengthen the accurate detection of anomalous traffic data in clusters. McGregor et al. (2004) proposed an EM-based probabilistic clustering method to aggregate packet header flows into clusters over networks. They selected both raw features (e.g., byte counts) and the statistical features (e.g., minimum/maximum packet size) of traffic flows in experiments.

7.5 Summary

In this chapter, we have demonstrated how to profile common network traffic using various data-mining and clustering methods. The huge amount of traffic flow impedes the understanding and identification of network behaviors, e.g., portscan. Extending the work on specific applications (e.g., scan detection), network traffic profiling characterizes the behaviors of hosts and their communications to support a high level of network monitoring. Hence, profiling extracts the dominant patterns in cyberinfrastructures. The profiling result will be included in a report to network administrators for further analysis and investigation. To facilitate further work, the profiling result has to be easily understandable for readers, e.g., visualization tools accompany research results.

Classic data-mining and machine-learning techniques classify or cluster network traffic flows with accuracy and/or computational speed. As shown in Application Study 5, the AutoClass algorithm generates a high degree of accuracy, but it takes a great deal of time to build a model. DBSCAN has a strong predictive power in several subsets of traffic clusters, but the overall predictive accuracy is poor. k-means is fast, but has poor classification accuracy and does not easily select parameter k. In addition, these techniques cannot provide a high-level report that is understandable. The SNN algorithm clusters network data into connection-related groups in MINDS. This method discovers clusters even when the traffic flows are distributed uniformly. However, it cannot cluster rare anomalous events and can overlook anomalous information when parameters are not properly selected.

The NETMINE framework consists of the extraction and generalization of association rules. It solves two problems when association rules mining and classification are applied in network traffic: the large number of rules that impede the interpretation and analysis of the embedding information, and the infrequent events that are pruned even if they imply critical knowledge of the network, such as anomalous event. Users can aggregate and extract rules through generating taxonomies. The generalized rules in networks facilitate monitoring network systems via the most relevant patterns.

The AutoFocus algorithm uses hierarchies in traffic clustering instead of Euclidean space in the classic clustering methods. It also uses compression association rules, which distinguish from classic association rules mining. Moreover, AutoFocus conveys compressed analysis results to network administers directly. Xu et al. built network traffic profiling through data mining and information theoretic methodology (2008). They attempted to discover significant traffic patterns and elucidate related behaviors to facilitate network monitoring. They characterized network traffic through RU based on entropy and along and across feature dimensions. The temporal properties also clustered behavior. The experiments showed the proposed method extracted and interpreted the novel behavior, and the authors determined that it could help the network administrator to take measures to combat detected anomalous resources.

While extensive work on intrusion detection and scan detection exists, researchers have spent little effort on generalizing or profiling network traffic patterns. The profiling of network behaviors is challenging due to difficulties in mining the huge amount of streaming data and the necessity of interpreting the profiling result in an understandable way. As shown in the application studies, most of the research has been to develop real-time (online) tools. The experiments for developing these tools have only been implemented offline. In addition, profiling requires good accuracy, sufficient coverage, and scalability in large-scale cyberinfrastructures. Feasible visualization tools are necessary to accompany the profiling result in a report to facilitate the monitoring and management of cyberinfrastructures.

References

Apiletti, D., E. Baralis, T. Cerquitelli, and V. D'Elia. Characterizing network traffic by means of the NetMine framework. *Computer Networks* 53 (6) (2008): 774–789.

Chandola, V., E. Banerjee et al. Data mining for cyber security. In: *Data Warehousing and Data Mining Techniques for Computer Security*, edited by A. Singhal. New York: Springer, 2006.

Cheeseman, P. and J. Strutz. Bayesian classification (autoclass): Theory and results. In: *Advances in Knowledge Discovery and Data Mining*, edited by G. Piatetsky-Shapiro, P. Smyth, and R. Uthurusamy U.M. Fayyad. Menlo Park, CA: AAI/MIT Press, 1996.

Erman, J., M. Arlitt, and A. Mahanti. Traffic classification using clustering algorithms. In: *Proceedings of the 2006 ACM SIGCOMM Workshop on Mining Network Data*, Pisa, Italy, 2006.

Ertöz, L., M. Steinbach, and V. Kumar. Finding clusters of different sizes, shapes, and densities in noisy, high dimensional data. In: *Proceedings of the Third SIAM International Conference on Data Mining*, San Francisco, CA, 2003, pp. 47–58.

Estan, C., S. Savage, and G. Varghese. Automatically inferring patterns of resource consumption in network traffic. In: *Proceedings of ACMSIGCOMM*, Karlsruhe, Germany, 2003, pp. 137–148.

Ester, M., H. Kriegel, J. Sander, and X. Xu. A density-based algorithm for discovering clusters in large spatial databases with noise. In: *The Second International Conference on Knowledge Discovery and Data Mining (KDD)*, Portland, OR, 1996.

Karagiannis, T., K. Papagiannaki, and M. Faloutsos. BLINC: Multilevel traffic classification in the dark. In: *Proceedings of ACM SIGCOMM*, Philadelphia, PA, 2005, pp. 229–240.

Lakhina, A., M. Crovella, and C. Diot. Characterization of network-wide anomalies in traffic flows. In: *Proceedings of the Fourth ACM SIGCOMM Conference on Internet Measurement*, Taormina, Sicily, Italy, 2004, pp. 201–206.

Lakhina, A., M. Crovella, and C. Diot. Mining anomalies using traffic feature distributions. In: *Proceedings of the 2005 Conference on Applications, Technologies, Architectures, and Protocols for Computer Communications*, Philadelphia, PA, 2005.

McGregor, A., M. Hall, P. Lorier, and J. Brunskill. Flow clustering using machine learning techniques. In: *PAM 2004*, Antibes Juan-les-Pins, France, 2004.

Xu, K., X.L. Zhang, and S. Bhattachayya. Internet traffic behavior profiling for network security monitoring. *IEEE/ACM Transactions on Networking (TON)* 16 (6) (2008): 1241–1252.

Chapter 8

Privacy-Preserving
Data Mining

The best weapon against an enemy is another enemy.

Friedrich Nietzsche

In Chapters 4, 6, and 7, we have focused on data-mining and machine-learning applications and on techniques for profiling cyberinfrastructures to safeguard cyberspace against the attacks from anomalous users. Data mining, machine learning, and related statistical methods help researchers to learn and mine user patterns from the information collected in cyberspace. These statistical methods mine the user information, and detection ability protects the privacy and security of the cyber communities. Ironically, malicious users can employ these powerful data-mining and machine-learning techniques to learn or mine the confidential information of private sectors, corporations, and national departments. Instead of stealing vital personal information directly, our adversaries can deduce the private information from information available on public databases. For example, Sweeney identified a previous governor of Massachusetts easily based on the anonymous data sets collected by Group Insurance Commission (GIC) and anonymous voter registration information from Cambridge, Massachusetts (Sweeney, 2002). Sweeney mined or identified the governor in the voter registration list, through his known information of birth date, gender, and five-digit zip code. Furthermore, Sweeney recognized the governor's medical record in GIC (see Figure 8.1).

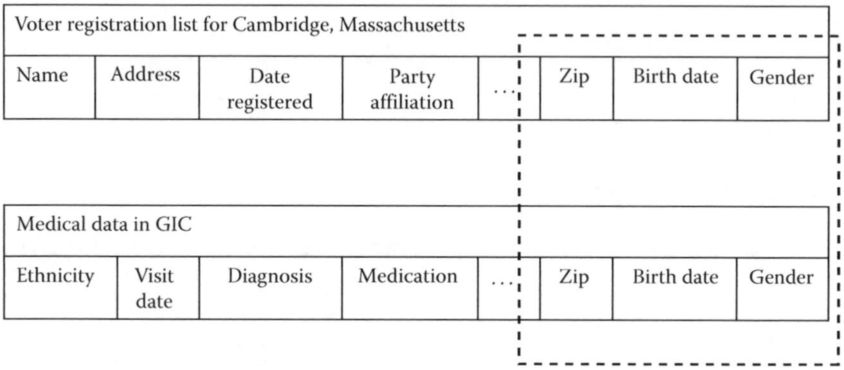

Voter registration list for Cambridge, Massachusetts							
Name	Address	Date registered	Party affiliation	...	Zip	Birth date	Gender

Medical data in GIC							
Ethnicity	Visit date	Diagnosis	Medication	...	Zip	Birth date	Gender

Figure 8.1   Example of identifying identities by connecting two data sets.

In the above example, Sweeney successfully identified the target of interest using three unique features in the identity information. To preserve privacy, people generally ask that private records be used in one of three ways: without disclosure of any information, with disclosure of some information, with disclosure of modified information (Aggarwal and Yu, 2008). In the above example, randomly swapped medical or voter data would have prevented Sweeney from deducing exact private information through the three features.

Preserving privacy is nearly ubiquitous in various informatics disciplines, including but not limited to bioinformatics, homeland security, and financial analysis. It influences cybersecurity significantly with the recent development of information collection and dissemination technologies. The unlimited explosion of new information through the Internet and other media have inaugurated a new era of research where data-mining algorithms should be considered from the viewpoint of privacy preservation, called privacy-preserving data mining (PPDM). The Online Security and Privacy Study of 2009 conducted among 2385 U.S. adults showed a 78% increase from 2007 respondents who choose to log on Internet browsers that protect private information, and a 62% increase in respondents who choose servers that provide built-in security (Online Security and Privacy Study, 2009).*

The ubiquitous applications of data-mining and machine-learning algorithms allow malicious users to employ data mining to obtain private information and, hence, raises the following questions: will data mining compromise privacy and should data mining be limited in some applications. This concern can be addressed from two aspects: ethical and technological. Legitimate use of private data would benefit the data-mining users and private owners. Various

---

* This survey was conducted by Harris Interactive, and was commissioned by Microsoft and The National Cybersecurity Alliance (Online Security and Privacy Study, 2009).

countries have produced regulations and legislation to protect the data owners, control the dissemination of private data, and regulate the accuracy of a database. A variety of issues have to be involved in these semantic systems, such as the definition of privacy, the compromise level in data mining, the accurate boundaries between data users and data owners, the responsibility of data users, etc. An elaborative privacy protection regulation can prohibit the misuse of sensitive information and avoid intrusion of human rights. While regulations can protect private data from misuse, the technological solutions can proactively provide solutions to the application of various data-mining algorithms without compromising privacy.

We will introduce privacy preservation techniques in Section 8.1 following the three ways mentioned in the last paragraph. These PPDM techniques attempt to modify or weed out sensitive private information from databases so that data miners cannot retrieve private information. Researchers regard these techniques as one new direction for data mining (Aggarwal and Yu, 2008). PPDM reduces unauthorized access of private information, while retaining the same functions as a normal data-mining method for discovering useful knowledge. Privacy-preserving methods generally alter the integrity of data, so that the generally employed data-mining methods cannot discover the same knowledge from the modified data as completely and correctly as from the original data. For example, scientists need private information from banks to mine for fraudulent activities. Modifying the client information can protect privacy, but can also cause normal data-mining and machine-learning methods to build the fraud statistical patterns improperly and to create unusable patterns in the detection of fraud clients. Hence, researchers design the PPDM methods to mine the privacy-preserved data.

In this chapter, we introduce PPDM. We discuss the privacy-preserving techniques in an extensive PPDM research area. We further analyze several PPDM applications and research studies to understand the details of the state-of-the-art methods for preserving privacy in data mining and machine learning. In Section 8.1, we will define PPDM and explain related research topics, such as privacy-preserving techniques, multiparty computation (MPC), cryptography, and the performance evaluation of PPDM algorithms. We will categorize privacy-preserving and PPDM methods according to data modification methods. In Section 8.2, we will outline the workflow of PPDM. We will discuss the difference between general data-mining and machine-learning techniques, and PPDM to understand why privacy leaks occur in data-mining and machine-learning applications. In Section 8.3, we will analyze several applications of PPDM in-depth and compare them to various machine-learning techniques, which face challenges of sensitive outputs. We will also briefly introduce other PPDM frameworks. In Section 8.4, we will summarize the advance in PPDM and explore its roles in cybersecurity.

8.1 Privacy Preservation Techniques in PPDM

8.1.1 Notations

For the convenience of description, we assume all data employed in this chapter is presented in the format as shown in the above Table 8.1. Each data set X has samples $\{S_1,\ldots, S_n\}$, while a set of feature values define a vector for each sample in the d dimensional feature space $\{f_1,\ldots, f_d\}$.

8.1.2 Privacy Preservation in Data Mining

The objective of PPDM is to prevent unauthorized users from accessing private information, such as private data-mining or machine-learning results. Privacy preservation and data mining worked in parallel, until Aggrawal et al. defined the specific research area in data mining concerning privacy protection in 2000. In PPDM, researchers adopt a large number of privacy preservation techniques in data-mining and machine-learning algorithms to preserve knowledge security. The complexity in PPDM algorithms raises several research topics other than privacy preservation and data mining. Verykios et al. (2004a) classified the existing PPDM techniques by considering five views: horizontal or vertical data distribution, data modification methods, data-mining algorithms, rule confusion, and privacy preservation. Most data distributions are horizontal or vertical.

Given the data set described, as shown in Table 8.1, we can partition a given data set in two ways: horizontally and vertically. Following the notations introduced in Table 8.1, we understand horizontal partitioning as splitting samples, while each sample has a complete feature set in the feature space. Respectively, vertical partitioning divides the feature space into multiple feature sets, so that each feature set has the same number of samples.

Data modification methods include perturbation (e.g., adding noise), blocking (e.g., replacing a feature value with *NaN*), aggregation (e.g., replacing several values with a statistical value), swapping (e.g., exchanging values between samples), and sampling (e.g., revealing part of the available sample data) operations on the data. Rule confusion refers to the balance between data hiding and data-mining

Table 8.1 Data Set Structure in This Chapter

	f_1	...	f_d
S_1			
...			
S_n			

efficiency or the function using hidden data. We will investigate this topic associated with data-mining algorithms in PPDM in Section 8.2. As data-mining and machine-learning methodologies have been explored separately, we will explain application studies in Section 8.3.

Let us define privacy and then review privacy violations. Privacy is the designation of confidential information for entities (e.g., personal) that is not supposed to be publicly known. There is no exact definition of privacy for any entities due to the complicated categorization of information in different situations by different entities. Similarly, we can attribute privacy breaches to various causes, such as data mining, inference from the legitimate responses to database queries, disclosed data in cooperative computations and analysis, and the poor privacy preservation systems. To solve the above privacy violations, respective solutions include PPDM (Du et al., 2004), privacy constraint processing (Du and Atallah, 2001), multilevel encryption (Hinke et al., 1997), secure multiparty computation (SMC) (Yao, 1982), and more advanced privacy protection systems (Vaidya and Clifton, 2004).

According to the definition of privacy and possible causes of privacy leaks, we summarize two purposes for privacy preservation: to keep private information anonymous or to control valid information leaks. Valid information counters sensitive information that represents the entity privacy. The sensitive information can be obtained directly from available data sets or inferred indirectly from computational methods, such as data mining or machine learning.

Verykios et al. classified privacy preservation techniques in PPDM into three groups: heuristic privacy preservation, cryptographic privacy preservation, and randomization/perturbation/reconstruction-based privacy preservation (Verykios et al., 2004a). Vaidya and Clifton surveyed two privacy preservation approaches in data mining: randomization/perturbation and SMC (Vaidya and Clifton, 2004). Researchers hybridize and implement various techniques in PPDM algorithms to obtain particular privacy preservation objectives, along with a variety of application-specific infrastructures. For example, in many MPC problems, researchers generally implement cryptography techniques on the original data before conducting randomization and permutation, and then share the hidden data with partners. We elucidate the detailed implementation in Section 8.3. Below, we briefly describe the categorization of privacy preservation techniques as examples of the common PPDM knowledge. Readers should refer to Verykios et al. (2004a) and Vaidya and Clifton (2004) for more information. We classify the PPDM methods into three groups according to data resource distribution. We do so in a way that is similar to the categorization used in Verykios et al. (2004a).

The first group of techniques includes centralized data resources; the second group includes distributed computation, or SMC; and the third group includes both data resources. Centralized data-based PPDM refers to data-mining or machine-learning algorithms that perform applications on the data resources collected at a single central repository. The data storage system can be violated for privacy easily from the inference or learned rules. The proposed solutions employ perturbation-based or blocking-based rule confusion methods to downgrade the rule mining results so that sensitive rules are buried in insensitive rules or insensitive information blurs sensitive data. Heuristic privacy preservation is also called downgrading privacy preservation, because the data modification leads to the downgrading of rules or the ineffectiveness of machine-learning classifiers. Data-mining or machine-learning algorithms must balance between mining or learning efficiency and privacy preserving. We explain evaluation criteria in Section 8.2.

Another solution to the centralized data system is to distribute data among multiple repositories and minimize the information leaks by applying SMC. SMC takes advantage of the proliferation of Internet technologies and cooperative computations on private data resources. Cooperative computation and communication of private data opens new vulnerabilities for attackers to breach privacy through data aggregation or other data-mining methods. For example, Alice holds a collection of hacker profiles for a cyberinfrastructure, and Bob detects a recent cyber attack in the system. Bob hopes to use Alice's database to find a signature match to the hacker's behavior and identify the hacker's ID, while preventing Alice from learning of the hacker's behavior because such a leak implies the vulnerability of his cyberinfrastructure. Meanwhile, Alice also prevents leaking the hackers' private information to Bob (Du and Atallah, 2001).

Cryptographic privacy preservation originated from the MPC problem. Yao introduced MPC in 1982 (Yao, 1982). In MPC, multiple participants, $P_1, \ldots, P_M$, compute a function $f(DS_1, \ldots, DS_M)$, given each participant P_i knows only the exact value of data set DS_i in database $(DS_1, \ldots, DS_M)$. Participant P_i only knows the exact data sets of $\{DS_j\}, j = 1, \ldots, M, j \neq i$ and his or her input and output in the function $f(DS_1, \ldots, DS_M)$. As shown in Figure 8.2, privacy preservation considers that individual participants can hold each part of the data set in one of two ways: horizontal or vertical.

By combining all of these individual data subsets into one complete sample data set, one can derive a more accurate data-mining or machine-learning model.

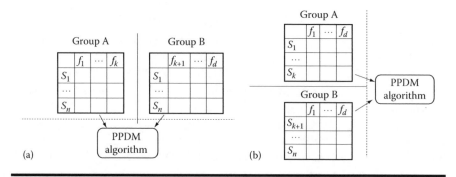

Figure 8.2 Two data partitioning ways in PPDM: (a) horizontal and (b) vertical private data for DM.

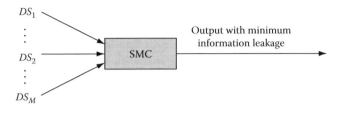

Figure 8.3   Workflow of SMC.

However, the combination of these individual data subsets requires sharing the data subsets between parties while causing private data leaks. A number of techniques have been proposed to conduct SMC in face of the privacy violations in MPC. As shown in Figure 8.3, the objective of SMC is to generate a global data model to characterize the union of the distributed data sets, while removing local sensitive information in the computation result.

Perturbation and reconstruction are paired techniques in PPDM. Perturbation, using randomization, attempts to preserve sensitive information using privacy preservation techniques, while reconstruction attempts to recover data distributions to obtain feasible and accurate data mining or machine-learning results (as shown in Figure 8.4). The randomization method is commonly employed in distorting the original data. Given the original data set $\{x_1, \ldots, x_n\}$ originated from the probability distribution of variable X, we attempt to hide these data values. Randomly drawing n data points $\{r_1, \ldots, r_n\}$ from the probability distribution of variable R, we can obtain a distorted data set $\{x_1 + r_1, \ldots, x_n + r_n\}$, which falls in the probability distribution of variable Y. Let the random distribution R have a variance large enough (e.g., three sigma) to perturb the original data values. The original data values $\{x_1, \ldots, x_n\}$ can be hidden securely by the added noise data $\{r_1, \ldots, r_n\}$.

The reconstruction methods attempt to recover the distribution of the data set $\{x_1, \ldots, x_n\}$ without exact data values. From the above information, we obtain $X = Y - R$ and can estimate the distribution of variable X based on the statistically approximated distribution of R. In practice, the distribution estimate is based on Bayes' rule, density-based machine-learning methods (e.g., EM), and sampling algorithms (Agrawal and Srikant, 2000). The reconstructed data distribution will

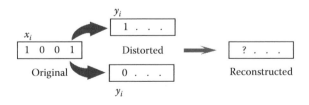

Figure 8.4   Perturbation and reconstruction in PPDM.

be the input for data-mining or machine-learning algorithms. As the commonly used data-mining or machine-learning algorithms are designed for data points as input, new data-mining or machine-learning methods have to be designed to deal with this difficulty. Another challenge lies in the reconstruction of the original data distribution in a way that does not disclose private data.

8.2 Workflow of PPDM

8.2.1 Introduction of the PPDM Workflow

As shown in Figure 8.5, PPDM methods consist of six procedures: modification of the original data for privacy preservation, collection of data, modification of the aggregated data for privacy preservation, PPDM algorithms, reconstruction of the mining results for individual data points, and performance evaluation of the PPDM result. The modification of the original data points attempts to avoid the breach of sensitive information in the individual data points or the privacy violation of participants. In contrast to the commonly employed data-mining or machine-learning methods, PPDM requires the input to be modified. After collecting the data, the aggregated data needs to be further processed so that the data source ID or other private information is blocked.

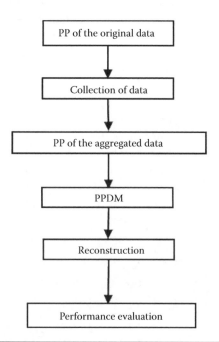

Figure 8.5   Workflow of PPDM.

8.2.2 PPDM Algorithms

PPDM algorithms focus on the privacy problems caused by data-mining results and methods. Vaidya and Clifton identified the use of unmodified data-mining and machine-learning methods as the primary cause of privacy leaks (Vaidya and Clifton, 2004). In these classic data-mining and machine-learning methods, centralized data are required as input. As explained in Section 8.1, malicious users violate the single data repository in a facile manner. The solutions to this problem include hiding all of the sensitive information in the data and distributing the data for computation, e.g., SMC. The former solution removes detailed information from the original data and reduces the completeness of input. The latter solution poses new challenges, such as how to reduce the computation and communication cost caused by the information flow in the distributed network, and how to preserve sensitive information in the net flow.

Another privacy issue is the possibility of data-mining results inferring privacy. This problem occurs in MPC and SMC. In MPC, each participant holds one subset of the whole data set, and hides its sensitive information in the collaborative computation. Given an accurate data-mining result in SMC, a participant is able to infer the other participant's private information.

To our knowledge, no unique framework solves all of these problems for various PPDM algorithms. This lack of unique framework is partly due to the complexity of data-mining algorithms and partly due to the requirement that privacy preservation be application specific. For example, the U.S. Healthcare Information Portability and Accountability Act (HIPAA) requires cooperation from clinics and hospitals to preserve personal data (Vaidya and Clifton, 2004). We will demonstrate the PPDM solutions in ubiquitous applications in Section 8.3. Along with the solutions, we present a possible way to evaluate the efficiency and effectiveness of privacy preservation. The performance evaluation of PPDM algorithms needs a set of parameters in terms of accuracy, privacy breaching, computational complexity, etc.

8.2.3 Performance Evaluation of PPDM Algorithms

With the influx of a huge number of electronic data in corporations, researchers have studied a variety of PPDM algorithms extensively to sanitize the information involved. A unique performance criterion cannot measure all of the quality aspects of various PPDM algorithms. For example, the strong data perturbation can enable users to protect their privacy 100%, but may compromise the mining of the insensitive information. While the preliminary requirements vary among PPDM applications, a set of quality measures can guarantee the most appropriate selection of PPDM algorithms for miners. Broadly speaking, these PPDM-related metrics characterize information security, mining accuracy, and computation efficiency.

Information security includes the privacy hiding quality and transversal preservation. To measure privacy hiding ability, we identify the possible vulnerabilities in PPDM operations. Referring to Figure 8.5, we consider the sensitive information leaks at three levels: the uncertainty of original data privacy preservation, the disclosure of aggregated privacy, and the privacy violation of mining results. The uncertainty of privacy preservation in original data originates in the limitation of data modification or hidden approaches, such as the privacy preservation techniques we described in Section 8.1.2.

A typical privacy preservation metric for this level is the measure of whether the original values can be estimated with a confidence level $c\%$ to fall into the confidence interval $[\beta_l, \beta_u]$. This method overlooks the underlying distribution of original data such that the aggregate information can cause high-level privacy leaks (Evfimievski et al., 2003). Entropy-based metrics were proposed to solve the problems in the above metric. Given two random variables X and Y, we measure the leaking information of variable X inferred from variable Y by $2^{H(X|Y)}$, where $H(X|Y)$ denotes conditional entropy. Readers should refer to Shannon (1949) for full descriptions of entropy and conditional entropy. Moreover, we measure the conditional probability of the privacy protection using $P(X|Y) = 1 - 2^{H(A|B)/H(A)}$. As the above metric calculates the average conditional information of variables, it considers their underlining probability distribution. Evfimievski et al. demonstrated that the average metrics could not capture the privacy leaks of specific properties, e.g., "worst-case" privacy breaches. Worst-case denotes the privacy breaches that occur when certain properties, such as a value or a subset in a randomized transaction, reveal the original values (Evfimievski et al., 2003). Using the randomization notations in Section 8.1.2, we present the breaching of a property $Q(X)$ given a randomized value y_i, $y_i \in Y$, as $P\big(Q(X)|Y = y_i\big) = \displaystyle\sum_{Q(x), x \to Q(x)} P\big(X = x|Y = y_i\big)$.

If $P(Q(X)) \le Th_1$ and $P(Q(X)|Y = y_i) \ge Th_2$, with $0 < Th_1 < Th_2 < 1$ and $P(Y = y_i) > 0$, and $Th_1 - \text{to} - Th_2$, then privacy breaching occurs. We take the example in Evfimievski et al. (2003) to explain such measures as follows.

Given private data values located in [0, 1000] for the random variable X, $X = 0$ occurs with 1% probability, while all other valid values occur individually and with uniform distribution at 0.0991% probability. We have $P(X = 0) = 0.01$, and $P(X = k) = 0.00099$, $k = 1, \ldots, 1000$. As shown in Table 8.2, Evfimievski, Gehrke, and Srikant listed three randomization results of $Y = R(X)$. The first randomization kept the variable Y_1 within the original values of X with 20% probability while preventing Y from falling into other values with uniform distribution at 80% probability. The second randomization used an addition operation by $Y_2 = X + R(mod\ 1001)$, where variable R distributes randomly in $[-100, \ldots, 100]$; the third randomization kept its probability distribution at 50%, the same as Y_2 and 50% in uniform distribution. Given prior values $Y_i = 0$, $i = 1, 2, 3$, the posterior probabilities of two properties for variable X were obtained: $Q_1(X) \equiv 'X = 0'$ and $Q_2(X) \equiv 'X \notin \{200, \ldots, 800\}'$. The initial randomization results released both properties $Q_1(X)$ and $Q_2(X)$ in high

Table 8.2 Analysis of Privacy Breaching Using Three Randomization Methods

	Probabilities (%) of $Q_1(X)$	*Probabilities (%) of $Q_2(X)$*
X	1	40.5
Y_1	71.6	83
Y_2	4.8	100
Y_3	2.9	70.8

Source: Reprinted from *Inform. Syst.*, 29, Privacy preserving mining of association rules, Evfimievski, A., Srikant, R., Agrawal, R., and Gehrke, J., 343–364, Copyright (2004), with permission from Elsevier.

probabilities when $Y_1 = 0$ was known. The second method revealed little information about property $Q_1(X)$, but disclosed property $Q_2(X)$ with 100% probability. The third method operated the best with the two lowest information breaches.

The disclosure of aggregated privacy is related to the statistical properties of the original or available data (Willenborg and DeWaal, 2001; Dinur and Nissim, 2003; Dwork and Yekhanin, 2008). Query restriction is a typical approach to control the statistical breaching of privacies. In this method, all allowed queries obey a designed structure so that unauthorized access will be blocked. Given a database $X = \{x_1, \ldots, x_n\}$, $x_i \in \{0,1\}$, $i = 1, \ldots n$, a query $q \subseteq [n]$ obtains answer Y_q. The perturbation of the answers can be captured by the distance measure $\left| Y_q - \sum_{i \in q} x_i \right|$. Using the captured perturbation information, the database can be recovered.

Unauthorized users can use the mining results of classifiers to infer the characteristics of original data (Verykios et al., 2004b; Kantarcıoglu et al., 2008). Assuming that sensitive data (S1) depends on publicly available data (S2) and unknown data (S3), unauthorized users have m pairs of S2 and S3 data points. Based on these data, we have a PPDM classifier C. Then, we obtain a classification model C2 on the m pairs of data points from S2 and S3. Combining the information of these pairs of data points from S2 and S3, and the classifier C1, we obtain the third classifier C3. If classifier C3 has a higher accuracy than C2, then classifier C1 has a privacy leak. The classifier accuracy is defined as

$$\sum_j P(C(x_i) \neq j \,|\, y = j) P(y = j), \qquad (8.1)$$

where
  x_i is the data point in data set $\{x_1, \ldots, x_n\}$
  $C(x_i)$ denotes the class label of x_i
  y indicates the true label of x_i

Transversal endurance refers to the endurance of a proposed privacy preservation technique when it is applied in PPDM algorithms. A privacy preservation technique, such as a sanitization algorithm, is initially developed in pairs with a specific data-mining or machine-learning method. Given a number of data sets, the transversal endurance measures the ability of privacy protection provided by a variety of PPDM algorithms using the same privacy preservation methods.

Accompanied by the protection of sensitivity information, we need to consider the accuracy of mining results impacted by the loss of insensitive information. We call this metric functionality loss, because the modification of the original input data and new data-mining or machine-learning algorithms may lead to the downgrading data-mining or machine-learning results. Fundamentally, the functionality loss presents the difference between the mining results using the original data and the privacy preservation mining results using the modified data. Thus, this metric depends on both data set and PPDM algorithms. Various concepts have been proposed to present this metric in terms of data set, including accuracy, completeness, consistency, and so on.* Readers should refer to Bertina et al. (2005) for more details about these concepts. For example, the following classification error E_C can present the total function loss of clustering algorithms:

$$E_C = \frac{1}{n} \sum_{k=1}^{K} \left| Cluster_k(X) \right| - \left| Cluster_k(X_M) \right|, \tag{8.2}$$

where $\left| Cluster_k(X) \right|$ and $\left| Cluster_k(X_M) \right|$ denote the cardinalities of cluster k with the original data set $X = \{x_1, \ldots, x_n\}$ and modified data set $X_M = \{x_{M_1}, \ldots, x_{M_n}\}$. With respect to association rules, function loss refers to the loss of nonsensitive rules. This loss results from the application of privacy preservation techniques that hides both sensitive and insensitive information.

Computation complexity evaluates the time requirements of privacy preservation algorithms. The proposed approaches include calculating the CPU time used by the algorithm measuring the operations needed for hiding the sensitive information and measuring computational cost by the degree of a polynomial. In SMC, we must include the communication cost in the final computation cost, which is caused by the amount of exchanged information between sites.

Scalability evaluates the efficiency of PPDM algorithms with the increasing amount of input data. The proliferation of information communicative techniques and data storage capabilities requires the development of more efficient PPDM algorithms to deal with the influx of data sets. Moreover, the increasing data dimensionality exacerbates the design of high-scalable PPDM methods.

---

* Completeness measures the loss of individual data information in the sanitized data; consistency measures the loss of correlation between data in the sanitized data.

8.3 Data-Mining and Machine-Learning Applications in PPDM

The objective of PPDM is to keep private data and private knowledge safe once the mining on the data has been completed. PPDM methods can be analyzed from the perspectives of data distribution, data modification, data mining algorithms, data or rule hiding, or privacy preservation (Verykios et al., 2004a). We categorize the principle PPDM methods in Table 1.1, according to data-mining algorithms and present their privacy preservation methods. In particular, the privacy preservation technique is the most important for the selective modification of the data, which are classified into three groups: heuristic-based techniques, cryptography-based techniques, and reconstruction-based techniques. For a more detailed analysis, readers should see Verykios et al. (2004a).

Researchers have investigated various data-mining algorithms in isolation of each other. Among them, the most important privacy preservation methods have been proposed for a number of data-mining algorithms, like support vector machines (SVM) classification (Yu et al., 2006), association rule mining algorithms (Evfimievski et al., 2004), K-means clustering (Vaidya and Clifton, 2003), decision tree inducers (Agrawal and Srikant, 2000), BN (Wright and Yang, 2004), KNN (Kantarcioglu and Clifton, 2004), ANN (Barni et al., 2006), and other statistical methods (Du et al., 2004). Readers should see Table 1.1 for our list of references on this topic.

8.3.1 Privacy Preservation Association Rules (Table 1.1, A.4)

Let us review the association rules as explained in Chapter 2. Let $E = \{I_1, I_2, ..., I_k\}$ be a set of items and X be a database consisting of n transactions $T_1, ..., T_n$, $X = \{T_1, ..., T_n\}$. Each transaction T_j, $\forall 1 \leq j \leq n$ is a subset of items with $T_j \subseteq E$. Each transaction T_j has support $s(T_j)$ in E, defined by the following conditional probability:

$$s(T_i) = \frac{\#(t \in X \mid T_i \subseteq t)}{n}. \tag{8.3}$$

Given a threshold *Th*, if $s(T_j) \geq Th$, we say transaction T_j is frequent; if we have another transaction $T_i \subseteq E$ and $T_j \subseteq T_i$, we say $s(T_j) \geq s(T_i)$.

Itemset I causes a privacy breach of level ρ, if we randomize transaction $T_j' = R(T_j)$, and we find that a frequent itemset I and the item $I_r \in I$ have the conditional probability

$$P\left(I_r \in T_j \mid I \subseteq T_j'\right) \geq \rho. \tag{8.4}$$

To solve this problem, Evifimievski et al. proposed randomization operators using "cut and paste" to insert "false" items to replace some true items (Evfimievski et al., 2002). Their method includes three steps as follows:

Step 1. Randomly select an integer number N between 0 and the cutoff Km.
Step 2. Randomly select N items in transaction T_j and put them in the empty transaction T_j'.
Step 3. Select items in the remaining set $E = \{I_{1'}, I_{2'}, \ldots, I_{k'}\}$ with probability ρ_m and continue to fill them in T_j'.

In the above, transaction T_j has size m, and two parameters Km and ρ_m are optimized based on the desired level of privacy.

Using the notations as defined above, itemset I and $X = \{T_1, \ldots, T_n\}$ were defined as $|I| = d$ and $|T_i| = m$, $i = 1, \ldots, n$. Then, using the definition of support given in Equation 8.3, the authors obtained partial support for itemset I as follows: $\vec{s} = (s_0, \ldots, s_d)$ and $s_l = \#\{T_j \in X | \#(I \cap T_j) = l\}/n$.

They proposed a transition matrix M, to transform the original support of itemset I, $\vec{s}$, to the randomized support of its subsets, $\vec{s}'$. Matrix M has d rows and m columns, and the following definition for each element at row l' and column l:

$$M_{l'l} = P\left[\#(T_j' \cap I) = l' \,|\, (T_j \cap I) = l\right]. \tag{8.5}$$

The transformation between $\vec{s}$ and $\vec{s}'$ is as follows:

$$E(\vec{s}') = M \cdot \vec{s}, \tag{8.6}$$

where $E(\vec{s}')$ denotes the expected value of the randomized partial support vector $\vec{s}'$ and $\vec{s}'$ follows multinomial distribution. Using Equation 8.6, the original partial support vector can obtain its unbiased estimator as

$$\vec{s}_{uest} = M^{-1} \cdot \vec{s}', \tag{8.7}$$

and the variance matrix for this estimator as

$$Cov(\vec{s}_{uest}) = \frac{1}{n}\sum_{l=1}^{d} s_l \cdot P^{-1} \cdot D[l](P^{-1})^T, \tag{8.8}$$

where matrix $D[l]$ has $k + 1$ rows and $k + 1$ columns, and each element $D[l]_{i_D,j_D} = P_{i_D,l} \cdot \delta_{i_D = j_D} - P_{i_D,l} \cdot P_{j_D,l}$, $i_D = 1, \ldots, d$, $j_D = 1, \ldots, m$.

Using the above randomization and randomized support analysis, the privacy preservation apriori association rules can be mined in the following steps:

Step 1. Initialize $k = 1$.

Step 2. Randomize the original data, and estimate partial support and variance σ^2 of each candidate set using Equations 8.7 and 8.8.

Step 3. Keep those candidate sets that contain support values above the minimum support threshold s_{min}.

Step 4. Form new candidate sets with all $(k + 1)$-sized itemsets that have k-sized sub-itemsets with all support values above $s_{min} - \sigma$.

Step 5. Return to Step 2 with $k = k + 1$ and repeat steps until no candidate remains or the estimator deviates from the expected value significantly.

As shown in Figure 8.6, Evifimievski et al. proposed a framework for privacy preservation association rules mining from transactions by randomization methods. They evaluated the privacy breach level by checking Equation 8.1 and obtained the conditional probability by

$$P\left(I_r \in T_j \mid I \subseteq T'_j\right) = \frac{\sum_{l=0}^{d} s_l^{+} \cdot P_{dl}}{\sum_{l=0}^{d} s_l \cdot P_{dl}}, \tag{8.9}$$

where $s_l^{+} = P\left(\#\left(T_j \cap I\right) = l, I_r \in T_j\right)$, $s_0^{+} = 0$.

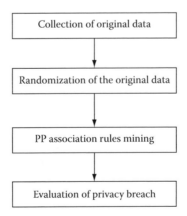

Figure 8.6 **Workflow of privacy preservation association rules mining method. (Reprinted from *Inform. Syst.*, 29, Privacy preserving mining of association rules, Evfimievski, A., Srikant, R., Agrawal, R., and Gehrke, J., 343–364, Copyright (2004), with permission from Elsevier.)**

They defined the lowest discoverable support (LDS) as the support of an itemset 4σ away from zero. Then, mutual interaction between LDS and the privacy breach level can demonstrate the relation between rules discoverability and privacy breach level. They used two real data sets in the experiments. The first (soccer) data set consists of the click stream log from the 1998 World Cup Web site. Each transaction denotes a session of a user's access to the Web site, and each item denotes an HTML request. The soccer data set includes 11,000 HTMLs and 6,525,879 soccer transactions. The mail order data set consists of order transactions from an online market. Each transaction denotes a sequence of items purchased by a single order. The mail order data set includes 96 items and 2,900,000 transactions.

As shown in Figure 8.7, where one transaction has five items, the LDS decreases when the privacy breach level increases by a great deal. This figure demonstrates that a higher breach level needs a much lower LDS for 3-itemsets. A higher breach level indicates a weaker randomization level or a lower hidden ability. A 3-itemset has a lower LDS than 1-itemset at higher privacy breach levels, e.g., from 65% to 90%. This phenomenon occurred because of the large number of false items involved in the randomization process. Because the 3-itemset involved fewer false positives than the 1-itemset at a higher breach level, discovering the 3-itemset became easier than discovering the 1-itemset.

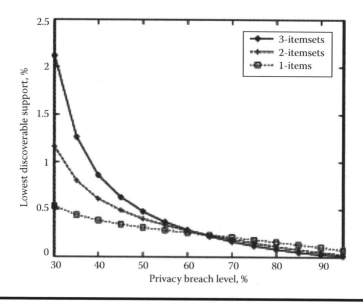

Figure 8.7   LDS and privacy breach level for the soccer data set. (Reprinted from *Inform. Syst.*, **29, Privacy preserving mining of association rules, Evfimievski, A., Srikant, R., Agrawal, R., and Gehrke, J., 343–364, Copyright (2004), with permission from Elsevier.)**

Evifimievski et al. experimented on both data sets by choosing a privacy breach level of 50% and a minimum support threshold of LDS. They reported high coverage of the predicted rules, a high true positive, and low false positive rates.

8.3.2 Privacy Preservation Decision Tree (Table 1.1, A.6)

Given a data set partitioned into two parts, Du and Zhan attempted to solve the MPC problems using a decision-tree classifier (DTC) (Du and Zhan, 2002). They built a protocol that allows two partners to classify the data set without compromising either's privacy.

Du and Zhan partitioned the data set into two feature sets: $\{f_1, \ldots, f_k\}$ and $\{f_k, \ldots, f_d\}$, and grouped the data composed by the feature set $\{f_1, \ldots, f_k\}$ into group A and the data composed by the feature set $\{f_{k+1}, \ldots, f_d\}$ into group B (see Figure 8.8). They denoted these two groups of data as S_A and S_B, respectively.

As noted in Section 3.3.5.1, decision-tree classification consists of two procedures: tree building and tree pruning. In the tree-building procedure, the splitting of nodes depends on the splitting criteria. The best split can equal the discovery of the largest information gain among features. To calculate entropy, Du and Zhan first estimated the probability of class j in sample data as follows:

$$P_j = \frac{\hat{P}_j}{|S|}, \tag{8.10}$$

where

$\hat{P}_j$ denotes the number of class j in data set S
$|S|$ denotes the cardinality of data set S

They obtained $\hat{P}_j$ using the following equations:

$$\hat{P}_j = V_A \cdot (V_B \wedge V_j) \quad \text{or} \quad \hat{P}_j = (V_A \wedge V_j) \cdot V_B, \tag{8.11}$$

where V_A, V_B, and V_j denote feature vectors of size d, respectively for S_A, S_B and the data in S belonging to the jth class. If data point S_i in group A (B) (see Figure 8.8)

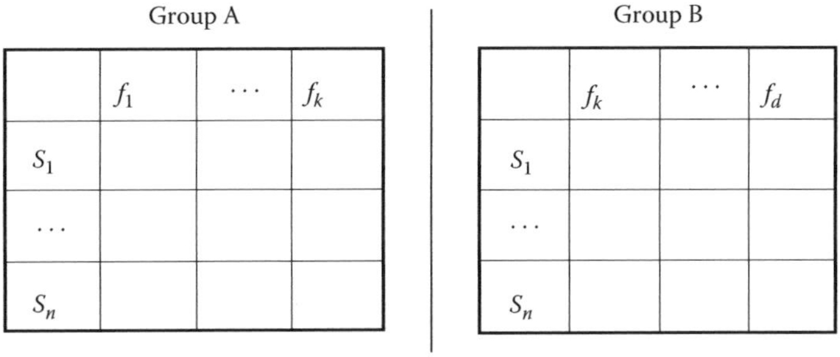

Group A				Group B		
	f_1	$\cdots$	f_k		f_k	$\cdots$	f_d
S_1				S_1		
$\cdots$				$\cdots$		
S_n				S_n		

Figure 8.8   Partitioned data sets by feature subsets.

satisfies the requirement that only considers group A's (B's) feature set, the vector $V_A(V_B) = 1$; otherwise, $V_A(V_B) = 0$. If data point S_i belongs to class j, then vector $V_j(i) = 1$; otherwise $V_j(i) = 0$. Using equations in Section 3.3.5.1, information gain can be calculated.

Using the above DTC, a data point $(A_1, ..., A_k, B_{k+1}, ..., B_d)$, where $(A_1, ..., A_k)$ and $(B_{k+1}, ..., B_d)$ denote the known part in group A and known part in group B respectively, can be classified as follows. Group A (B) traverses the tree separately. In the tree traverse by group A (B), for any node split by the feature in group A (B), its respective child will be traversed according to the data value; for any node split by feature in group B (A), all children of the node are traversed by group A (B). All the leaf nodes that are reached by group A (B) are recorded in a respective vector T_A (T_B).

Since finding a trusted third party to combine the groups is unfeasible, Du and Zhan solved the problem using the commodity server (CS) model. In this model, the third party is not allowed to participate in computation, not allowed to gain knowledge of private data and computation result from A and B, and not allow to collude with both sides. Based on these assumptions, they computed the scalar product of the private data sets belonging to group A and B, respectively. Given private vector V_A from group A and private vector V_B from group B, the scalar product was calculated between V_A and V_B as follows:

$$V_A \cdot V_B = \sum V_A(i) \cdot V_B(i). \tag{8.12}$$

The scalar product protocol using CS consists of the following steps:

> *Step 1.* CS generate random vectors V_{RA} and V_{RB} and random numbers r_A and r_B for group A and group B, respectively, where $V_{RA} \cdot V_{RB} = r_A + r_B$.
> *Step 2.* Group A (B) sends $V_A' = V_A + V_{RA}$ ($V_A' = V_B + V_{RB}$) to group B(A).
> *Step 3.* Group B sends $V_A' V_B + r_B$ to group A.
> *Step 4.* Group A derives $V_A \cdot V_B$ from $(V_A' \cdot V_B + r_B) - V_{RA} \cdot V_B + r_A$.

The proposed framework is efficient, but the assumption that the third party should not collude with either source poses challenges for implementation. The proposed algorithm may cause an information breach in two ways: the scalar product results or design of the privacy preservation framework. They also did not test the proposed scheme in real and complex data sets.

8.3.3 Privacy Preservation Bayesian Network (Table 1.1, A.2)

Using the vertically partitioned data of two groups S_A and S_B, in Section 8.3.2, we discuss the technique of privacy preservation Bayesian networks (PPBN). In PPBN, the objective is to learn Bayesian network (BN) structure on the combination of data sets S_A, held by Alice, and S_B, held by Bob, and prevent privacy leaks between Alice and Bob. Each participant, Alice or Bob, only receives knowledge of the BN structure but no confidential information from the other partner.

Yang and Wright (2006) presented a protocol to construct a BN for vertically partitioned data. We use the notations and definitions presented in the Section 3.3.6.1 BN classifier to simplify the description of PPBN. Two research topics exist in the BN classifier: the recognition of BN structure and the training of BN model. Wright and Yang employed the K2 algorithm (Yang and Wright, 2006) in learning the BN structure and modified the scoring function in the K2 algorithm. Given a set of v variables or nodes, $X = \{x_1, \ldots, x_i, \ldots, x_v\}$, the K2 algorithm attempts to maximize the score function $f(x_i, parent(x_i))$ in the sequence of parent candidates (nodes) up to a maximum of u (the number of upper bound) parents for a node. K2 consists of the following steps.

Step 1. Initialize parent set *parent* (x_i) to be empty for each node, $i = 1, \ldots, v$.

Step 2. Update $f(x_i, parent(x_i))$ with $f(x_i, parent(x_i)) \cup (cparent(x_i) - parent(x_i))$, if $f(x_i, parent(x_i)) < f(x_i, parent(x_i)) \cup (cparent(x_i) - parent(x_i))$; otherwise stop adding parents to node x_i, where $cparent(x_i)$ refers to the pool of possible parents of node x_i and $parent(x_i)$ refers to the pool including the selected parent nodes.

Step 3. Iterate Steps 1–2 until node x_i has obtained u parents.

Step 4. Iterate Steps 1–3 until all nodes in the BN have been added as parents.

In the original K2 algorithm, the score function has the following definition for binary attributes:

$$f(x_i, parent(x_i)) = \prod_{j=1}^{q_i} \frac{P_{ij0}! P_{ij1}!}{(P_{ij0} + P_{ij1} + 1)!}, \tag{8.13}$$

where q_i denotes the number of unique parents of variable x_i, $P_{ijk, k = 0 \ or \ 1}$ denotes the number of occurrences of variable x_i taking value k and its *parent*(x_i) taking the jth unique value. To preserve privacies in BN computation, Wright and Yang proposed a new score function as follows:

$$g(x_i, parent(x_i)) = \sum_{j=1}^{q_i} \frac{1}{2} \left(\ln P_{ij0} + \ln P_{ij1} - \ln(P_{ij0} + P_{ij1} + 1) \right)$$
$$+ \left(P_{ij0} \ln P_{ij0} + P_{ij1} \ln P_{ij1} - (P_{ij0} + P_{ij1} + 1)\ln(P_{ij0} + P_{ij1} + 1) \right). \tag{8.14}$$

Yang and Wright obtained this score function via the operation of a natural log on the score function in Equation 8.13 and simplified processing with respect to Stirling's approximation. The log function and approximation have no effects on the ordering of the parent nodes in the K1 algorithm, while the operations preserve the original score information in the new score function. Following the example above, we will use Alice and Bob to illustrate the authors' point. In the implementation of the g score function in the K2 algorithm, Alice and Bob jointly solved the maximum g scores associated with the parent nodes. In the proposed PPNB method, privacy-preserving protocols were employed on scalar products, computations of P_{ijk}, score computations, and score comparisons. Alice and Bob shared the intermediate values of the above four computation results.

Wright and Yang designed a privacy-preserving scalar product protocol as follows. Given private vector V_A from Alice and V_B from Bob, the proposed scalar product protocol consisted of the following steps:

Step 1. Alice generated an encryption key and a decryption key using an encryption algorithm, and shared the encryption with Bob.

Step 2. Alice encrypted her private data elements in V_A, $E(V_{A1}), \ldots, E(V_{An})$, and shared the encrypted data with Bob.

Step 3. Bob encrypted a random number R, obtained the encrypted R, $E(R)$, and shared the encrypted data $E(R) \cdot \prod y_i$ with Alice, where if $V_{Ai} = 1$, $y_i = E(V_{Ai})$; otherwise $y_i = 1$.

Step 4. Alice derived $R + V_A \cdot V_B$ from $E(R) \cdot \prod y_i$.

In the above, Wright and Yang demonstrated that $E(R) \cdot \prod y_i = E(V_A \cdot V_B + R)$ in Step 3, such that Alice could obtain $R + V_A \cdot V_B$ using the description key while Bob only maintained R. With respect to the computations of privacy-preserving parameters P_{ijk}, both Alice and Bob generated a respective n-length vector compatible with i, j, k. Then, both partners obtained the shared parameters P_{ijk} via the above private scalar product protocol. The output was the random shares of parameters P_{ijk}.

In private score computation, Wright and Yang referred to Yang and Wright (2006) for computing random shares of $\ln P_{ijk}$ and $P_{ijk} \ln P_{ijk}$. With respect to $(P_{ij0} + P_{ij1} + 1) \ln (P_{ij0} + P_{ij1} + 1)$, they let Alice and Bob separately compute random shares. Then, Alice and Bob selected the maximum values among the m shared score values. Yang and Wright (2006) evaluated the proposed g score function on two data sets. The first (Asia) data set included eight features such as Asia, smoking, tuberculosis, lung cancer, bronchitis, either, x-ray, and dyspnoea. The second (synthetic) data set consisted of 10,000 data points and six features denoted 0–5. Wright and Yang compared the performance of the g and f score functions in both data sets and observed that the g score function approximated the f score function sufficiently for the K2 algorithm, e.g., all g scores fall into 99.8% of $ln(f)$. They noted several causes of information leaks: known structure of BN, sequence of edges included in BN, and parameters of BN model, which were associated with particular features.

8.3.4 Privacy Preservation KNN (Table 1.1, A.7)

As explained in Section 2.3.2.3, KNN classifies a query data point x_{query} into the majority class of its neighborhood. This neighborhood is defined by a distance function $d(x_j, x_{query})$ and the k nearest neighbors measured by the distance to the query data point. In an SMC problem, the entire data set $\{x_j\}$, $j = 1, \ldots, n$, is composed of multiple data sets located at different sites *site* 1, …, *site* N. As shown in Figure 8.9, each site i, where $i = 1, \ldots, N$, holds a part of the horizontally partitioned data S_i. Hence, the whole data set can be expressed as $S = \cup_i S_i$. Without considering the privacy-preserving issues, the k closest neighbors can be found in S for the query data point x and the majority class among the k neighbors labels data point x. In privacy preservation KNN calculation, each site prevents its private data from leaking to the other sites while serve as a participant in obtaining the k nearest neighbors for the query data.

Kantarcioglu and Clifton (2004) presented a framework using a privacy-preserving KNN method to mine horizontally partitioned databases. Hence, the feature space remained the same among all participants. They assumed each set of databases is able to conduct KNN separately. They attempted to find the local KNN results most similar to the global KNN results, and to obtain most of the global KNN results. The third party, C and O in Figure 8.9, is a not trusted but is a non-colluding party.

In the proposed privacy preservation KNN method, Kantarcioglu and Clifton first obtained $N*k$ local nearest neighbors among all of the N partners in an untrusted site C. Second, they combined the local KNN results, and obtained the final global classification result, which they then sent to site O. The private information considered in the procedures included original location of the local nearest neighbors and their distance values, and the global class labels assigned to the data points.

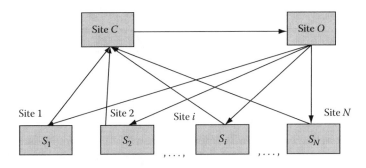

Figure 8.9 Framework of privacy preservation KNN.

The proposed privacy preservation KNN method included the following steps:

Step 1. Generate public encryption keys E_C and E_O for site C and site O, using the confidential key encryption algorithm owned by site i, $i = 1, \ldots, N$.

Step 2. Obtain local k nearest neighbors at each site i, and randomize the distance and local KNN result X_{ij}, $j = 1, \ldots, k$, at each site i.

Step 3. Generate the encrypted local clustering result for each site i, as follows: $R_i(id, d, Eo(c)) = \bigcup_{j=0}^{k-1} \left(E_K(ik + j), X_{ij} \cdot d \| E_u(ik + j), E_o(X_{ij} \cdot c) \right)$, where $E_K(ik + j)$ denotes the encrypted identifier of the jth nearest neighbor at site i, K denotes the key that each site generates using the key generation function E_K, $d\|E_u(ik + j)$ denotes the encrypted identifier of the jth nearest distance at site i, u denotes the key that each site generates using the key generation function E_u, and $E_o(X_{ij} \cdot c)$ denotes the encrypted local KNN results obtained at site O.

Step 4. Build comparison vectors ER_i at site i using share-splitting method in SMC: for $\forall R_i(id, d, E_o(c))$, $v = \cup (R_{hj} \cdot id, \text{share of } f(d, R_{hj} \cdot d) \text{ at site } i)$ if $id < R_{hj} \cdot id$; $v = \cup (R_{hj} \cdot id, \text{share of } f(R_{hj} \cdot d, d) \text{ at site } i)$, if $id > R_{hj} \cdot id$. The encrypted comparison results are assigned to set ER_i for site i by $ER_i = \cup (id, E_c(v), E_o(c))$, where E_C is the encryption key assigned by site C, and function $f(R_{hj} \cdot d, d)$ obtains the secure comparison result as follows: if $R_{hj} \cdot d > d$, $f(R_{hj} \cdot d, d) = (1 \oplus r, r)$ otherwise, if $R_{hj} \cdot d < d$, $f(R_{hj} \cdot d, d) = (0 \oplus r, r)$ where r is random share for each participant (site) and "$\oplus$" denotes the exclusive-or function of the shares.

Step 5. Permute $ER = \bigcup_i ER_i$ and send the permuted result to site C.

Step 6. Select the k nearest neighbors among the encrypted comparison result ER: decrypt the encrypted shares in ER and find the global k nearest neighbors, $NN_i = E_o(c_i) \oplus r_i$, where r_i is random number, using the secure comparison results obtained in Step 4.

Step 7. Site C sends global KNN result to site O, and site O determines which class is in majority: first site C operates Blum–Goldwasser encryption (Kantarcioglu and Clifton, 2004) on each class c_i to get the k nearest neighbors in the form of $NN_i = (\dot{r}, c_i \oplus r \oplus r_i)$. Given $\dot{r}$, site O is able to decrypt r and obtain $c_i' = c_i \oplus r_i$. Finally, the class of the neighbors can be obtained by using the circuit evaluation function: $maj\left(c_1' \oplus r_1, \ldots, c_k' \oplus r_k\right)$.

A salient advantage of the proposed method is that it can balance between accuracy, efficiency, and privacy through multi-round protocols. The method assumes two parties, O and C, have no collusion, which pose challenges in practical computation. From the viewpoint of computation cost, privacy level depended mainly on the amount of encryption operations, and the communication and comparison cost between sites.

8.3.5 Privacy Preservation k-Means Clustering (Table 1.1, A.3)

Vaidya and Clifton (2003), introduced a privacy preservation k-means clustering method for MPC, when different sites contain different attributes for a common set of entities. Each site learns the cluster of each entity, but learns nothing about the attributes at other sites. As explained in Section 2.3.2.1, a k-means clustering algorithm clusters data points into the k-closest clusters. Each cluster has a center point, and data points are nearer to this center than to any other cluster. Centers are clustered within this cluster. Given a set of vertically partitioned data, each site holds a subset of the feature space, e.g., the two partitioned subsets of the whole feature space $\{f_1, ..., f_d\}$ in Section 8.3.2. The data set $\{x_i\}$, $i = 1, ..., n$, is composed of multiple sites, and each site has the same number, n, of data points, while the feature vectors between sites are different. We assume N sites: $\{S_j\}, j = 1, ..., N$, exist. We denote the data set in site j as $\{x_{ij}\}$.

The objective of privacy preservation k-means is to cluster the combined data and obtain k-means and their associated clusters. To preserve private information, each participant is allowed to know only the clustering centers that involve his or her own feature set and final clustering result of the data points. As shown in Figure 8.10, Vaidya and Clifton proposed a privacy preservation k-means clustering framework consisting mainly of three procedures: compute the distance vector for each point in every data site corresponding to each cluster, find the closest cluster securely for each data point, and check the distance between the new centers of clusters and old centers using the threshold for algorithm termination decision.

In the first module, Vaidya and Clifton defined a distance vector $\vec{D}_j, j = 1, ..., N$, for site j as follows:

$$\vec{D}_j = \left[D_{1j} ... D_{gj} ... D_{kj} \right]^T, \tag{8.15}$$

where $D_{gj} = dist(x_{ij}, u_{gj})$ refers to the distance between the gth cluster center and ith data point in site j. At each site j, they obtained distance vector $\vec{D}_j$, which serves as

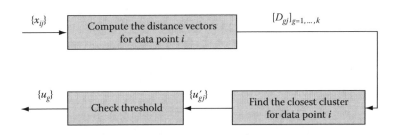

Figure 8.10 Workflow of privacy preservation k-means in Vaidya and Clifton (2004). (Vaidya, J. and Clifton, C., Privacy-preserving data mining: Why, how, and when, IEEE Security Privacy. © 2004 IEEE.)

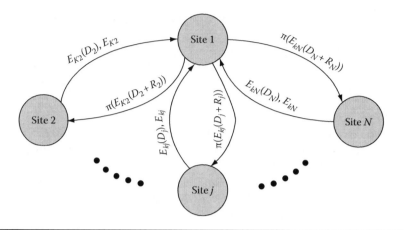

Figure 8.11 Step 1 in permutation procedure for finding the closest cluster.

the input for the second module. In the second module, three sites are trusted not to collude: site 1, site 2, and site N. This module consists of four steps. In the first step, site 1 generates a random matrix R_{kN} and permutes the vectors $\vec{R}_j, j = 1, ..., N$, corresponding to the columns in matrix R_{kN}. As shown in Figure 8.11, each site j, $j = 1, ..., N$, has a vector $\vec{D}_j$ and random vector $\vec{R}_j$. Site $j, j = 2, ..., N$, generates a public–private keys E_{kj}, and encrypts vector $\vec{D}_j$ into $E_{kj}\left(\vec{D}_j\right)$.

In Step 2, site $j, j = 2, ..., N$, sends $E_{kj}\left(\vec{D}_j\right)$ and key E_{kj} to site 1 and receives the permutation result $\pi\left(E_{kj}\left(\vec{D}_j + \vec{R}_j\right)\right)$ from site 1 (see Figure 8.12). Then, site j decrypts the permutation results using its public key and private key, and obtains the permuted result $\pi\left(\vec{D}_j + \vec{R}_j\right)$. The above permutation algorithm is based on the homomorphic property in encryption: $E_{kj}\left(\vec{D}_j\right) * E_{kj}\left(\vec{R}_j\right) = E_{kj}\left(\vec{D}_j + \vec{R}_j\right)$. The reader should consult Vaidya and Clifton (2003) for a more detailed analysis. In the second step, each site $j, j = 1, 3, ..., N - 1$, sends $\pi\left(\vec{D}_j + \vec{R}_j\right)$ to site N and

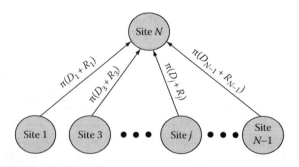

Figure 8.12 Step 2 in permutation procedure for finding the closest cluster.

obtains summation result $\vec{Y} = \sum_{j=1,3,\ldots,N-1} \pi\left(\vec{D}_j + \vec{R}_j\right)$. In Step 3, each cluster g, $g = 1, \ldots, k$, makes the secure comparison of $Y_g + \pi(D_{gj} + R_{gj})$ with another cluster, and finds the minimum result in $Y_g + \pi(D_{g2} + R_{g2})$ and identifies the minimum label g_m. In Step 4, site N sends the minimum label g_m to site 1, and site 1 identifies the original value g_m, which corresponds to the nearest cluster the point i.

After finding the nearest clusters for all the data points in the data set, $\{x_i\}$, each cluster can obtain the mean of every individual feature value u'_{gi} for all the data samples falling into the cluster. Using these mean values, the check threshold algorithm attempts to search for the stop criteria for the whole algorithm. The algorithm stops when the difference between new means and old means is smaller than a defined threshold.

Assuming no collusion exists between the multiple sites, Vaidya and Clifton demonstrated, theoretically, that the proposed algorithm could ensure that the private information will be not disclosed even if disclosing the point clustering at an iteration. As site 1 and site N hold most of the computation and communication information, such as the permutation result, random matrix and comparison result, the collusion between site 1 and site N will leak information for the calculation of distances between data points. Vaidya and Clifton analyzed the legalistic and technical countermeasures against such collusions in practice. Readers should see the detailed analysis in Vaidya and Clifton (2003). They analyzed that the computation cost was in linear polynomial order. The communication cost depended on the number of iterations required for convergence.

8.3.6 Other PPDM Methods

Agrawal and Srikant developed the first PPDM method for preventing privacy leaks (2000). They perturbed sensitive information in the original centralized data using uniform or Gaussian randomization, so that miners could not access the precise records (Agrawal and Srikant, 2000). Then, they built a DTC based on the perturbed data, where they proposed to reconstruct the distribution of the perturbed data to retrieve the original data. Lindell and Pinkas constructed a privacy preservation decision-tree model for horizontally partitioned data sets and first designed cryptographic protocol for PPDM methods (2002).

In Du et al. (2004) and Kantarcioglu and Clifton (2004), multivariate statistical analysis methods were suggested to solve "Secure 2-party multivariate linear regression problems" and "Secure 2-party multivariate classification problems." Their practical security model serves as the basis for a number of building blocks for solving these two problems. In Barni et al. (2006), the problem of secure data processing by means of ANN was addressed. Two levels of protection were considered: in the first level, only ANN weights were protected, whereas the node activation functions were also protected in the second level. This work includes a description of an efficient way of implementing the proposed protocol by means of the recently proposed multiparty computation techniques. Yu et al. (2006) presented a privacy-preserving linear SVM classification algorithm, based on the optimization formulation of the proximal SVM on horizontally partitioned data.

8.4 Summary

As we discussed above, a number of data-mining and machine-learning algorithms have to be redesigned to address growing concerns with privacy protection. Although not all data-mining and machine-learning algorithms are exhaustively studied for privacy protection, we believe the current PPDM algorithms present the most employed data-mining methods. Due to the specific data requirements and particular data-mining and machine-learning algorithms, researchers have developed PPDM methods for individual data-mining techniques. We have presented the applications of privacy preservation association rules, privacy preservation decision-tree model, privacy preservation KNN, privacy preservation k-means clustering, and privacy preservation BN. The privacy preservation concerns mostly concentrate on the reformation of original input data, the redesigning of the data-mining algorithm for the hidden data source and for the prevention of information leakage during computation and communication of data sharing, and privacy preservation of the data-mining results.

The modification of original data causes information loss and blockage, whereas the early data protection ensures the original data known by fewer people. Most of the data protection protocols fall into the categories of anonymization, blocking, cryptography, and perturbation. To retrieve the original information, the corresponding reconstruction procedures have to be designed before the PPDM algorithms. These procedures concern the discovery of useful knowledge for data mining, e.g., data distribution, while protecting the individual sensitive information. The definition of sensitive information differentiates, e.g., data owners who are concerned about sensitive data points in horizontally partitioned data sets, may disagree about which information is most important, and be more concerned about different sensitive feature subsets in vertically portioned data sets.

Because PPDM techniques are not infallible, researchers are concerned about the privacy leaks in computations and communications even while running PPDM algorithms. The sensitive information is not directly related to the original data values but is possibly caused by data structures, inferred information, and problematic frameworks. For example, in SMC collaborations, any information leak from a third party can compromise the privacy of all participants. The PPDM results can leak privacy if further privacy protection processes are not implemented. The data modification methods and permutation algorithms can hide the sensitive rules or induction information effectively. For example, association rules elusively present the correlation between items. Any additional information in the rules, such as the resources of the items, may cause privacy leaks.

Various PPDM methods have not been built in a general framework due the complications and various privacy protection techniques and various motivations for using privacy preservation. However, the performance of PPDM algorithms focuses on several metrics: privacy leakage level, mining accuracy, computational cost, scalability, and endurance privacy protection techniques for several data-mining algorithms. PPDM algorithms are designed along with a set of parameters for evaluating the privacy leakage level. Normally, the privacy leakage levels are evaluated in each computation and communication procedure. Subsequently, after several steps of privacy protection, the PPDM results cannot exactly match the data-mining results of the original data and original data-mining algorithms. Hence, the evaluation of PPDM algorithms needs to balance between mining accuracy and privacy leakage level. Computational and communication cost also need to balance with the privacy leakage level. More encryptions cause high privacy protection and high computation complexity. Expensive computation cost along with a high dimensional data set, requires PPDM algorithms to have sufficient scalability. Few scientists have researched and evaluated PPDM endurance, because PPDM is still new and underdeveloped, and every PPDM algorithm concentrates solely on one data-mining or machine-learning method.

We also find most PPDM algorithms have been proposed theoretically, and few of them have been implemented in real-world situations or tested using a real data set, making it difficult to definitively determine the level of security that the algorithms will provide users. However, we can provide several research directions based on the reviewed PPDM techniques. First, we need to search for optimal solutions to balance the mining accuracy and privacy breach level of PPDM algorithms. The existing quantifications of privacy and proof methods have not sufficiently explored the strength of the PPDM algorithms. A small improvement of the constraints on the PPDM can increase algorithm accuracy up to the potential boundary of the algorithms. Second, it is challenging to search for the trusted third party in SMC. Participants are often concerned that benefits can entice the third party into collusions with unauthorized parties. A third party can secretly secure the privacy information stored in machines. The privacy data will decay completely if the machines are open. One example of such machines is the IBM secure coprocessor. The limitations of these machines are their limited computation speed, insufficient storage size, and possible communication with suspicious systems.

Third, a monetary evaluation of private data can leverage the accuracy and the cost of a PPDM algorithm. Such costs include privacy leakage, computation cost, and scalability. The monetary value of data brings PPDM users and private data owners into another trade-off between profit and privacy. The more accurate data contribute expensively to mining accuracy and lower the computation and communication cost in privacy protection. Fourth, PPDM in network monitoring and profiling techniques are emerging as the influx of huge online private information, such as healthcare and medical records. The huge number of records, high-dimensional feature set, and dynamic nature of network traffic flows make privacy protection network monitoring much more challenging than other applications.

References

Agrawal, R. and R. Srikant. Privacy-preserving data mining. In: *Proceedings of the ACM SIGMOD Conference on Management of Data*, Dallas, TX, 2000, pp. 439–450.

Aggarwal, C.C. and P.S. Yu. *Privacy-Preserving Data Mining: Models and Algorithms*. New York: Springer, 2008.

Barni, M., C. Orlandi, and A. Piva. A privacy-preserving protocol for neural-network-based computation. In: *Proceedings of the Eighth Workshop on Multimedia and Security*, Geneva, Switzerland, 2006, pp. 146–151.

Bertina, E., I. Nai Fovino, and L.P. Provenza. A framework for evaluating privacy preserving data mining algorithms. *Data Mining and Knowledge Discovery* 11 (2) (2005): 121–154.

Dinur, I. and K. Nissim. Revealing information while preserving privacy. In: *Proceedings of the 22nd Symposium on Principles of Database Systems (PODS)*, San Diego, CA, 2003, pp. 202–210.

Du, W. and M.J. Atallah. Secure multi-party computation problems and their applications: A review and open problems. In: *Proceedings of New Security Paradigms Workshop*, Cloudcroft, NM, 2001, pp. 11–20.

Du, W. and Z. Zhan. Building decision tree classifier on private data. In: *Proceedings of the IEEE ICDM Workshop on Privacy, Security and Data Mining*, Maebashi City, Japan, 2002.

Du, W., Y.S. Han, and S. Chen. Privacy-preserving multivariate statistical analysis: Linear regression and classification. In: *Proceedings of SIAM International Conference on Data Mining (SDM)*, Nashville, TN, 2004.

Dwork, C. and S. Yekhanin. New efficient attacks on statistical disclosure control mechanisms. In: *Proceedings of the 28th Annual Conference on Cryptology: Advances in Cryptology*, Santa Barbara, CA, 2008, pp. 469–480.

Evfimievski, A., J. Gehrke, and R.J. Srikant. Limiting privacy breaches in privacy preserving data mining. In: *Proceedings of the ACM SIGACT SIGMOD SIGART Symposium on Principles of Database Systems*, San Diego, CA, 2003, pp. 211–222.

Evfimievski, A., R. Srikant, R. Agrawal, and J. Gehrke. Privacy preserving mining of association rules. In: *Proceedings of the Eighth ACM SIGKDDD International Conference on Knowledge Discovery and Data Mining*, Edmonton, Alberta, Canada, 2002.

Evfimievski, A., R. Srikant, R. Agrawal, and J. Gehrke. Privacy preserving mining of association rules. *Information Systems* 29 (4) (2004): 343–364.

Hinke, T.H., H.S. Delugach, and R.P. Wolf. Protecting databases from inference attacks. *Computers and Security* 16 (8) (1997): 687–708.

Kantarcioglu, M. and C. Clifton. Privately computing a distributed k-nn classifier. In: *Proceedings of the Eighth European Conference on Principles and Practice of Knowledge Discovery in Databases*, Pisa, Italy, 2004, pp. 279–290.

Kantarcioglu, M., J. Jin, and C. Clifton. When do data mining results violate privacy? In: *Proceedings of the 2004 ACM SIGKDD International Conference on Knowledge Discovery and Data Mining*, Seattle, WA, 2008, pp. 599–604.

Online Security and Privacy Study. A report from Harris Interactive 2009. http://www.whitehouse.gov/files/documents/cyber/National%20Cyber%20Security%20Alliance%20-%

Shannon, C.E. Communication theory of secrecy systems. *Bell System Technical Journal* 28 (4) (1949): 656–715.

Sweeney, L. K-anonymity: A model for protecting privacy. *International Journal of Uncertainty, Fuzziness and Knowledge-Based Systems* 10 (5) (2002): 557–570.

Vaidya, J. and C. Clifton. Privacy-preserving K-means clustering over vertically partitioned data. In: *Proceedings of the Ninth ACM SIGKDD International Conference on Knowledge Discovery and Data Mining*, Washington, DC, 2003.

Vaidya, J. and C. Clifton. Privacy-preserving data mining: Why, how, and when. *IEEE Security and Privacy* 2 (2004): 19–27.

Verykios, V.S., E. Bertino, I.N Fovino, L.P. Provenza, Y, Saygin, and Y. Theodoridis. State-of-the-art in privacy preserving data mining. *ACM SIGMOD Record* 33 (1) (2004a): 50–57.

Verykios, V.S., A. Elmagamid, E. Bertino, Y. Saygin, and E. Dasseni. Association rule hiding. *IEEE Transactions on Knowledge and Data Engineering* 16 (4) (2004b): 434–447.

Willenborg, L. and T. DeWaal. *Elements of Statistical Disclosure Control, Lecture Notes in Statistics*, Vol. 155. New York: Springer, 2001.

Wright, R. and Z. Yang. Privacy-preserving Bayesian network structure computation on distributed heterogeneous data. In: *Proceedings of the 10th ACM SIGKDD International Conference on Knowledge Discovery and Data Mining*, Seattle, WA, 2004.

Yang, Z. and R.N. Wright. Privacy-preserving computation of Bayesian networks on vertically partitioning data. *IEEE Transactions on Knowledge and Data Engineering* 18 (9) (2006): 1253–1264.

Yao, A.C. Protocols for secure computations. In: *Proceedings of the Third Annual IEEE Symposium on Foundations of Computer Science*, Chicago, IL, 1982.

Yu, H., X. Jiang, and J. Vaidya. Privacy-preserving SVM using nonlinear kernels on horizontally partitioned data. In: *Proceedings of the 2006 ACM Symposium on Applied Computing*, Dijon, France, 2006.

Chapter 9

Emerging Challenges in Cybersecurity

> Fear nothing but what thy industry may prevent; be confident of nothing but what fortune cannot defeat; it is no less folly to fear what is impossible to be avoided than to be secure when there is a possibility to be deprived.

Francis Quarles, 1592–1644, British Poet

Information technologies facilitate human activities, including communication, commerce, travel, study, work, voting, and policy dissemination. Cyberspace is no longer a place that exists on the fringe of society. We live in cyberspace, and it seems every activity has a paired terminology starting with e- or cyber-, such as cyber crime, cyber attack, cyber thieves, and e-commerce. As with our physical world, we benefit and suffer from activities conducted in cyberspace. Cyberinfrastructures may provide us with access to faster and more convenient modes of communication; likewise, we can suffer from cyber crimes and cyber warfare. In Chapters 3 through 8, we have mentioned many cyber protection techniques to combat malicious cyber activities. However, we cannot cover all levels of cyber attacks and prevention, as the area is vast, complex, and constantly growing. To broaden readers' views of cyberspace in the years ahead, we summarize the emerging challenges in cybersecurity, focusing on cyber threats, network monitoring and privacy protection, and network intrusion detection.

This chapter contains an overview of emerging topics and recent cases in cybersecurity, such as botnet attacks, economic cyber crimes, privacy protection in cyber monitoring systems, cyber warfare, and intrusion detection for multi-level wireless communication systems. These challenges motivate us to increase cyber defense levels against malicious users, hackers, cyber criminals, and political adversaries (Tikk, 2008; *Virtual Criminology Report 2009: Virtually Here: The Age of Cyber Warfare*, 2009). In this chapter, we first summarize the emerging threats in various attack methods in Section 9.1. In Section 9.2, we present several privacy-preserving (PP) problems in cyber monitoring and profiling infrastructures, including PP data, PPDM, legislation, and PP traffic in networks. We illustrate a framework, PRIvacy-aware Secure Monitoring (PRISM), to help readers understand the solutions. In Section 9.3, we present the challenges of using network intrusion detection systems (IDSs), which are caused by the fast aggregating network traffic flows. We highlight the difficulties in designing and validating efficient IDSs. In Section 9.4, we summarize the challenges ahead and recommend research directions for data-mining and machine-learning applications in cybersecurity.

9.1 Emerging Cyber Threats

Mustaque et al. (2008) reported five emerging cyber threats that will challenge cybersecurity in the years ahead: malware, botnets, cyber warfare attacks, threats to mobile communication, and cyber crimes using various attack methods. We describe these cyber threats in this section.

9.1.1 Threats from Malware

Hackers use malware programs, such as phishing scams, to steal private information or for other malicious purposes. They deliver malware by leveraging the vulnerability of Web site structures, social network systems, and document transmissions that do not scan for such threats. With the widespread use of social network tools such as MySpace, MSN Messenger, and Facebook, social networking systems are becoming the dominant targets for malicious users. For example, MSN Messenger links users via the Internet, and video messages shared between MSN Messenger users can be convenient conduits for cyber attacks and malware. If the recipient tries to open a video, a popup may ask him or her to install a video plug first. If he or she continues to install the software, he or she will actually install malware in the computer and link the computer to a botnet. Taking advantage of the vulnerabilities of the computer systems, the malware will be able to track and record the user's keystrokes, spy on the user's browsing habits, alternate any browsing page to a phishing Web site, and send private information, such as a social security number, to an attacker. To repair the vulnerable points in the software, a number of software vendors provide patch-update versions of their software periodically.

9.1.2 Threats from Botnets

Botnets are a group of bots, which make use of bots that attackers can run in groups using remote control systems.* The master communicates with the bots to launch the botnet attack like an army. The bots' mechanisms and their capabilities can be updated via this communication to evade intrusion detection. The Georgia Tech Information Security Center (GTISC) reported that the number of botnet-infected computers increased, approximately, from 10% to 15% of online computers from 2008 to 2009 (Mustaque et al., 2008). As shown in Table 9.1, Damballa, a cybersecurity company, reported that millions of computers in the United States were infected by botnets in 2009 (Messmer, 2009). Computer and Internet users suffer privacy breaches, financial losses, loss of valuable data, and damage to computer systems caused by botnets.

The *Botnet Research Survey* composed by Zhu et al. shows that botnet research is still in its early stages (Zhu et al., 2008). Most antivirus software is signature-based detection technology, which cannot detect subtle behaviors between bots. Researchers have proposed to understand botnets from two perspectives: specific-bot behavior analysis at a network level, such as an HTTP bot and a P2P bot, and aggregation study of botnets, such as botnet size and statistical features of specific bots.

One possible method of detecting botnets is to collect malware and track botnets so that the master and bots can be destroyed or blocked. However, this approach requires a system capable of understanding and responding to the request and command in a group of bot syntax. The growing and enriching features in the syntax, especially the incorporation of anti-detection techniques, execrate the difficulties of tracking the bot masters. The other solutions require monitoring the network systems and detecting the anomaly behavior of botnets through learning the patterns of network traffic flows. The biggest impediment to the accurate and efficient monitoring of network traffic lies in the huge amount of streaming data that must be processed. We have discussed possible data-mining and machine-learning solutions to this problem in the book.

We briefly summarize the possible applications of these methods for botnet detection. Feature selection or extraction techniques can reduce redundant data and improve the efficiency and effectiveness of the implementation of data-mining and machine-learning algorithms. Signature-based detection methods can find the suspicious traffic flows generated by bots, e.g., by matching the flows with a botnet infecting dialog syntax. The inability to detect new features of attacks limits the capacity of this type of detection methods. The useful features involved in botnet detection include the connection duration, start time, end time, and types of messages. As botnets work in groups and each group of bots shows similar patterns, data-mining and machine-learning algorithms are able to detect the anomaly

---

* Bot is the short name of a software robot. It performs various tasks automatically, such as deep web search and game playing.

Table 9.1 Top 10 Most Active Botnets in the United States in 2009

Rank	Botnets	Infected Computers	Threats
1	Zeus	3.6 M	Using fake Internet banking login pages to steal customer bank account numbers, user IDs, and passwords
2	Koobface	2.9 M	Using video links to entice users to install additional software, which is malware
3	TidServ	1.5 M	Spreading via spam and connecting remote bot master via backdoor ports
4	Trojan. Fakeavalert	1.4 M	Downloading malicious software and arising false alarm
5	TR/Dldr. Agent.JKH	1.2 M	Executing commands from remote masters
6	Monkif	520 k	Downloading and installing unsolicited applications and exploiting security flaw
7	Hamweq	480 k	Propagating via movable disks and stealing private data
8	Swizzor	370 k	Spreading unnoticed by users through manually executing malicious programs
9	Gammima	230 k	Spreading via movable drives and aiming to steal login IDs and passwords in Internet games
10	Conficker	210 k	Spreading through Internet, downloading, and promoting malicious programs

Source: Adapted from information presented in Messmer, E., America's 10 most wanted botnets, Damballa, Atlanta, GA, 2009; *PRIvacy-aware Secure Monitoring.* http://fp7-prism.eu/index.php?option=com_content&task=view&id=20&Itemid=29 (accessed 2010).

behaviors statistically among traffic flows by using clustering, classification, or correlation methodologies.

These anomaly detection techniques classify any abnormal behavior in network flows as anomalous, which generates a large number of false alarms. Hybrid IDSs attempt to combine the advantages of signature-based and anomaly detection methods to detect unknown attacks while reducing false-alarm rates. The accuracy and speed of the detection results of hybrid methods depend on the ability of the user to combine those detection methods effectively. Along with anomaly detection techniques, hybrid detection techniques have been implemented infrequently in practical usage. Profiling networks can potentially explore large-scale botnets, although our review of the profiling research implies that this research domain is in a preliminary stage. The influx of huge amounts of traffic data hampers the application of a number of machine-learning methods. Another challenge for researchers is how to address the dynamic characteristic of traffic data. The spatiotemporal transmission matrix can only solve dynamic programming issues when the data volume is reasonable and computable by the available computation resources in practice. Scalability must also be considered when detecting the botnet traffic flows, because an analysis of botnet attacks requires days or weeks of monitoring the communication in the network of interest.

9.1.3 Threats from Cyber Warfare

Cyber attacks are critical military actions. Instead of physically engaging in combat, attacks may come from cyberspace. The rapid development of digital information technologies makes national infrastructures, such as financial structures, utility transmission, and media communication, run efficiently in cyberspace. This dependence on cyberinfrastructures leaves a large number of vulnerabilities for cyber warriors to exploit for military activity. Cyber warfare has accompanied physical war in the past, and may come from sources that are not organized enough to fight a physical war. The most recent example of cyber warfare occurred during the Russia/Georgia conflict of 2008.

During the conflict, Russian hackers blocked almost all network traffic flows at gateways, segregating Georgia's local networks from those of other countries. They also accessed confidential information from the Georgian government and intruded on Georgian communication networks to phish state secrets. A similar event occurred when rebel hackers shut down Estonia's cyber communications (Tikk et al., 2008; *Virtual Criminology Report 2009: Virtually Here: The Age of Cyber Warfare*, 2009). However, this act was not accompanied by physical war.

Whereas traditional, physical warfare is expensive and closed to many members of a society, cyber warfare is inexpensive and is open to anyone who can launch a malicious program. Therefore, cyber defense against cyber attacks is an inevitable but challenging goal of military forces around the world. An efficient cyber defense requires collaboration between countries, states, institutions, and industrial societies, because cyber attacks can be launched through various routes at a large number of optional sites. The variety of attack options also discloses vulnerability in a cyber world that has no established rules of conduct. The lack of international cyber laws makes cyber defense challenging.

9.1.4 Threats from Mobile Communication

Researchers have put a great deal of effort in combating cyber attacks in terms of silent data types. They use silent signals to represent voices, images, and other media information. Mobile devices are linked to the Internet to facilitate everyday communications and activities, such as making purchases and checking bank balances. A variety of companies can provide services through mobile networks, including the traditional mobile phone and Voice over Internet protocol (VoIP) infrastructures. The good calling quality and reliable service entices more companies to offer mobile services and attract more customers to use them. The investigations have shown that even financial transactions appear in mobile services. These services on mobile devices provide a number of opportunities for hackers to steal valuable information from the digital voice communication. We discussed PPDM in Chapter 8. Mobile attacks include stealing and/or mining private data. Similarly, private data can be unveiled in digital voice communication systems. Research institutions are developing reliable intrusion prevention methods to solve voice fraud and phishing. Antivirus software is another solution to mobile attacks although the drain on battery life hampers its practical application. Google's Android promises better security, since users are able to use the normal security algorithm as mobile security solutions.

9.1.5 Cyber Crimes

Cyber fraud, stealing, phishing, and other malicious behaviors are enriching the terminologies of cyber crimes in the years ahead. The term cyber crime does not have a set definition because of the evolution of cyberspace and its subsequent problems. For example, the constant evolution of cyberinfrastructures makes it difficult to identify and catch cyber criminals. Different jurisdictions define cyber crimes as they correlate to local situations. As we discussed above, ubiquitous cyber tools facilitate everyday life along with a large number of cyber services via computers, mobile devices, wireless networks, and so on. Cyber crimes refer to the malicious activities to block, read, or interfere with these services. The motivations of cyber criminals include gaining economic benefit, compromising cyberinfrastructure (e.g., in cyber warfare), and self-satisfaction.

Undoubtedly, prosperous e-commerce or online business entices cyber criminals. Motivated by huge profits, cyber criminals can purchase malware tools from professional cyber experts and conduct economic crimes, such as gaining credit card and social security numbers, and electronic money laundering. The cooperation between the owners of cyber attack platforms and cyber criminals promotes malware delivery in networks. Vulnerabilities in the e-commerce or online services provide opportunities for cyber crimes in the economy. Combating cyber crimes requires more than updating patches for vulnerabilities. Many cyber crimes leave no detectable evidence, since cyber criminals can easily destroy evidence before being captured. Because of the lack of evidence, cyber police cannot quantify malicious behaviors. In some cases, cyber criminals have encryption and concealment tools to cover up their malicious activities. It is also challenging to aggregate corroborative evidence from the third parties in cyber crimes. Moreover, the borderless cyber world and its limited number of laws constrain the analysis and determination of cyber crimes. Thus, combating cyber crimes requires effort in two perspectives.

First, uniform cyber laws need to be enacted. Second, advanced intrusion detection technology based on data-mining and machine-learning methods need to be developed to defend against criminals. While new laws can protect victims, computer and mobile phone users can also implement self-protection methods. Furthermore, highly developed intrusion detection techniques can help cyber police detect crime evidence.

9.2 Network Monitoring, Profiling, and Privacy Preservation

In Chapter 8, we discussed privacy preservation in data mining and machine learning. In practice, attackers are interested in more than the data communicated between users. For example, attackers can learn an individual's or a group's intent when they observe the communication between parties. PP network traffic monitoring and profiling is emerging as a new research direction in cybersecurity. In this new research domain, monitoring and profiling programs attempt to collect traffic traces in the cyberinfrastructures to perform routine administration and operations and detect anomalous behavior in traffic flows. However, such programs are responsible for preserving the private information of network users in traffic flows. Thus, the PP processing has to take effect in the data collection process, of the monitoring and profiling of personal traffic flows, and the sensitive profiling results.

9.2.1 Privacy Preservation of Original Data

First, protection of private data by cryptographic, anonymous, and any other effective operation plays a preliminary but always effective role in privacy preservation. The earlier the users implement protective operations on the sensitive data, the less possible it is that attackers will breach user privacy. We discussed these privacy-preservation techniques in Chapter 8, and found the data modification process cannot always ensure abstract privacy preservation in various specific applications, such as different data-mining or machine-learning methods. Researchers develop a variety of PPDM frameworks with respect to the separate data-mining and machine-learning algorithms.

Privacy-preservation methods are also specifically designed for different data types, e.g., the vertically and horizontally portioning of data sets in SMC. In literature, the proposed privacy preservation methods solve specific problems one-by-one, but maintain no preparation for the upcoming specific data breaching issues. PPDM researchers have started investigating a general framework for privacy preservation solutions among applications, but most of them focus on bio-related data protection, finance or business privacy preservation, or privacy preservation within other specific domains. Network data protection can also provide a solution to cybersecurity. In applications, monitoring and profiling programs collect partial header-related packets for data mining to reduce the data amount involved in data analysis. This data preprocessing also produces opportunities to remove the sensitive features and sample data from the data set, although this process cannot replace privacy preservation procedures, because no sensitive information or data contributes to the monitoring and profiling.

9.2.2 Privacy Preservation in the Network Traffic Monitoring and Profiling Algorithms

Second, we need to re-devise the monitoring and profiling programs for the privacy-preservation data. As we showed in the application studies in Chapter 8, data-mining and machine-learning methods are adapted to various privacy preservation data types, as a preprocessor of monitoring and profiling programs. How to extract the desired knowledge from the encrypted data poses the first challenge. Network traffic flows differentiate from normal PPDM data types in the dynamic streams and huge amount of influx. The scalability and computation requirements for the monitoring programs exacerbate the difficulty in designing applicable privacy-preservation monitoring methods.

We have presented several recent applications of network monitoring and profiling methods in Chapter 7. These limited sources show that cyber experts and data-mining researchers have started building network traffic monitoring and profiling frameworks. The discussions within these sources focus on what mining or learning information the data-mining algorithms should provide, and how detailed the monitoring and profiling results should be. The proposed methods for pattern description include graphic-based traffic descriptors, entropy-based information flow, volume-based traffic evaluation, and traditional clustering or machine-learning algorithms. None of these algorithms has addressed privacy-preservation issues, because network traffic monitoring and profiling research only started recently.

As a new field, network traffic monitoring and profiling has challenging problems, such as the accuracy of mining, the coverage of profiling, and the scalability and computation complexity in face of the huge and streaming network traffic flows. However, privacy preservation and PPDM remains a cybersecurity issue. We have demonstrated in Chapter 8 that researchers have to redesign PPDM algorithms for a corresponding data-mining or machine-learning method almost from scratch to involve privacy-preservation functions. The complexity of designing a PPDM algorithm is as much as or even more than the difficulty of designing a data-mining or machine-learning algorithm. Thus, the earlier we involve the privacy preservation issue in network traffic monitoring and profiling, the less effort we need to spend redesigning the programs.

9.2.3 *Privacy Preservation of Monitoring and Profiling Data*

Third, we need privacy preservation algorithms to process the monitoring and pro-filing results of network traffic data. Similar to PPDM algorithms, original moni-toring, and profiling rules, or learned models, indicate a correlation between users or hosts in the network. Sensitive rules or patterns have to be removed or hidden for privacy preservation. Network traffic monitoring and profiling poses a similar problem, as explained in Section 9.2.2. The huge amount of traffic flows result in a large number of rules, and we must determine which of these rules are sensitive and how to identify and preserve them before reporting. To accurately monitor and profile cyberinfrastructures, the rules should be elucidative and representative. For privacy preservation, the results should not disclose any informative clues for malicious users to know the rules and their correlations. To solve this dilemma, researchers need to find a balance between privacy breach-level and monitoring and profiling accuracy. Achieving this balance also poses a problem of how to evaluate privacy-preservation results of monitoring and profiling.

9.2.4 *Regulation, Laws, and Privacy Preservation*

Regulatory and laws limit the development and application of privacy-preservation techniques (see Section 9.1.4). The United States and European countries have acknowledged the protection of private data as a fundamental human right in legislation (Bianchi et. al., 2007; *Data Loss Prevention Best Practices: Managing Sensitive Data in the Enterprise*, 2007), whereas the emerging privacy breaches call forth the elaborative definitions and legislation specific for PPDM and privacy-preservation network monitoring and tracking. The powerful data-mining and machine-learning techniques offer criminals not only the chance to invade private databases, but also the tools to discover the network user profiles. Hence, related regulation has to address the elaborative degree of network monitoring and profil-ing tools. Conversely, a reasonable elaboration of user behaviors supports network administrators in detecting malicious users.

As we discussed in Section 9.1.4, an elaborative intrusion detection result can help police detect criminals and find evidence. The elaborate results may relate to the log history of criminals or other malicious users. This evidence col-lection raises two more privacy issues: how long the log records should be kept for users and how much information should be included in the records. A long history and detailed information in the log files can cause problems with privacy preservation on two fronts: Its length can challenge both the data repository capability and can provide more chances of security breach. On the other hand, a short log file does not provide sufficient evidence of criminal activity and, thus, does not provide enough information for administrators and authorities to profile a criminal or malicious user with good accuracy. Additionally, deli-cate regulation has to address the restrictions on the access of network data storage, the repository locations, the strict authorization on the access of repositories at different confidential levels, the traceable but protective log records of malicious users, etc.

9.2.5 Privacy Preservation, Network Monitoring, and Profiling Example: PRISM

As discussed above, privacy preservation network monitoring and profiling pose problems not only in scientific solutions, such as data mining and machine learning, but also in social life. Consequently, the solutions require collaboration from multiple partners. For example, researchers from several European countries collaborate on the FP7 IST project, PRISM (*PRIvacy-aware Secure Monitoring*, 2010), to produce solutions for privacy-preservation network traffic monitoring and profiling. PRISM is the first attempt at a complete and operational network monitoring solution that technically integrates PP solutions. As shown in Figure 9.1, PRISM consists of three principal components: a front-end traffic probe, a back-end monitoring and storage module, and a privacy-preserving controller (PPC).

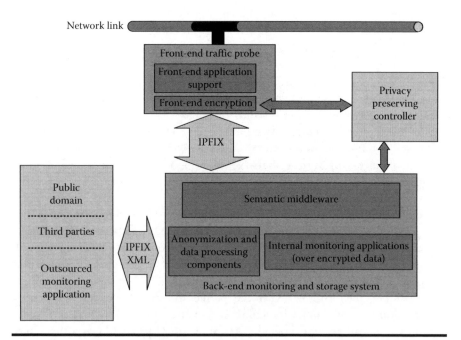

Figure 9.1 Framework of PRISM. (Bianchi, G. et. al., Towards privacy-preserving network monitoring: Issues and challenges, in: *The 18th Annual IEEE International Symposium on Personal, Indoor and Mobile Radio Communications*, Athens, Greece, 2007. © 2007 IEEE.)

The front-end traffic probe attempts to protect the original network flows as early as possible after capturing the packets from the monitored network. Meanwhile, the preliminary operations project the privacy preservation preprocessed data into the separated subspaces with respect to a variety of application specific purposes, such as intrusion detection and profiling. This partitioning process allows the specific applications to see the required details in the protected traffic data while restricting the contents in a security style, such as using statistical aggregation.

PPC can control the network independent of other components in the system. Authored operators administrate and control the regulations and rules in the PPC. The rules restrict the data access rights of users, the data applicable environments, the data-processing purposes, the access level of users, and other data management related to privacy preservation. As original traffic flows have been privacy preservation processed in the front-end component, PPC cannot access and provide original data.

The back-end monitoring and storage module processes and stores the encrypted traffic flows obtained from the front-end component. The back-end module consists of three components: semantic middleware, anonymization and data-processing mechanisms, and internal monitoring applications. Semantic middleware extends and adapts the privacy-restricted access control to the stored data corresponding to the monitoring application scenarios. The scenario information in the middleware includes the application of data, the usage of the data, the request types of data, and the legislation of the requested data. Anonymization and data-processing mechanisms perform further data protection procedures before outsourcing the data to the third parties for monitoring. The internal monitoring applications collaborate with the PPC module to process the front-end encrypted data with more functionality but little compromise.

The IPFIX protocol is standard for the transmission of anonymized network traffic flows between a back-end and a front-end module and other deployment across standard interfaces. IPFIX provides flexibility to choose exported data fields according to application requirements.

The PRISM framework addresses privacy-preservation network monitoring issues from the security of cyberinfrastructure and traffic-packet levels. The designed two-tier architecture enforces privacy preservation for the original data at the front-end tier, and conducts privacy-aware access control on the front-end privacy preservation processed data. The external operators conduct PP control through the module, PPC, on back-end module to reverse the data-preserving mechanisms. The combined reversion composes the privacy-aware access control in the back-end module. The PRISM framework produces privacy-preservation traffic data for third-party monitoring processing. PRISM provides solutions for privacy preservation in network traffic monitoring operations. Its modular design of PPC allows legalistic operations on the privacy data. Meanwhile, anomaly detection can prevent privacy intrusion when original data are partitioned for separate purposes.

9.3 Emerging Challenges in Intrusion Detection

In this book, we have discussed a variety of data-mining and machine-learning techniques to improve intrusion detection and prevention. These techniques secure cyberinfrastructures ranging from specific applications to various scales of operating systems, such as host-based or network-based IDS. Researchers have formulated these systems in data-mining and machine-learning models, or in other mathematical forms, based on specific assumptions on the anomalous data and normal data. These assumptions have facilitated the formulation of intrusion detection problems with regard to the objective of detection and the constraints on the data description in the formulation.

Most commercial products contain signature-based detection techniques. These techniques work, because all malicious or misuse behaviors have been profiled in signatures in a set of features. Extracting or selecting the features among the given data set promotes signature matching. However, missing features or insufficient profiling can cause these techniques to miss unknown attacks. The likelihood of missing unknown attacks hampers the abilities of these techniques to combat the miscellaneous novelties of cyber attacks. Anomaly detection techniques, including hybrid systems involving signature-based techniques, have occupied the research domain of intrusion detection in the past years. These techniques assume that, given the profile of all normal behaviors in cyberinfrastructures, outlying behaviors are anomalous. Such profiling techniques statistically aggregate the normal data into feature subsets or data clusters, which enable the flexibility and adaptability of anomaly detection to novel attack paradigms. Unfortunately, such techniques depend on accurate and precise boundaries between normal and anomalous data points.

The current machine-learning classification and clustering methods result in a high false-alarm rate when applied in anomaly detection systems. The high false-positive rate hampers the application of anomaly detection techniques in real-world data sets. The high false-alarm rate can make an anomaly detection system ineffective. When an IDS detects more false alarms than true attacks, the true attacks are easily lost. In worst-case scenarios, the detected alarms are all false instead of true attacks. Axelsson recommended the upper boundary of the effective false-alarm rate should be around 0.001% (Axelsson, 2000). The low requirement makes the task of reducing false alarms more challenging, especially with the large number of streaming traffic data.

Researchers have discovered a number of anomaly detection techniques in ubiquitous applications that reduce false alarms while maintaining acceptable true positive rates. Most of these techniques focus on specific applications and are restricted in preliminary studies. We attribute their limitations to several challenges emerging in cyberinfrastructures and the underlining restriction of the current researches, such as the lack of a theoretical framework for anomaly detection, the lack of sufficient evaluation data sets, and incomplete evaluation techniques. We will discuss these challenges in the IDS, especially in anomaly detection systems.

9.3.1 Unifying the Current Anomaly Detection Systems

Since anomaly detection techniques were motivated by various normal and anomalous characteristics in an unstructured way, researchers have not provided a unified framework of anomaly detection systems. Without a structured understanding of the normal and anomalous data sets, the detection problems can be biased, or the formulation may describe the given data set insufficiently. For example, the patterns of network traffic data have been described in traffic flow volume, entropy, traffic matrix, connection frequencies between the hosts of interest, etc. Each description presents an opportunity to discover various parts of the data characteristics, but no researcher has determined a unified description that is invariantly stable in face of a variety of anomalous data sets. The limitation of the ordinary intrusion detection or analysis systems lays in the lack of fundamental comprehension of the nature of the given cyberinfrastructures and of the data obtained in these systems.

This limitation also leads to the disordered theoretical framework in anomaly detection systems. Due to this limitation, few researchers have tried to combine the strengths of data-mining and machine-learning techniques into IDS. This theoretical framework also requires the fundamental discovery and analysis of the correlation between various data-mining and machine-learning techniques, so that an efficient hybrid method is explored. We have discussed similar issues in hybrid detection systems. We also categorized the existing hybrid detection techniques into serial, parallel, and mixture models. From the application studies, we know that no hybrid detection system can guarantee a better detection result than a single misuse-based detection system or anomaly detection system. An accurate hybrid detection system originates from the comprehensive understanding and combination of the proposed framework and the given data set. The statistical and combinatorial study of the designed workflow needs the investigation of data characteristics in depth. Thus, future research should include finding the optimal hybrid of various data mining, machine learning, or detection techniques, correlating machine-learning techniques for different detection objectives, and designing and analyzing intrusion detection evaluation data sets.

9.3.2 Network Traffic Anomaly Detection

As described in Section 9.2, cyber crimes and other malicious uses have emerged as a major concern in cyberspace. To help prevent these uses, researchers monitor networks using techniques such as network anomaly detection, as a part of IDSs to combat cyber attacks. Successfully updating network traffic techniques requires that the network profiling algorithms to be fast and highly scalable. The same requirements apply to the emerging network traffic anomaly detection systems and the solutions to suppressing the false-alarm rate. The wireless networks, VoIP, and mobile communications pose a variety of novel challenges to the traditional network traffic detection techniques, in terms of the flexibility and adaptability to the particular characteristics of the traffic data. The peculiar characteristics include, but are not limited to, multimedia data, heterogeneous data from multi-standard cyberinfrastructures, an influx of high streaming traffic flows, novel noises largely involved in traffic traces, and the short period for updating of cyberinfrastructures.

The network detection systems need to operate across multiple infrastructures including sensor wireless networks, cellular digital packet data (CDPD), general packet radio service (GPRS), multichannel multipoint distribution service (MMDS), and worldwide interoperability for microwave access (WiMAX). To adapt to the new challenges above, simply restructuring the current data-mining and machine-learning techniques for IDS may not solve the anomaly detection issues. Network engineers consider network security issues when they design the new generation of networks, so that security concerns are addressed across the cyberinfrastructure layers. Following the network systems from the first step of designing, the corresponding IDS systems can adapt to the updating of cyberinfrastructures.

Network engineers also investigate the vulnerabilities of the networks. The understanding and analyzing of vulnerabilities in the updated networks help the engineers not only improve the security level of networks through patches, but also facilitate the designing of anomalous detection systems by deducing the possible malicious patterns that these vulnerabilities can cause. Anomaly detection techniques, coupled with the network traffic monitoring and profiling system, will compose the IDS framework in the future. These techniques require novel validation data sets and tools to run successfully on the heterogeneous networks and deal with the online traffic flows.

The design of new IDS also needs to consider the malicious events across various cyberinfrastructure levels, such as network level and application level. To keep costs low, tolerance levels or alarm classes can be assigned to the network levels corresponding to different attacks. The current network shuts down completely when its IDS detects anomalous behavior in the system. For example, some parts occupy trivial roles in the operation of networks, and the intrusion on these parts compromise nothing or little of overall network system in the allowable time. Hence, an adaptive anomaly detection and alarm system can reduce the damage caused by of false alarms and improve the effectiveness of detection.

9.3.3 Imbalanced Learning Problem and Advanced Evaluation Metrics for IDS

Researchers have used a variety of evaluation methods, including detection rate, false-alarm rate, ROC curve, and F-score. None of these metrics can completely measure the various intrusion detection techniques in an acceptable quantification. We attribute the cause of such failures to three perspectives: imbalanced data, inappropriate machine-learning methods, and bad evaluation metrics.

Each data-mining and machine-learning method has its special cost function, which measures the learning error differently such that its evaluation should be a respective metric. We discussed the classic machine-learning classification methods in Chapter 2, and noted that most of the machine-learning algorithms perform well when data are balanced. Anomalous data cover a small part of the audit log records or network traffic flows. The imbalanced learning has the respective solutions, such as one-class learning, cost-effective machine learning, sampling methods, and feature selection filters (Stolfo et al., 2000; He and Garcia, 2009). Cost-effective machine learning relies on the assignment of costs to the four detected types: TP, FP, TN, and FN, to obtain the balanced objective function.

The challenge in using this technique is to determine how to find the appropriate cost parameters, and the assignments are strongly application dependent. Sampling methods attempted to provide balanced validation data such that normal machine-learning methods can be effective. The result implies overfitting or smaller coverage due to the repetition of minor samples or the reduction of major samples. We investigated several one-class anomaly classification methods, such as one-class SVM in Chapter 4, and showed these methods can reduce the false-alarm rates fairly, but lead to a low detection rate. Compared to the other proposed imbalanced learning algorithms, the one-class method has no significant advantages.

To address imbalanced learning, many researchers employed ROC and AUC to consider both the false-alarm rate and the true positive detection rate in one curve. However, both of methods may be misleading and incomplete, as we discussed in Chapter 2. A more accurate methodology is needed to evaluate the intrusion systems, especially in imbalanced learning.

9.3.4 Reliable Evaluation Data Sets or Data Generation Tools

To evaluate an IDS or compare the performances of IDSs, we need trusted data sets or data generation tools. Few public available data sets exist for examining IDS application studies. Furthermore, the generation of these data sets has not been reliable in the past. For example, MIT DARPA 1998 and 1999 are the most employed among them. The evaluation has showed that the DARPA data sets are not appropriate to simulate actual network systems or the data set generation tools (McHugh, 2000). The lack of proper evaluation data sets hampers the fair evaluation of IDS detection ability. The design of appropriate evaluation data sets and data generation tools should consider both the normal network traffic conditions and the anomalous traffic flows stealth in the traffic traces.

9.3.5 Privacy Issues in Network Anomaly Detection

As discussed in Section 9.2, privacy issues in network anomaly detection can be approached from two methodologies: the identification of useful encrypted traffic packets and/or the privacy preservation problems in distributed anomaly detection.

Cryptography techniques have been applied in networks to solve privacy preservation problems, as well as randomization, permutation, and other data protection methods. Privacy protection processed data, such as encrypted traffic packets, prevent malicious users from accessing private information. The traditional anomaly detection techniques lack the ability to decrypt the encrypted packets. Since the traditional anomaly detection techniques cannot read these valuable encrypted packets, they will remove them and reduce the useful traffic information for anomaly detection. A desired solution would be to maintain these data without compromising the detection ability of IDS.

As discussed in Chapter 8 and in Section 9.2, especially related to MPC and SMC, we can regard privacy preservation as a particular topic in SMC. The distributed sensor networks and collection of data across the network for anomaly detection motivated the development of the privacy-preservation network distributed anomaly detection (Valdya and Clifton, 2004; Zimmermann and Mohay, 2006). Although PPDM and anomaly detection appear as isolated topics in this book, these issues are not separate. Such a privacy-preservation issue originates in the centralized data requirement for the traditional anomaly redetection algorithms. The adaptation of PPDM methods, especially in SMC, to network traffic flows, can potentially solve the privacy-preservation problem in distributed anomaly detection. In the PRISM project (Bianchi et al., 2007, 2008; *PRIvacy-aware Secure Monitoring*, 2010) (see Section 9.2), this issue was solved in a privacy-preservation network traffic monitoring system. In Pokrajec et al. (2007), techniques have been proposed to assign anomaly scores to test data points and update the anomaly detection system. Practical testing and evaluation are needed for the above-recommended methods.

9.4 Summary

With the unprecedented advances in cyber data collection and utilization, humans face unprecedented challenges in cybersecurity and privacy protection. These challenges extend throughout cyberspace because of the continuous advancements in information techniques. As we present in the book, researchers have proposed a number of cybersecurity solutions using data-mining and machine-learning techniques. These techniques have to be improved to incorporate the emerging challenges in the years ahead. We also found that we must consider cybersecurity and privacy-protection issues when we design and promote innovative tools in cyberspace. We believe that, in the near future, new tools and legislation for privacy protection will significantly enhance the challenges and opportunities for data-mining and machine-learning techniques for cybersecurity.

References

Axelsson, S. The base-rate fallacy and its implications for the difficulty of intrusion detection. *ACM Transactions on Information and System Security* 3 (2000): 186–205.

Bianchi, G. et al. Towards privacy-preserving network monitoring: Issues and challenges. In: *The 18th Annual IEEE International Symposium on Personal, Indoor and Mobile Radio Communications*, Athens, Greece, 2007.

Bianchi, G., S. Teofili, and M. Pomposini. New directions in privacy-preserving anomaly detection for network traffic. In: *Proceedings of the First ACM Workshop on Network Data Anonymization*, Alexandria, VA, 2008, pp. 11–18.

Data Loss Prevention Best Practices: Managing Sensitive Data in the Enterprise. A report from IronPort Systems, San Bruno, CA, 2007.

He, H. and E.A. Garcia. Learning from imbalanced data. *IEEE Transactions on Knowledge and Data Engineering* 21 (9) (2009): 1263–1284.

McHugh, J. Testing intrusion detection systems: A critique of the 1998 and 1999 DARPA intrusion detection. *ACM Transactions on Information and System Security* 3 (2000): 262–294.

Messmer, E. America's 10 most wanted botnets. Damballa, Atlanta, GA, 2009.

Mustaque, A., A. Dave et al. Emerging cyber threats report for 2009. Georgia Tech Information Security Center, 2008 GTISC security summit—Emerging cybersecurity threats.

Pokrajec, D., A. LAzarevic, and L.J. Latecki. Incremental local outlier detection for data streams. In: *Proceedings of the IEEE Symposium on Computational Intelligence and Data Mining*, Honolulu, HI, 2007.

PRIvacy-Aware Secure Monitoring. http://fp7-prism.eu/index.php?option=com_content&task=view&id=20&Itemid=29 (accessed 2010).

Stolfo, S.J., W. Fan, and W. Lee. Cost-based modeling for fraud and intrusion detectors: results from the JAM project. In: *DARPA Information Survivability Conference & Exposition*, Hilton Head, SC, 2000, pp. 120–144.

Tikk, E., K. Kaska, K. Rünnimeri, M. Kert, A.M. Talihärm, and L. Vihul. *Cyber Attacks against Georgia: Legal Lessons Identified.* NATO, 2008.

Valdya, J. and C. Clifton. Privacy-preserving outlier detection. In: *Proceedings of the Fourth IEEE International Conference on Data Mining*, Brighton, U.K., 2004, pp. 233–240.

Virtual Criminology Report 2009: Virtually Here: The Age of Cyber Warfare. McAfee, Santa Clara, CA, 2009.

Zhu, Z., G. Lu, Y. Chen, Z. Fu, P. Roberts, and K. Han. Botnet research survey. In: *Annual IEEE International Computer Software and Application Conference*, Turku, Finland, 2008, pp. 967–973.

Zimmermann, J. and G. Mohay. Distributed intrusion detection in clusters based on non-interference. In: *Proceedings of the Australasian Workshops on Grid Computing and E-Research*, Hobart, Tasmania, Australia, 2006, pp. 89–95.

Index